BY TANK INTO
NORMANDY

So it is; yet let us sing
Honour to the old bow string!
Honour to the bugle-horn!
Honour to the woods unshorn!
Honour to the Lincoln green!
Honour to the archer keen!
Honour to tight Little John,
And the horse he rode upon!
Honour to bold Robin Hood,
Sleeping in the underwood;
Honour to Maid Marian,
And to all the Sherwood clan!

JOHN KEATS

BY TANK INTO NORMANDY

A MEMOIR OF THE CAMPAIGN IN NORTH-WEST EUROPE FROM D-DAY TO VE DAY

STUART HILLS MC

CASSELL

Cassell Military Paperbacks

an imprint of Orion Books Ltd,
Orion House, 5 Upper St Martin's Lane,
London WC2H 9EA

An Hachette Livre UK company

British Library Cataloguing-in-Publication Data
A catalogue record for this book is available from the
British Library

ISBN 978-0-3043-6640-8

Printed and bound in Great Britain by
CPI Cox & Wyman., Reading, RG1 8EX

The Orion Publishing group's policy is to use papers that
are natural, renewable and recyclable products and
made from wood grown in sustainable forests. The logging
and manufacturing processes are expected to conform
to the environmental regulations of the country of origin.

www.orionbooks.co.uk

CONTENTS

ILLUSTRATIONS AND MAPS

Major Chris Sedgewick and Lt Col Stanley Christopherson

Trooper Arthur Hinnitt

Sergeant 'Nev' Hinnitt

Keith Douglas

Lt Dick Holman

Major Jack Holman

Major Tim Olphert

The author in 1945

Lt Denis Elmore

MAPS

ACKNOWLEDGEMENTS

The author gratefully acknowledges the help he has received from Helen Burra-Robinson, Ken Ewing, Peter Hills, Bert Jenkins, Richard Lane, Ernie Leppard, Willy Lieber, Jimmy McWilliam, Peter Mellowes MC, Tim Olphert, Hans Pol, David Render, John Semken CB MC and Harry Wijchersen.

The extract from 'The Aristocrats' by Keith Douglas is from his *Collected Poems*, and other extracts by Keith Douglas are from his *From Alamein to Zem Zem*; reprinted by permission of the publishers Faber and Faber Ltd.

The extract from 'The Wilderness' by Sidney Keyes is from *Collected Poems* (Routledge, 1945).

The extracts from *To War with Whitaker* by the Countess of Ranfurly, published by Heinemann, are reprinted by permission of the Random House Group Ltd.

The extracts from *Normandy 1944 – From the Hull of a Sherman* by Arthur Reddish are reprinted by kind permission of Ken Ewing Publications.

The extracts from *The Man who Worked on Sundays* are reprinted by kind permission of the author the Reverend Leslie Skinner.

FOREWORD

War memoirs, like wine, do well to be kept in store for a while. Stuart Hills's account of that extraordinary year between June 1944 and May 1945 comes more than half a century after the experience, and in my judgement is all the better for it. That is partly because, as we grow older, we see such events in better perspective; partly because there are now so many folk who have no recollection at all of how, against all the odds, the Second World War was won. I think some of us may have bored our children with stories of what we did in those years – for while they were growing up, we were still suffering from that war's consequences.

Our grandchildren form a different audience. Many of them are genuinely eager to know what happened – and why it happened. The history of those times puzzles them. Why did we have to go to war again so soon after 1914–18? Why did the French, who had fought so tenaciously in that war, collapse in 1940?

That last question takes us towards the heart of Stuart Hills's story. As all of us who were soldiers in the late summer of 1940 knew in our hearts, to win that war we would somehow have to storm our way back across the English Channel and into a Europe heavily fortified by

Germany. There were many heroic battles between 1940 and 1945. But as a feat of arms, the invasion of France by the Allied Armies in June 1944 stands by itself.

The 8th Armoured Brigade to which Stuart Hills and I belonged was often at the sharp end of that invasion. His was the more gallant part, I must hasten to add, because, as you will read, the tanks of his regiment played a crucial role on D-Day itself. The motor battalion, to which I belonged, was crowded out on that day. We landed a few days later. But essentially those of us who belonged to that brigade were colleagues in arms during the Battle for Europe. I look back on it all now, as I am sure Stuart does, with a profound sense of gratitude.

We survived, for one thing! And we survived partly because we were in the hands of capable senior officers. The casualties of the First World War led to a torrent of criticism of the higher command – not all of it altogether fair. We simply could not afford to have casualties on that scale barely a generation later. Even so, my own records show that between June 6 1944 and May 5 1945 8th Armoured Brigade lost 54 officers and 372 other ranks killed, another 10 officers and 163 other ranks missing, and 175 officers and 1,226 other ranks wounded. So, although *By Tank into Normandy* may sound a fairly safe way to go, it was not all that safe!

By any measurement of history the conquest of Europe was a military triumph, something of which to be justly proud, a story to remember and to tell. Nobody is better qualified to tell it than a man who fought from start to finish with the Sherwood Rangers.

Lord Deedes KBE MC PC DL

AUTHOR'S FOREWORD

For far too many years I was too lazy to set in some sort of order the mass of papers which I accumulated in connection with my, and my regiment's, activities in North-West Europe during the war. Apart from my own war diary, much of which was written at the time and contained photos, sketch-maps, press cuttings and obituaries, I also had most of the letters I had written to family and friends during the campaign.

It was only recently, while watching cricket with David Walsh, a housemaster and historian at Tonbridge School, that he persuaded me to hand these papers over for scrutiny. To my surprise, he considered it worthwhile to set them all in order, so that they would provide a fitting chronicle for others to read.

Having given me a mass of prep to do, David then went ahead with this hefty assignment. Once the pattern was set and further research completed, we combined our efforts in composing a narrative which my family enjoyed.

I hope the reader will too.

Stuart Hills

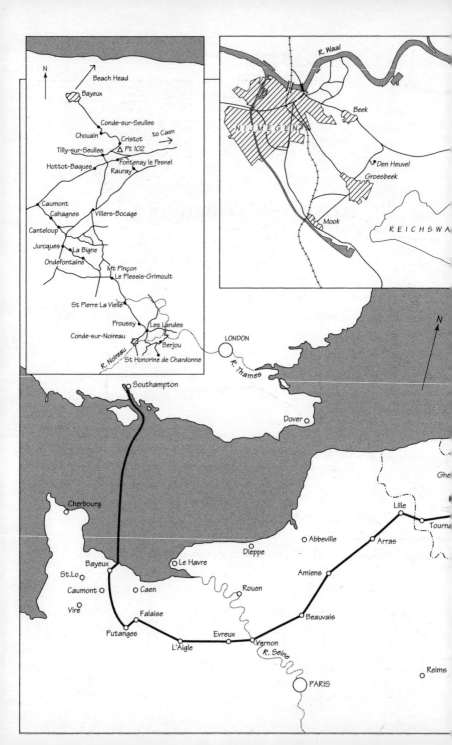

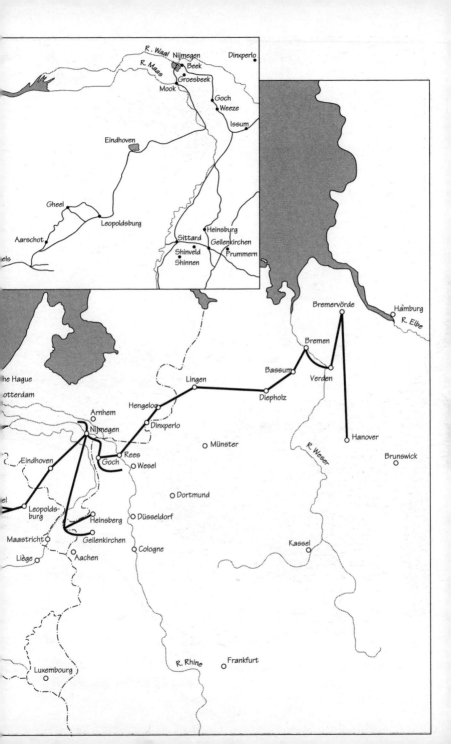

CHAPTER ONE **PRELUDE**

It was 6.45 a.m. on Sunday June 4 1944 in a wood near Calshot, on the western shore of Southampton Water, and the Brigadier was casting a disapproving eye in my direction. I was stripped to the waist in the early morning sunshine outside a tent I shared with Tim Olphert, one of my fellow troop leaders in C Squadron, and I was writing a letter to my brother Peter. The Brigadier obviously thought I should be more formally occupied, but he said nothing and I resumed my letter, saying that I was working hard but, for security reasons, could say little more. Later that afternoon, in weather that still seemed favourable, we drove our tanks down to the nearby quay, just where Southampton Water meets the Solent, and boarded Landing Craft Tanks (LCTs) belonging to 15 and 40 LCT Flotillas. Ours was numbered 442. We moved out into the Solent, taking care to avoid the myriad vessels plying back and forth, and slowly headed out towards the sea. We had little idea that General Eisenhower, in his SHAEF Headquarters at Southwick Park near Portsmouth, had already taken the decision to postpone Operation Overlord for twenty-four hours because of worsening weather conditions.

My confidence was lifted by the presence around me of men who were already familiar with the horrors and excitement that war can bring. I was a twenty-year-old newcomer and unblooded, while they were veterans of the successful campaign in the North African desert. It had been in January 1944 that I had joined the Nottinghamshire Sherwood Rangers Yeomanry fresh from 100 OCTU (Officer Cadet Training Unit) at Sandhurst. The Regiment had only then recently returned from three years in the Middle East, a period during which it had been involved in every major engagement of the desert war, including El Alamein and the breaking of the Mareth Line before Tunis. Tim Olphert never spoke about the desert or the heavy casualties the Regiment had suffered, although his tank had been knocked out there. I was therefore unaware how he and the others felt about what lay ahead. All I knew was that I must not let them down.

Ours was the last tank to reverse carefully up the narrow ramp on to the LCT, which meant we would be the first off when the signal was given to launch. Arthur Reddish, my twenty-three-year-old lap gunner and co-driver, picked up a small pebble from the beach as a last reminder of England, and I thought at the time that maybe he knew something that I did not. On the whole, however, the loading was achieved without fuss or ceremony, and with just a little banter here and there. I cannot remember anyone wishing each other luck, and I could not conjure up any appropriately heroic words or feelings myself. In some craft the words of Henry V before Agincourt might well have been uttered, but here I just felt myself among professionals who had a job to do and were determined to see it through properly. It did not occur to me that I might not see some of them again. And what I did not know then was that I was to be the only troop leader in the Regiment who would emerge unscathed from the whole North-West Europe campaign.

On our LCT were five Sherman DD tanks, 'swimming tanks' as they had come to be known. The tanks of Sergeant Sid Sidaway and Sergeant Kirby Tribe, both desert veterans, made up my troop of three and we were joined by those of Captain Bill Enderby, the C Squadron second-in-command, and Sergeant-Major Robson. The LCT moved through the Solent and steadily out to sea. As the land disappeared over the horizon, so the weather began to worsen. The wind picked up, the light rain became heavier and the sea began to get rougher. Just then the word came through to us that the operation had been postponed, but although many vessels did return to port, our flotilla remained anchored outside Southampton Water. There we stayed all through that night of June 4/5 while we waited for the Supreme Commander to meet again with his staff to review the weather conditions. The forecast of Group Captain Stagg and the other meteorological experts was now more favourable, with wind in the assault area of not more than Force Three, and so at four o'clock in the morning of June 5, Eisenhower made the fateful and irrevocable decision that D-Day would be on Tuesday June 6.

CHAPTER TWO **CHILDHOOD**

Journeys in ships were something with which I was not unfamiliar. My father Herbert was an electrical engineer who had joined Jardine Matheson and Company in Hong Kong in 1910 but had been based mainly in Shanghai, working on electricity and railway projects in China as far north as Harbin. He told me it had been very cold there and that he remembered reading *The Count of Monte Cristo* by the open fire. When the Great War broke out, he joined the Hong Kong Volunteers and then transferred to the Reserve of Cavalry in 1916 so that he would have a chance to get into the war. He saw service at Salonika in mid-1917 and then found himself attached to the Nottinghamshire Sherwood Rangers Yeomanry in Egypt, Palestine and Syria. By 1918 he was a captain and Adjutant of the Regiment and he took part in the great campaigns against the Turks which were effectively the last time the British cavalry was able to display its effectiveness as a fighting force.

In May 1918, the Sherwood Rangers were part of the 5th Cavalry Division as it swept into the Jordan Valley from Jerusalem to Jericho and Nazareth, and then on to Haifa and Acre, capturing Damascus in September. By the time of the Turkish surrender in late October, the Sherwood Rangers and their Indian allies had reached Aleppo. In twenty-seven days they had travelled 529 miles, and the Commander of the Egyptian Expeditionary Force was to write in his final despatch: 'The Desert Mounted Corps took some 46,000 prisoners during the operations. The complete destruction of the 7th and 8th Turkish Armies depended mainly on the rapidity of the cavalry's movements.'

While my father was thus occupied, three of his brothers were serving on the Western Front. Second Lieutenant Frederick Mervyn Hills had been killed in action near Ypres on July 27 1917 at the age of 34, while serving with the Northamptonshire Regiment. Two other brothers had been wounded. There is a remarkable book called *Tonbridge School and the Great War* which chronicles not only all the dead but lists the records of all those who served. It was compiled by H. R. Stokoe, a housemaster at the school, in tribute to his son, who had been killed in 1915 near St Eloi 'by the premature explosion of a rifle grenade'. Frederick Hills's life shows the tremendous range of exciting opportunities in life open to that generation. From the Royal Irish Constabulary, he had gone to the United States to become a civil engineer, excavated a subway under the Hudson River, built railways in British Columbia and explored north to find an outlet for the headwaters of the Chilliwack River. He had been killed by a shell that struck battalion headquarters.

My father had met my mother Edith in the Middle East, where she had served as a nurse at Gallipoli and in Egypt. They duly married in Hong Kong in 1919, after my father had returned to the colony to rejoin Jardine Matheson. Their house was 29 The Peak, where I was born in 1924. Harlech and Lugard Roads led from the upper tram station, circling The Peak at a height of 1,200 feet above sea level. They joined up about halfway round at Number 29, which was built in 1922 and was some 300 feet below the Governor's summer residence. The only traffic possible from the Upper Tram Station was by rickshaw via Harlech Road, and we had two rickshaws of our own – the coolies wearing smart uniforms of blue with white trimmings. In 1951, when I was employed with the Malayan Civil Service and was studying Chinese in

Macau, I was persuaded to sell the site, which had been destroyed by the Japanese when they invaded in 1941. I duly sold on my mother's behalf for a pittance, only to discover months later that the Harlech Road side had now been opened to cars, at which point the value of the site rocketed and the new owner profited hugely.

Twenty-nine The Peak appeared to be set rather precariously on the steep slope of the hillside, but the rock foundations and retaining walls were sound enough to cope with possible landslides. The view overlooking the western side of the harbour and Stonecutter's Island was breathtaking unless, as was sometimes the case, it was partially obscured by fog. The ground floor of the house included two drawing rooms, a conservatory, verandah, dining room, study, kitchen and cloakroom, while on the first floor there were three large en suite bedrooms and a dressing room.

The servants' quarters accommodated eight. The senior ranking of these was the No. 1 Boy, Ah Jhen, who was paid HK$31 a month. No one in the Colony was allowed to pay more than the Governor, who paid his own No. 1 Boy HK$32. (The value of the HK$ at that time was one shilling and three pence.) The lowliest in the servant hierarchy was the wash *amah* who received five dollars. The remainder – *amah*, cook, No. 2 Boy, gardener and the two rickshaw coolies – were paid various sums in between. As far as these servants were concerned, my mother was sensible enough to accept 'squeeze' – a term covering what she allowed them to take from household purchases of food, drink and other items. For example, when the gardener demanded a new broom, she would give him the money for it, knowing full well that he just went up the hillside to cut the necessary twigs. She knew, and he knew that she knew. On this basis we kept our servants for years, whereas others who did not follow the practice lost theirs.

I have wistful memories of those early days. At the weekends, when my father was at home, we spent time on the many lovely beaches, followed the hunt in the New Territories, watched the horse races at Happy

Valley or joined lunch parties in the surrounding bays. My sister Helen and I visited a governess every morning by rickshaw while in the afternoons we drew with the chalk we found on the side of Harlech Road. (The chalk was of various colours – pink, white and a tinge of blue – and it proved a useful medium in which to pursue my early artistic efforts. These culminated later in some amateur, and briefly, professional success, although my younger brother Peter outstripped me in this regard: he often exhibited at the Royal Academy, mainly as a sculptor, and taught art at Tonbridge School for some twenty-eight years.) On Sundays we always attended St John's Cathedral, which was in those days a conspicuous landmark, as were the Barracks, the Hong Kong Club, the Courts of Justice and the Cricket Club. Some of these have either been rebuilt or have simply disappeared among the forest of modern skyscrapers that is now Hong Kong. Cathedral services were usually combined with a military church parade and I remember particularly the Scottish regiments marching past in great splendour with a swirl of tartan and a skirl of pipes. It was here, I think, that my interest in the Army was first aroused.

But this idyllic childhood in Hong Kong was about to end. It was the custom for most expatriate parents in Hong Kong, India or wherever to despatch their children back to England as soon as they were ready for preparatory school. In my case that meant when I reached the age of seven in 1931. The South of England positively teemed with small boarding schools, especially seaside watering holes such as Seaford, Broadstairs, Bexhill and Eastbourne. The school chosen for me was Upland House (now Cottesmore), between Crawley and Horsham in Sussex. I was accompanied back to England by Helen, who was then nine, and my brother Peter, who was only five, and both of them went off to North Foreland Court in Broadstairs, which was principally a girls' boarding school but also took boys up to the age of seven.

I stayed at Upland House from 1931 until 1937. The house itself was originally known as Buchan Hill, just behind the quaintly named hamlet of Pease Pottage, which is on the main London-to-Brighton road. It was built by the Saillard family in the 1880s and is described by Mark Girouard in *The Victorian Country House* as 'large and florid, and everything that a Victorian nouveau-riche house should be'. The outside was imposing, a combination of red brick and yellow sandstone, and the interior had some exquisite wooden panelling, a minstrel's gallery and much oak carving. The park in which it stood was huge, with lakes and woods, and there is now a fine thirty-six-hole golf course in it. Upland House itself was to close at the start of the war, like many schools which found themselves in what was a potential war zone, and it never re-opened.

The memory one has of some teachers is always strong. At Upland House I remember with particular affection Gerry Moll. Apart from being an excellent teacher of English with a sharp eye for the exactitudes of grammatical expression, he had been and still was a fine sportsman who held the Public Schools' High Jump record for a number of years. He was a very useful cricketer and drilled into me the virtues of playing with a straight bat, but his greatest success was in teaching me to box. Boxing is of course now banned in schools, no doubt for good medical reasons, but in the 1930s, however, there was no such thing as the nanny state, and being taught how to defend yourself and deliver a good straight left was deemed a good thing. Gerry Moll's maxim, 'Hit first, hit straight and hit hard', was to stand me in good stead later at school and in the Army.

Much emphasis at Upland House was placed on good manners, particularly at meal times. We were instructed on how tables should be laid and the correct handling of cutlery. No request was allowed for vegetables or condiments to be passed during meals: to be served, one merely had to wait upon the services and good manners of others. Any infringement of these rules was punished by banishment for a day or more (the duration dependent on the degree of the offence) to a Pig's Table where only bread and water were provided.

Physical chastisement was the ultimate punishment for bad behaviour, though the writing of lines was more common. The overall curriculum was intensive, beginning with cold showers, breakfast and Chapel, followed by lessons, games and evening prep. There were half holidays on Wednesdays and Saturdays, and on Sunday a longer Chapel service and the obligation of writing home to our parents. We were allowed bicycles to ride in the grounds and occasionally went shooting game and rabbits with the gamekeeper, who rewarded us with threepence for every mole we trapped. We bathed in one of the lakes closest to the school.

One of the drawbacks of being sent to school in England was that one saw one's parents very infrequently. Nowadays children fly home to Hong Kong every holidays and often for a week's half-term too, but ours were different times. My parents came back in 1933 together, then my mother on her own in 1934 and again in 1937 to fetch us back to Hong Kong for a few months, and finally they both came in 1939 just before the outbreak of war, only then to hurry back to the colony. That was the way it was, and consequently we had to spend our school holidays with guardians. This sounds a frightfully deprived existence, but in fact it was rather fun.

The first of these guardians were Miss Laura and Miss Mary Emtage, who were joint headmistresses of my sister and brother's school, North Foreland Court in Broadstairs. They were formidable but kindly. Summer was enjoyable because of the proximity of the beaches and a large garden, while in winter we slept in an unheated dormitory, and the fire in the schoolroom, which was our living space, was never lit until 4 p.m. sharp. The cold north wind made for a healthy existence, to say the least. One pretty young thing who looked after us had played cricket for the England Ladies XI, but the curriculum was somewhat monotonous, involving on weekdays walking a bad-tempered dog to the lighthouse and then amusing ourselves in the schoolroom. I did not enjoy Sundays because I had to wear an Eton collar to church and then had to illustrate texts from the Bible and write to my parents. Nevertheless we were happy and became very good at amusing ourselves – reading, drawing, painting, doing fretwork and even learning to knit.

We always spent one week of each holidays in Maidstone with our maiden aunts, whom my future house master at Tonbridge, David Somervell, described as 'a breath from the Victorian age'. There was also Aunt Ethel, who had married Bernard Haynes, a local businessman and trader who had played football for Wolverhampton Wanderers. She always gave us a treat each winter such as a visit to Bertram Mills' Circus at Olympia or seeing *Peter Pan* at the theatre. In 1939, when my parents and sister returned to Hong Kong and the Emtages had retired from North Foreland, my brother Peter and I were given a new guardian, Mrs Cornish Bowden, who taught at Peter's new preparatory school, Marlborough House at Hawkhurst. She lived in a house near and belonging to the school and this arrangement worked well for two years, until she moved to Uppingham. Then – this was now 1941 – in an inspired moment, I sent a telegram to the Emtages, who were now running a boarding house in Dorking called Bracondale. 'Can we come and stay in the holidays?' I enquired. 'Delighted,' came back the reply, so the link was re-forged. The boarding house was filled with aged folk to whom the Emtages referred as 'the inmates'. We learned to play bridge, to do crosswords and to amuse the inmates with charades. And we went for runs, invited over our Tonbridge friends and even discovered pubs. Miss Em did the cooking, a cigarette constantly in her lips and dropping ash into the saucepan, but it seemed not to do either us or the inmates any harm.

At the end of my last summer term at Upland House in 1937, my father decided that he was too busy to return on leave and that we should come out to Hong Kong instead. My mother was therefore despatched to pick us up and return us to England by Christmas – each time by P&O Line. On the way out I remember playing a lot of ping-pong with the Princes Chula and Bira of the Royal House of Siam. The former was the quieter of the two and gave me a book, *Wheels at Speed*, which he had written about his brother's motor-racing career. The latter, chatty and effervescent, regaled me with stories about his two ERA cars, Romulus and Remus. The princes were invariably dressed immaculately, Prince Bira wearing his conventional blue cravat with white spots in which he raced.

We arrived in Hong Kong on September 3 1937 and were greeted that evening by probably the worst typhoon the colony has experienced. Our house at 29 The Peak was almost totally destroyed (it had to be painstakingly rebuilt over the following weeks) and the colony itself suffered terrible damage. One 20,000-ton vessel, the Japanese *Asama Maru*, finished up on a beach, and a tidal wave at Aberdeen claimed some 10,000 victims. But one of the joys of this visit was the chance to spend time at home in the company of my parents for the first time since 1931, although sadly it would also be the last time. My parents were certainly loving and caring, and we loved them very much too, but they belonged more to the Victorian world. They were always concerned that we should do our duty, as they had done in the Great War. My father was an outstanding engineer who tried me out with Meccano at an early age. I found this rather uninteresting so, perhaps to show me how useless I was, whenever I came down in the morning he had usually built edifices which more resembled the Forth Bridge or Eiffel Tower. Both he and my mother were careful about money, although they had no great reason to be, and expected the same of their children. Once, when my mother was in England, I urgently needed money for a model aeroplane which had been advertised in *The Wizard* magazine for one shilling and nine pence. We were allowed threepence a week pocket money, one penny of which was for the church collection, but I diligently saved the necessary amount, went back to the shop, longingly watched the plane being wrapped and handed over my money, only to be told that the price was now one shilling and eleven pence. Disappointed, I went back to my mother to ask for the extra twopence, only for her to say, 'You will of course have to wait until next week.'

My father was a keen cricketer who had played for the Tonbridge 2nd XI and he followed my own fortunes with a degree of pride. (The only two innings of mine he ever saw were in 1939, when I made 82 and 102 not out for a Hampshire Boys' XI.) He and my mother were taller than average and reasonably good-looking, and they were much involved in Hong Kong's social life, which was rather hectic, though perhaps less so than that of the more cosmopolitan Shanghai. My mother was a very keen bridge player and on one occasion, when my father returned late one afternoon from work to find a ladies' bridge session going on in his drawing room, he turned to me and said, 'Come on, let's get out of here, I hate the smell of warm drawers.' He was meticulous in his work as an exchange broker and always ensured that he kept his accounts in credit with all the major banks so that they were unable to squeeze lower discounts on transactions. He often worked late in the evenings in his study so that I saw little of him during the working week. But I always made the effort to have breakfast with him when, for some reason or other, he introduced me to the practice of putting mustard on my bread and butter. I rather stood in awe of him, although he had a jolly sense of humour and there were only a few occasions when I suffered corporal punishment. He was a heavy smoker of cigarettes – perhaps another lesson he taught me – and during his internment under the Japanese in Stanley Camp he picked up dog-ends with a friend who had been the manager of the Hong Kong Shanghai Bank and, after laying the salvaged tobacco on blotting paper, re-smoked it. My mother, as she again displayed later, after the Japanese capture of the Colony, was a brave woman. Once her finger was crushed in a car door, but to avoid upsetting us she said nothing until we realised that blood was dripping on to the floor.

When I left Hong Kong in late 1937 to come back to Tonbridge after passing Common Entrance, I had no idea I would not see the place again until 1951. My parents came back on leave to England in the summer of 1939, but when war broke out, they decided to hurry back while ships were still available. My father was by now running an exchange broking business in Hong Kong and could not afford to be away for long. He waved me farewell from the touchline in late September 1939 when I was playing rugby for a Tonbridge team. I was not to see him again until 1946. My mother followed him back there soon afterwards, taking my sister Helen with her. Peter and I had to be left at school in England.

On Monday December 8 1941 my father looked out of his window in our house on The Peak to see shells bursting in the harbour below. The Japanese had attacked Hong Kong and by December 18 they had landed on Hong Kong Island itself. It was always a hopeless battle. Just six battalions of British, Indian and Canadian troops were there to defend the island, without hope of relief or reinforcement, against over 60,000 Japanese troops from the mainland. The imperial battalions fought gallantly, supplemented by the civilian soldiers of the Hong Kong Volunteer Defence Corps, in which my father, as an old soldier, served as a private with special responsibility for radio communications. My mother nursed in Rosemary Hill and St Theresa's Hospitals, both of which were bombed and shelled. Hong Kong surrendered on Christmas Day when General Maltby decided that no further useful military resistance was possible, but not before the Imperial Japanese Army had disgraced itself with the barbaric massacre of doctors, nurses and prisoners of war.

My mother, in fact, was lucky to survive. During the fighting she nursed a Japanese soldier, who died of his wounds, but she made sure he was properly buried, wrapped in the Japanese flag. When the Japanese took over the hospital at the end of the fighting, my mother, the doctor and ward sister were tied up and taken down to the courtyard because the Japanese suspected the dead soldier might have been murdered. Machine-guns were trained on them while the body was disinterred, and only when the Japanese saw the body wrapped in the flag did they accept what had really happened and release my mother and the others. My father was taken immediately to the notorious Stanley Camp, but my mother was allowed to continue nursing at the hospital for about six months before joining him there. Here they suffered terrible privations of hunger and ill treatment at Japanese hands. When my mother went into Stanley, she hid her rings in her abundant hair, one of them being a large diamond solitaire. At one point she heard that the Jardine Matheson prisoners were anxious to supplement their meagre diet through a black market which existed between the Japanese guards and the local Chinese and Indians outside the camp. The senior Jardine's representative duly came to an arrangement with her by giving her an IOU on a scrap of paper for £1,000 in exchange for the ring, which he then used to buy additional food. My mother kept the IOU and, when she finally returned to England, she visited Mathesons in London, who promptly paid up.

My sister Helen and my mother had gone by ship to Australia in October 1941 to stay with my aunts. When my mother then returned to Hong Kong in late November, my sister stayed in Sydney. She decided to risk returning to England on the Blue Funnel Line vessel *Ulysses*, but the ship was torpedoed off South Carolina. She and other survivors were picked up by a destroyer and taken to Charleston, thence to New York and Halifax, from where, after embarking in the hold of a small cargo ship, they were taken in convoy to Glasgow. On her arrival, she came straight down to see me at Tonbridge, where the kindly Somervells, of whom more later, put her up. She soon afterwards joined the WAAF (Women's Auxiliary Air Force).

From Christmas 1941 until a British naval squadron sailed into Hong Kong to accept the Japanese surrender on August 30 1945, we had virtually no news of our parents, except for a few brief messages via the Colonial Office. They of course had no news of us, and I can only imagine the anguish for them of being in that terrible place, not knowing if their daughter had safely escaped or what either of their sons might be doing. Peter and I, of course, spent the whole period of the war out of effective contact with our parents, first at school and then in the Army. My uncle Bernard paid for our education and guardianship needs from a fund established for this purpose by my father before he left. We just had to get on with things, and although guardians and friends were very kind, it did not make life any easier. In recording it all later, my mother could only write: 'We remained there for three and a half years, and the least said about those years the better.' When they were finally released, my mother resembled a skeleton and my father was in an even more terrible condition, suffering from tuberculosis and beri-beri among other things. My mother came back to Britain to see the children she had not seen for six years and my father was put on a hospital ship to New Zealand and then in 1946 invalided back to Britain, where he died in 1947. When he arrived back here, I was due to go out to South Africa. We had not seen each other for seven long years, and the son he had left on the Tonbridge touchline had grown into a man who had himself been to war. I think he was very proud that I greeted him in my Sherwood Rangers uniform and our mutual reticence meant that we did not know whether to kiss or hug. In the end I think we did both, but I then set off soon afterwards for Johannesburg, little knowing how ill he really was. My parents did not want me to change my plans and agreed not to tell me, a characteristic decision on their part. I was not to see him again, although my mother lived to the ripe old age of 91.

Our trip back to Hong Kong in late 1937 meant that I started at Tonbridge a term later than I would otherwise have done, and so I duly presented myself at the school in January 1938. Tonbridge School was then, and still is, an excellent educational establishment. Perhaps lacking the social cachet of the palaces of the Thames Valley and northwest London, it has always delivered a fine all-round education for its curious mixture of boarders and day boys. Founded in 1553 by Sir Andrew Judde, who endowed the school generously, it has been well managed ever since by the Skinners' Company. It has turned out literary luminaries as diverse as E. M. Forster, Frederick Forsyth and Vikram Seth, and sportsmen, in the widest sense of the word, as outstanding as Colin Cowdrey. My father, grandfather, great uncle and four uncles had all preceded me to Tonbridge, and I was happy to be there too.

Schoolboys make their mark at a school (or not, as the case may be) and then move on, but the memories linger of the unbridled and often irresponsible pleasures of youth, life and love in the company of friends of a similar disposition – moments, alas, that now are only recaptured in dreams. In my case, the sudden transition from school to army and then to war makes those memories all the more poignant, because I had to grow up so fast between the ages of eighteen and twenty-one that I felt in some way cheated. Added to that, my domestic circumstances and holiday arrangements meant that school was as much home to me as it was educational establishment. I owe Tonbridge a great deal.

My memories of the school revolve around the things I enjoyed doing and the people I came to know there, masters as well as boys. I was placed in Judde House, which was then under the fatherly and unique eye of the housemaster, D.C. Somervell. DCS or David Somervell was a Tonbridge institution. Appointed to teach history in 1919, he spent thirty-one years at the school. Another Tonbridge historian, Owen Chadwick, later Master of Selwyn College, Cambridge, wrote this about him in his obituary: 'He was unquestionably a great teacher . . . occasionally in this vale of tears you meet folk who tell you that history at their school was a mountain of useless lumber, a waterless sand, and a heap of dusty skeletons. Whenever I hear such reminiscence, I listen to my own inside and hear a secret whisper of gratitude to Somervell that I cannot understand what they are talking about.' DCS was not only a great teacher, but an historian of genuine scholarship with many publications to his name, including his crowning glory of abridging the ten volumes of Toynbee's *Survey of History* into one. Supposedly he was the model for the dotty bicycle-riding history teacher in the film *If*. With his immense height and curious voice, he was a prolific source of anecdote and recollection, and a target apparently simple, but in fact very elusive, for any mimic – and he could certainly never be dull.

We knew him as housemaster, reclining in his deck-chair on hot summer nights in 1940 while we were cooped up in the air-raid shelter. Or illustrating at lunch the Battle of Marengo by using all the salt pots, forks et cetera within reach. One of us had pushed an enormous slug out of his lettuce on to the table. DCS merely pushed it into the middle saying, 'This can be Napoleon,' and went on lecturing. As he spoke, he often used to pick up bits of food from the table and swallow them. The slug went down as the rest of us stared, too hypnotised to speak. He never read notices in the Common Room. 'If it is important enough, someone is bound to tell me,' he would say, and he usually threw away most of the papers in his pigeon-hole. He occasionally strolled past the cricket ground, though he never took games himself. 'What a particularly stupid shot!' a spectator once said as the captain got out. 'It's not surprising, he's a particularly stupid boy,' said DCS. 'Oh, I'm his father,' the man protested. 'Well, that accounts for it then,' said DCS and strolled on. His eccentricities we loved, and both he and his wife Dorothea were always great fun. She mothered us and, in spite of war rationing, she always fed us better than any other houses.

The life of a new boy in any school at that time was not for the fainthearted. Because I had started a term later than planned, I found myself junior to almost everyone. Those who had arrived the term before in Judde appeared unwilling to welcome any intruder and I had to endure some rough treatment at their hands, led as they were by an archetypal Flashman who, I am glad to say, died of drink at an early age. Fagging was part of the system, involving many kinds of menial tasks, but it was occasionally rewarded with a tip from a senior boy for carrying his books to school or whatever. Beating by the Head of House was the usual form of maintaining discipline, and I can remember some painful moments at the hands of Jack Rampton, who had the strong wrist of an Oxford squash blue and went on to a distinguished career in the

Civil Service. It is perhaps true of any institution that there is a natural pecking order and you do not want to find yourself at the bottom of it for too long; certainly life improved considerably at Tonbridge the older you became.

My efforts in the classroom were competent but not inspired. 'He does enough to get by' might have been my school report, but I did well at Art and won two school prizes, so my early efforts on the pavement at Harlech Road in Hong Kong had not been wasted. I did, however, come into contact with two of the most distinguished intellects of my time at Tonbridge. The first was Maurice Wiles, who spent the war breaking Japanese military codes at Bletchley Park and later became Regius Professor of Divinity at Oxford and a Fellow of the British Academy. The work he did at Bletchley is well described in *The Code Breakers*, edited by F. H. Hinsley, and to my mind was worth more than any number of infantry divisions. He was also a goodish cricketer, a leg spinner and a useful bat, playing with me in the 1941 First XI. He told me in a recent letter that he went on playing the game until 1990. Indeed, a curious thing happened a year or so ago when I was watching television one evening and a young figure appeared on the screen who looked familiar. The programme was about the proving of 'Fermat's Last Theorem', a problem that had eluded the world's greatest mathematicians for 358 years. In this figure I recognised a likeness to Maurice, and I was not far wrong because it was his son Andrew, who had achieved the proof of what many had regarded as impossible. So there must be something in the gene theory.

The second figure was Sidney Keyes, and thereby lies a remarkable coincidence. If anyone were asked to name the two greatest poets of the Second World War, they would probably mention Sidney Keyes and Keith Douglas. The one I was at school with, while the other I served with in the same regiment and was very close by when he was killed. Sidney Keyes came to Tonbridge a year or so before I did and left with a history scholarship to Oxford in 1940. For a time we went to tutor together with Tom Staveley, who taught English and later wrote a very moving tribute to Sidney in *The Listener* in 1947. I would have to say that my contributions to these sessions were limited to say the least, but I enjoyed listening to the two of them arguing about poetry and discussing life in general. I learned a very great deal which I would otherwise not have thought about. Sidney Keyes was quietly spoken and appeared to live in a higher world. On one occasion he was chosen, quite inappropriately, to run for his house in the Cras, the school cross-country race. He did not do very well, and it was rumoured that he had stopped for several minutes trying to remember a line from *Paradise Lost*. Tom Staveley recognised his genius in the poems he wrote and passed to him for critical discussion, writing later: 'He had that rare hallmark of poetic genius, his capacity to hit the ear and eye at once with the impact of a single image.'

Sidney Keyes's first book of poems, *The Iron Laurel*, was published in 1942 and he won the Hawthornden Poetry Prize in 1943. His stay at Oxford was confined to just eighteen months before he was commissioned into the Queen's Own Royal West Kent Regiment in September 1942. Posted to the Eighth Army in North Africa, he was killed on April 29 1943 in the final drive to Tunis and is buried in the Massicault War Cemetery, twenty-five miles south of Tunis. He was not yet twenty-one. Tom Staveley remarked of him: 'His attitude towards the craft of poetry was one of furious urgency and energy. Like all metaphysical poets, he felt death everywhere about him.' One of Keyes's most famous poems, 'The Wilderness', seems to presage his death:

> The red rock wilderness
> Shall be my dwelling-place.
> Where the winds saw at the bluffs
> And the pebbles fall like thunder
> I shall watch the clawed sun
> Tear the rocks asunder.

As Sidney Keyes died in that rocky Tunisian desert, so Keith Douglas and the Sherwood Rangers must have passed him, driving the German army back to Tunis and the surrender of North Africa.

I may not have been much of a poet, but I could play cricket reasonably well. Tonbridge has always prided itself on the quality of its cricket. It possesses perhaps the best school cricket ground in the country, known as 'The Head', situated right at the heart of the school and levelled in 1838. Barry Orchard, a much-loved master, Old Tonbridgian and chronicler of the school, once found a lady visitor staring at The Head. 'I have lived all over the world,' she said, 'and this is the most beautiful spot on earth. I always come back to it.' There are many who know what she means. In recent years Tonbridge cricket has been very strong and I have spent many happy hours on the bank above The Head watching it. The Old Tonbridgians have by far the best record of all schools in the prestigious Cricketer Cup competition, and cricket is always played at the school in a positive and exciting way. We have much to thank Colin Cowdrey for in the way that Tonbridge and cricket have become indissolubly entwined, but it should not be forgotten that Tonbridge cricket was very strong before Colin even set foot in the school just after the war. For this we were indebted to the legendary C. H. (John) Knott as cricket master.

I loved cricket and watched the First XI whenever I could. In my second summer at the school, in 1939, we had as good an all-round side as Tonbridge has ever had, but one that was tinged with tragedy. The captain, P. G. C. Wood, who also captained the Public Schools XI, was killed in action as a bomber pilot over Cologne in August 1941. T. R. R. Wood (no relation) also joined the RAF and was killed in June 1942. G.R. Leahy was yet another killed in the RAF, again in 1942. C. H. Pillman was killed in action as a lieutenant in the 4th/7th Dragoon Guards in Normandy in June 1944, and C. L. Welford, who also won the Public Schools' squash and the half-mile and captained Oxford at squash, died in November 1941. Let no one tell me that our generation suffered less than those at school before 1914. The slaughter of air crew in Bomber Command particularly was as bad as anything that happened to young subalterns on the Western Front.

I had no inkling, as I watched that 1939 cricket XI through June and July, that life was about to become very different. Young boys find it difficult to take much notice of events around them, and I cannot say that episodes such as the Munich Crisis or the British guarantee to Poland particularly seized my attention. The only visible sign of coming trouble was the building of an air-raid shelter on land opposite Judde House in the year's respite after Munich but, apart from that, life continued as it had always done. My parents were home on leave in the summer holidays of 1939, and term did not actually begin until the second half of September, so I was already back at school when they departed for Hong Kong with my sister. Through that first winter the only noteworthy events were the requirement to carry gas masks and the evacuation of Dulwich College to Tonbridge to share our facilities. This was not entirely satisfactory, and I enjoyed the answer in a recent school history exam for first-year boys. Question: 'Which event caused the most damage to Tonbridge School in the Second World War?' Answer: 'When Dulwich College was evacuated here.' The winter of the Phoney War was extremely cold, but for the most part we wondered what the fuss was about.

All this was to change at the start of the Summer Term 1940. By now air-raid shelters had been built for all the boarding houses, numbers in the school were down because of our proximity to the war zone, and a boarding house had to be closed. The Dunkirk evacuation took place in the first half of the Summer Term, and suddenly Tonbridge had become a key defensive point on the River Medway if the Germans invaded. The town became a fortress, with pill-boxes all over the place and an anti-tank trench alongside The Head. The school was on twenty-four hours' notice to evacuate and plans had been made to go to Oxford, but the Chief of the Imperial General Staff, Field Marshal Ironside, was an Old Tonbridgian and his advice was: 'Have everything ready to go, but don't go; if I have any reason to change my mind, I will let you know.' It was not needed.

We saw the Battle of Britain being fought overhead and, in the balmy days of that summer of 1940, watched with great excitement the circling and diving manoeuvres of the Spitfires and Messerschmitts in the glorious blue skies above us. I spent part of my holidays hop-picking in late August and, out in the fields, I could sometimes hear the rat-a-tat-tat of the machine-guns way above us and, very occasionally, one of the aircraft would swoop low enough for us to be able to make out its markings. Once or twice I saw a plane trailing smoke and there would be a low boom in the distance as I strained my eyes to look for the white canopy of the parachute. I cannot in all honesty say that I realised how vital a moment I was witnessing in our country's history, but they were days that nonetheless remain etched on the memory.

Later that year, during the Michaelmas Term, it was possible at night to see the red glow of the Blitz over London. We trooped dutifully into our air-raid shelters until it became clear that Tonbridge was not a target. One bomb landed near the Chapel, but our nights were disturbed only by sporadic anti-aircraft fire and the need for senior boys to do ARP work or serve in the Home Guard. We did have to undertake a lot of agricultural work as a large area of the playing fields were turned into allotments, and weeding became a regular punishment routine, though not necessarily a very efficient one. The school's iron gates and railings were taken away to be melted down into tanks and aircraft, paper was also in short supply and the average age of the teaching staff increased as the younger ones were called away to the war. Much of this was just seen by us as minor inconveniences at worst, but there was also a sense of excitement and a feeling that we were living on the edge. We participated more wholeheartedly in the Officers' Training Corps in the knowledge that the real thing was looming ever closer.

Throughout this period, I do not believe that as schoolboys we were unduly worried about the tragedies and catastrophes unfolding around us. We believed that all would be all right and that Churchill had matters well in hand. The masters certainly never drew our attention as to how serious things were, encouraging us to think that keeping a straight bat and concentrating on our work were more important. At Sunday Chapel the names of those Old Tonbridgians who had been killed were read out, but they mostly meant nothing to us, although I realise now that the older masters were picturing the faces as they sat and listened in the back pews.

My own enjoyment of school through all this time was greatly enhanced by my friendship with Denis Elmore. Since I did not find the company of my own year in Judde House particularly congenial, I sought and found friendship with boys in other houses and with day boys. Denis Elmore was one of the latter, living in nearby Hildenborough, and he and I hit it off from the start. His parents were also old China hands who had lived and worked for many years in Shanghai, where Denis and his sister Sheila had been born, before retiring back to Kent. In Shanghai they had been formidable tennis players, winning the local mixed doubles championship for years on end, and they were really friendly people who helped look after me when my parents had gone back to Hong Kong. Denis was one of those boys lucky enough to be good at everything. He had won an entrance scholarship to Tonbridge and was to leave with a prestigious Smythe Exhibition, awarded for top academic distinction to those about to go on to university. It will come as no surprise, therefore, that he and I were not often to be found in the same classroom. But Denis was also a fine all-round games player, excelling at cricket, tennis, fives and winning the Victor Ludorum for athletics in 1942. So it was on the games field that we regularly came together and this helped to develop a strong and lasting friendship.

He had been at a local prep school, where he had been nicknamed 'Birdie' because of his spare and somewhat threadlike form, his long legs and arms. His quiet and friendly demeanour was in contrast to the more rowdy elements among us, but he could hold his own with anyone by the sharpness of his repartee and the quickness of his wit. He had no malice in him and my brother Peter remembers how friendly and encouraging he was to him at school, even though there was two years' remove between them – a considerable gulf in the hierarchical structure of a 1930s boarding school. He was always neat and tidy, and this was to serve him well in the Army, when he frequently escaped guard duty after the guard commander judged him the best turned out cadet. I hope I do not give the impression that he was too good to be true, for he was as ready to take a few schoolboy risks as anyone and many were the scrapes we found ourselves in. Once, I remember, we were hauled up in front of the Head Boy and School Games Committee for leaving the Colts' cricket gear out overnight. We were probably for it anyway, but under intense questioning both Denis and I could barely conceal our amusement at what seemed an absurdly petty offence, and painful retribution followed for what was perceived as undue arrogance by junior boys.

Denis had the ability to cheer me up whenever I felt low, as I certainly did after the fall of Hong Kong became known, and no time spent in his company could ever be dull. There was a more serious and reflective side to his nature, and I remember him asking me once: 'Have you ever considered why we are in this life at all?' I think he was a little hurt when I replied with some flippant remark. But what pleased me more than anything was that in our final term at school, the Summer Term 1942, we both won a place in the First XI. I had played in the side the year before, as an off-spinner and batsman, and we ended our season with a fine victory at Lord's against our old rivals Clifton. I also made the Rugby XV that winter, but my main successes were in the boxing ring, where I remained unbeaten in all bouts against other schools by remembering Gerry Moll's instruction. We had a decent cricket season in 1942, and against Haileybury Denis and I had a partnership of over a hundred with both of us getting fifties. We did come a cropper against Dulwich, who had a formidable bowling partnership of Trevor Bailey and Tony Mallett, but we went to Lord's with high hopes.

Denis and I arrived at Lord's together in somewhat murky weather and under a sheltering umbrella of barrage balloons. It was July 27 1942, interestingly about two weeks before the Dieppe Raid, the last attempt to invade northern France before D-Day. By another coincidence the President of MCC that year, whom we met before the game, was called Stanley Christopherson and his nephew, who had the same name, was to become my commanding officer and friend. Lord's in wartime hosted a multiplicity of different matches, including Eton Ramblers v The Forty Club, Surrey Home Guard v Sussex Home Guard and Royal Australian Air Force v an RAF XI, but these school matches were a traditional part of the scene. Sad to say, I did not have a very successful game, being caught twice off my gloves for 2 and 2, though I did take some good catches and three wickets in each innings, with the Lord's slope benefiting my off-spin. Denis played superbly for 78 in the first innings. Clifton had batted first, making 198, to which we replied with 171. Their second innings of 226, slowly compiled, left us to make 254 for victory in two and a half hours. This was in reality too much to chase, and perhaps we should not have made the attempt, for we were bowled out for 174. However, at least when I sit and watch the Test Matches now on television, I can turn to my grandchildren and say, 'You know, I played at Lord's twice.'

By happy chance this was not the last time I was able to sit in one of the players' dressing rooms at Lord's. In 1946, the cricket master at Tonbridge School – C.H. (John) Knott – asked me to ensure that the press did not harry his youngest player, the thirteen-year-old Colin Cowdrey, during the match against Clifton. I duly sat with Colin in the dressing room before play started. However, his two scores of 75 and 44, plus eight wickets, kept him on the field for most of the game and left me sitting on my own.

Lord's was literally the final act of my school career. Tonbridge had given me much for which I am grateful, and I enjoyed reading the words of Lord Home in replying to the question of what his own school, Eton, had given him. He wrote: 'An introduction to life in a large and various company; a sniff of the value of independence; tolerance; self-discipline accepted as infinitely superior to orders; responsibility shouldered lightly; a perception of the fun of living; a recognition that power and authority had to be exercised with restraint.' I could not have put it better. It was time now, however, to put away childish things and prepare for sterner tests. The Clifton match ended on the evening of July 28 1942. Denis and I travelled down together to the home of my Uncle Bernard in Maidstone that night and early the next morning together enlisted in the Army. It had to be early in the morning because my uncle, who was Chairman of The Mote Cricket Club, wanted us to play a game that afternoon. When my final school report arrived a few days later, I found that the headmaster had written: 'If I was back in the Army as in the last war as a Company Commander, I should like Hills with me as a Platoon Commander, especially in a tight corner.' I like to think that he could not have given me a more glowing testimonial, and it made me more determined than ever not to let him down.

CHAPTER THREE **TRAINING**

Less than a month after we had enlisted, Denis Elmore and I reported to the 30th Primary Training Wing at Bovington Camp, near Wareham in Dorset, on August 20 1942. Conditions were fairly spartan – on arrival we had to fill our palliasses with spiky straw to sleep on – but from the first moment I enjoyed things enormously and felt that I had found my niche. We were a mixed bunch in No. 4 Platoon, but the former public schoolboys among us had perhaps become more used to the privations and discomfort of boarding life. We also possessed the advantage of having had rudimentary military training in the Officer Training Corps so knew something about drill, map-reading, rifle-shooting and, in my case, proficiency in signalling and Morse code.

To my guardians the Emtages I wrote in a letter: 'We are worked very hard, but the life suits me down to the ground and I simply love it now. The food is excellent and the pay (17s 6d a week) does me beautifully ... you would love to see us on parade here – we are really very smart, the drill is most efficient and I get a terrific kick out of it all ... Denis and I both did well in the sports. He won the high jump and I won the javelin ... We had the most awful day the other day – up at 5.30 a.m., breakfast at 6.30 and then, in full battle order, we were taken off in lorries to the shooting range and shot from 7.45 until 2.30 when they gave us a sandwich and a piece of cake and marched us twelve miles home across country, with manoeuvres included, in three hours. I felt absolutely dead at the end of it but good fun all the same.' Writing to my brother Peter at the same time, I reported: 'You've no idea what you don't appreciate in civvy life until you join the Army. Just you think as you get into bed sometimes – between sheets and blankets – that we have to sleep on straw palliasses with no pillows unless we use our kit bags. However things aren't too bad and one soon gets used to petty discomforts like shaving in cold water and no bog bumph.'

We were allowed a long weekend's leave during this period, which caused some problems as the only place I could stay was at Tonbridge School, where I could visit my brother. We had a three-mile walk to catch the London train, but from there we could only get down as far as Sevenoaks, so that we then had a seven-mile walk, Denis to Hildenborough and I a little further to Tonbridge. The return journey was just as bad. We also took leave in London, meeting up with my sister Helen and Denis's sister Sheila, who was married to Robert Hobbs, an Old Tonbridgian. We would go to a show and an expensive dinner, and Denis became fond of Helen, as I did of my own girlfriend Elisabeth, who was in the WRNS, but neither of these friendships developed into anything more serious. In fact, sitting in an orchard near Hottot in Normandy in June 1944, I read in the *Daily Telegraph* that Elisabeth had become engaged to a colonel. I could not match that.

From Bovington Camp we moved in early October to 36 Troop of the 58th Training Regiment, Royal Armoured Corps at Stanley Barracks, Bovington. Here conditions were worse. We slept in doubledecker bunks, thirty-four to a room. I lost the toss to Denis and got the top bunk, which consisted of wooden slats with a straw palliasse. We only had a small locker each and had to keep the whole place spotlessly clean. It was freezing cold and the rule was that windows had to be kept wide open all night, whatever the weather. We had to get up at 6 a.m. and parade at 7.45 after breakfast and having made beds, swept the floor, scrubbed the benches, polished our boots and cap badges, shaved and washed. Then there was kit inspection; everything had to be laid out perfectly, right down to the smallest needle and thread (we called it 'bullshit'). After parade it was drill, PT, digging, blancoing equipment and sport. Soon we started on specialist courses, such as 'Petrol Internal Combustion and Diesel Engines' or 'Introduction to Gunnery'. We learned too to drive lorries and then tanks – Churchills or Covenanters – both in convoy and across country. Then in December we went to Lulworth to learn how to fire tank guns.

This training started in rather Heath Robinson fashion, with the trainee gunner sitting behind a gun-sight of a cut-down air-gun fixed on a mounting. Facing him was a miniature theatre stage across which the instructor would, at varying speeds, wind little models of tanks fixed on a wire at which one was required to shoot. This was not entirely effective, but I suppose it was a start. The next stage, limited by the need to save ammunition, was to sit in a bona fide Matilda tank, armed with a 6-pounder gun, shooting at life-size wooden silhouettes of tanks at various distances. To sit in a tank like this for the first time gave me the feeling that real action could not be too far away.

My main recreation through all this was rugger. Denis and I were joined in the Regimental rugger team by Dick Holman, who had been scrum half at Sherborne. I also resumed boxing, after an attack of mumps, and won three tournaments before in March 1943 I passed the War Office Selection Board for Officers and was sent to No. 1 Pre-OCTU at Alma Barracks in Blackdown, where there was further training, including learning to ride motor-cycles. During this period Denis fell ill and consequently, when I joined Sandhurst, he was a month behind me.

So far my training had been rigorous and for the most part interesting, but I had not felt that I was really getting near the actual business of warfare. Sandhurst was to be my finishing school. We started by going over some old ground – general military training, driving and maintenance, gunnery and wireless. But then I moved on to more specialised training on the latest tanks, which in my case were Churchills, and to a week's battle training in Wales. This was the toughest week I had spent so far in the Army. It poured with rain and the wind blew a gale the whole time. We camped out for four nights in one of the bleakest spots on the Welsh mountains, with one blanket each, sodden boots and clothes, and had to do all our own cooking. We had to get up every morning at 4 a.m. and did exercises the whole day with live ammunition and explosives, and at times it was extremely dangerous. However, our troop sustained no casualties, which was unique. On the fifth day, on Snowdon, my Troop Officer, an Old Tonbridgian called Lieutenant J. W. Stone, said that he would take me down a different and more difficult way after our forced ascent. This involved a very narrow ridge, where two women had been killed the week before, and three pinnacles. It was an exciting if nerve-wracking experience and I was glad to reach the bottom intact. I returned from Wales seven pounds lighter and in perfect training.

I felt that I had done well, so I was a little miffed to receive a report from Stone which said: 'A very fit and athletic young man, who has in him the makings of a good officer, though as yet he is somewhat lifeless and lacking in authority. He thinks slowly and is apt to be hesitant when faced with a strange situation and I feel he dissipates his energies over too wide a field ... ' I took some exception to Stone's insinuation that I played too much cricket. Since it was the College who asked me to play, I decided to seek clarification from the CO before the rugby and boxing season started. This I duly did and I was able to play what I wanted. My boxing for the College served me well since it involved me in special training and thus released me from early morning PT, which others had to attend. By this time I was a light-middleweight and had a number of successful fights against the Grenadier Guards and others, before finishing up with a combined OCTU team against the RAF contingent at Regent's Park. It was the first time I had fought in a large arena in front of a big crowd and I was distinctly nervous. Although I managed to win a close points decision against the runner-up of the RAF Tournament, my opponent was right in whispering afterwards in my ear, as we shook hands, that he would have slaughtered me if there had been a fourth round.

At Sandhurst the time had come to find a regiment. My original hope was that I might be able to secure a regular commission in the Indian Cavalry, which was by then of course mostly mechanised and armoured. However, one day I was interviewed by Major Trotter, a former officer of the Sherwood Rangers. He was perhaps swayed by my father's former association with the Regiment, and I found myself accepted. Even better, Denis and Dick Holman were accepted too, although they were in a different troop. Thus my pre-Commission training ended and I was granted an Emergency Commission as a Second Lieutenant on January 9 1944. I was well aware that the war was now going our way, but that it could only be brought to a successful conclusion by the invasion of Northern Europe and the military defeat of Germany. It seemed only too clear that I was going to play a part in this, a prospect that stimulated my youthful bravado.

On January 19 1944 I joined the Sherwood Rangers near Newmarket at Chippenham Park, which was no more than a mass of Nissen huts surrounded by a sea of mud. The taxi mistakenly dropped me a mile or so away, so that by the time I had walked through the mud to report to the Adjutant my shoes and trousers were in a somewhat filthy condition. At dinner that night I had to sit next to the Colonel, Lieutenant-Colonel Ian Spence, MC, who had brought the Regiment home from the Middle East in December 1943 after four years or more abroad. It was quite an ordeal for a nineteen-year-old newcomer. The Mess itself was no more than another Nissen hut, so there was none of the silvered and polished splendour customarily found in regimental barracks. There was no regimental dress either, merely service dress for officers (only the Duty Officer wearing a Sam Browne) and battle dress for the waiters.

Cutlery, crockery and glass were only of War Department standard, as was the food. I was, however, surrounded by plenty of bonhomie and lively chat, and although no mention was made of the battles which had been fought in the desert, a strong sense of the importance of 'regiment' prevailed, and by everyone from the Colonel down I was made to feel very much at home.

The Nottinghamshire Sherwood Rangers Yeomanry was a remarkable Regiment. It is not easy for an outsider to understand the ethos of the Yeomanry. Their origins lie in the old County Militias, raised by the Lords Lieutenants in times of emergency. The Yeomanry were the cavalry arm of these militias, and their officers were generally of a higher social standing. In the Haldane Army reforms of 1907 the Yeomanry became part of the Territorial Force, retaining a degree of independence, but played their part nobly overseas in both the Boer and the Great War. In the 1930s some Yeomanry regiments were mechanised, but as the fourth most senior in order of precedence, the Sherwood Rangers remained as horsed cavalry, a privilege welcomed by the land-owning and hunting class from whom the officers tended to be drawn. On mobilisation in September 1939, the Regiment moved to Brocklesby Park, near Grimsby, the home of its Commanding Officer, Lord Yarborough. Another of its officers was the Earl of Ranfurly, whose wife the Countess of Ranfurly has left a vivid picture of this time in her book *To War with Whitaker*, writing on September 3 1939: 'Awaiting us was a telegram from Dan's Yeomanry saying he must report immediately at Retford in Nottinghamshire. After reading this Dan asked Whitaker (his valet) if he would like to go with him. The old fatty looked over the top of his spectacles and said, "To the War, my Lord? Very good, my Lord." Then we started to pack … We piled camp beds, saddle and saddle bags into the back of the Buick and started: Dan in uniform, Whitaker in his best navy pinstripe suit and myself in a fuss.'

In January 1940, the Sherwood Rangers went overseas to Palestine to relieve infantry on internal security duties. They were accompanied by their horses, and the officers by both their horses and their wives. The Countess of Ranfurly went too, and there was time for a lively social life. Then, after months of relative inactivity, she wrote in July: 'Dan told me the Sherwood Rangers are moving north to Haifa and broke it gently to me that the horses are not coming.' The days of horsed cavalry were over and their new job was the manning of coastal artillery. It was not very exciting, but new vistas were about to open up in March 1941, when orders were received that they were to become an armoured regiment, commanded now by the local Member of Parliament, Lieutenant-Colonel 'Flash' Kellett, who was to be killed on the Mareth Line in 1943.

The transformation from exclusive horsed cavalry to successful armoured regiment was now to take place. Training completed, the Sherwood Rangers joined 8th Armoured Brigade in time to take part in the Battle of Alam Halfa at the end of August 1942, an engagement which successfully blocked Rommel's drive into Egypt. They were then in the thick of the fighting at El Alamein in October and November of that year and joined the pursuit of the beaten German army through Libya and Tunisia, still as part of 8th Armoured Brigade. When the campaign ended in May 1943, the Regiment was still in the vanguard of the advance. In the process, fourteen officers and seventy-eight other ranks had been killed, including the commanding officer, Colonel Kellett, and Colonel 'Donny' Player, who succeeded him. Its story in this period is vividly portrayed by one of its officers, Keith Douglas, in his book *Alamein to Zem Zem* and there is no doubt that it had become a fine fighting force. Now it was not to Italy that the Regiment would go, but back to England to prepare for the Second Front. In December 1943 it disembarked on Clydeside and moved to Newmarket.

It was hardly surprising that I viewed my new posting with a certain amount of trepidation. At Sandhurst I had been able to compete on equal terms with my contemporaries of the same age. Now I was like the most junior boy in school, surrounded by men who were

experienced in the art of war, all older than me and all socially confident. I was expected to catch on quickly in the duties to be performed,
the main one in my case being to lead No. 4 Troop in C Squadron, but
the other officers, with their Africa Star medals and many with MCs,
gave me plenty of reassurance as they plied me with questions about
my background and training. The gentrified ethos of the Regiment had
become a little diluted by this time, so the fact that I was not an Etonian
caused less surprise than it might have done in 1939. The officers were
much more interested in the kind of armoured training methods used
in Britain since they had been abroad. They were impressed by the
emphasis on physical fitness and the need for new officers to learn all the
aspects of fighting a tank, namely driving, maintenance, gunnery and
wireless communication, at all of which I was now proficient. Whether
they themselves were all au fait with these functions was open to question, and in this respect perhaps I was more up-to-date than some
of them.

Foremost among those who looked after me was Stanley Christopherson, who commanded A Squadron and had already won the MC
and Bar. I stood in awe of him, and his paternalistic interest in me helped
me cope with my own father's absence. Even after the war, when I shared
digs with him in South Africa, I still could not bring myself to call him
anything other than 'Colonel'. He had been at Winchester, in the house
of the great cricket sage H. S. Altham, whom he was to visit at the College the Sunday before D-Day. He had rugged good looks and charmed
women of all ages with his debonair approach to life. In South Africa he
would charge into the house we shared shouting, 'Come on, we're due
at the Country Club in half an hour – it's a black tie affair.' Then, fully
dressed in an instant, he would bring me a dry martini in the bath. He
loved his cricket and founded a club in Johannesburg called The Stag-
gerers, who are still going strong. In battle he was a tower of strength,
his voice over the air always giving me enormous confidence and making me determined to do my best. When he came to command the

Regiment, he was often in the front line and fully exposed to danger, and his wartime record of two DSOs, two MCs and the American Silver Star really speaks for itself.

I also made the acquaintance of Keith Douglas, who was second-in-command of A Squadron. Someone must have seen me with my sketchbook and told Keith that I did a bit of drawing because, about two weeks after my arrival, he suddenly arrived unannounced at my hut with a handful of his own drawings under his arm. He showed them to me as he talked and they were spectacular – battle scenes, tanks ablaze, huddled tank crews and the general devastation of war. He had an artist's eye for its horrors and absurdities, and I stared fascinated at what he set before me. There was also an intense self-portrait that I remember. He was warm and welcoming, aware of my nervousness and lack of immediate confidence in such a regimental setting, and he talked to me as artist to budding artist, staying for a couple of hours. I had picked up comments in the Mess about him and knew that he was a writer as well as an artist, but I just regarded him at the time as a fellow officer, with lots of battle experience, who took more trouble over me than most.

Keith Douglas was clearly something of an unusual character within the Regiment. His Christ's Hospital and Oxford background was some-what different from that of the landed gentry officers with which the Regiment had gone to war. Consequently, when he had first been posted to the Sherwood Rangers in Palestine, he was like a fish out of water. This was made worse by his determination to stand his ground and not allow himself to be overawed by the social graces and confidence of his peers. Desmond Graham, a lecturer in English at Newcastle University who edited and wrote the introduction to *Alamein to Zem Zem*, wrote that Douglas found 'an enclosed, anachronistic and extraordinary social and military milieu', while it found him 'insufferably knowledgeable and recklessly outspoken'.

Douglas, however, from his Oxford days had mixed aestheticism and soldiering; while writing poems and painting pictures, he had also been a member of the cavalry section of the University Officer Training Corps. He really did enjoy soldiering and, when he was posted away from Palestine to the Staff, he yearned to return to the Regiment, which he managed just before second El Alamein in October 1942. To do this, he absented himself from Cairo and drove up to the desert to find the Regiment, prompting the celebrated remark from his delighted batman: 'I like you, sir, you're shit or bust, you are.' Here and in the subsequent advance he proved himself outstandingly brave, leading a troop almost constantly in action and eventually being badly wounded when he stepped on a mine.

Stanley Christopherson remarked of Douglas: 'When he joined the Regiment he appeared to have a grudge against the world in general and particularly those of his fellow Yeomanry officers who had been with the Regiment before the war and consisted of wealthy landed gentry ... he was a complete individualist, intolerant of military convention and discipline, which made life for him and his superior officers difficult ... I recall many occasions at various conferences and order groups having to upbraid him for drawing on his map instead of paying attention. In action he had undaunted courage and always showed initiative and complete disregard for his personal safety. At times he even appeared foolhardy – maybe on account of his short-sightedness, which compelled him to wear large thick-lensed glasses.' John Semken, who was also in A Squadron and knew Douglas well from the desert, concurred with this assessment: 'He was intelligent, well educated, very well-read (and contemptuous of any of his seniors who were not), energetic (particularly in pursuit of girls), brave, self-centred with no team spirit and full of little resentments. In short he was a pain in the neck, but he was "family" and I was fond of him.'

Keith Douglas is, of course, best known as one of the finest poets of the Second World War, but if there is a better piece of prose writing about that war than *Alamein to Zem Zem*, then I have yet to read it.

Apart from its vivid descriptions of what it was like to fight in a tank in the desert, it also has some marvellous pen portraits of those who fought with him, many of whom were now my fellow officers. He gave them all nicknames and Colonel 'Flash' Kellett became 'Piccadilly Jim'. Many must have been the clashes between the impetuous and outspoken Douglas and Kellett, who had, as Douglas put it, 'that assumption of superiority, that dandyism, individuality and disregard of the duller military conventions and regulations that made the regiment sometimes unpopular, but always discussed and admired'. Yet, when Kellett is killed – 'as one might say typically, while he was standing up in his tank shaving under shellfire' – Douglas makes it clear how much he really admired him.

One of Douglas's most famous war poems is 'Aristocrats', first published under the title 'Sportsmen', and written in Tunisia in 1943. It recaptures brilliantly the love-hate relationship which Douglas had with the Sherwood Rangers, and the 'Peter' of the poem is the much admired Colonel 'Donny' Player, who had been killed at Enfidaville in Tunisia in April 1943:

> The noble horse with courage in his eye
> clean in the bone, looks up at a shellburst:
> away fly the images of the shires
> but he puts the pipe back in his mouth.
>
> Peter was unfortunately killed by an 88:
> it took his leg away, he died in the ambulance.
> I saw him crawling on the sand; he said
> It's most unfair, they've shot my foot off.
>
> How can I live among this gentle
> obsolescent breed of heroes, and not weep?
> Unicorns, almost,
> for they are falling into two legends

in which their stupidity and chivalry
are celebrated. Each, fool and hero, will be an immortal.

The plains were their cricket pitch
and in the mountains the tremendous drop fences
brought down some of the runners. Here then
under the stones and earth they dispose themselves,
I think with their famous unconcern.
It is not gunfire I hear but a hunting horn.

Yet Douglas craved acceptance and respect from 'this gentle obsoles-
cent breed of heroes', and by the end of the desert campaign he had
achieved that through his courage and resourcefulness as a soldier.
When he returned to England with the Sherwood Rangers in December 1943, he had identified himself strongly with the Regiment and was
in fact one of its more experienced officers as it prepared for the opening of the Second Front. By this time, of course, the Regiment's social
composition was changing, largely because of the casualties it had sustained in North Africa, and it had transformed itself into an increasingly professional and battle-hardened armoured force, ready to take
the lead in the coming battle.

The command of the Regiment was soon also to change. Colonel
Spence, beside whom I had sat at my first dinner in the Mess, was taken
away to a staff job in London, and in his place came Lieutenant-Colonel
John Anderson. It is clear from both the Regimental History and Stanley Christopherson's own diary that this was not wholly welcomed.
The History talks of Colonel Anderson 'descending from the heights
of a full Colonelcy on the Staff ... He was appalled by our Middle East
habits, and introduced us to early rising, PT in the morning and
"Inglese" clothes with boots and gaiters. ["'Inglese' clothes" meant the
conventional uniform attire of the Home Forces rather than the suede
desert boots and scarves which were worn in Africa.] It was trying for
all, but we had learned to suffer.' Christopherson's sense of irony also

shows through. He talks of Anderson descended 'from the Gods of the Staff. He had been a regular cavalry officer and, appalled by our unsoldierly appearance and lack of dress discipline, he determined, quite rightly, to make it clear that we were no longer in the Middle East.' Anyway, he later became General Sir John Anderson, GBE, KCB, DSO, Deputy Chief of the Imperial General Staff.

The Second-in-Command of the Regiment was Major Michael Laycock, whom Keith Douglas christened 'Sweeney Todd'. Laycock was an Etonian of very distinguished military stock whose estate was at Wiseton, near Doncaster. His father was a general and house guest of the Ranfurlys on the day war broke out. His brother Robert was a real dare-devil; he was the first CO of No. 8 Commando when it was formed in June 1940 and later became a major-general and Mountbatten's successor as Chief of Combined Operations. Michael Laycock served with distinction right through the North African campaign, winning the MC at Alam Halfa. He was both an institution and a character within the Regiment, a 'true bull in a china shop' according to Douglas. I found him slightly intimidating and certainly demanding in what he expected of young officers. He was quick to anger, hence his other nickname 'Black Mike', but his anger melted away quickly and we knew that it derived from his determination to get things right. He was devoted to the Regiment, which had been part of his life since well before the war, and he longed to command it. He was absolutely straight and honest – a man who led by example rather than words.

Our very short time at Chippenham was uneventful. Those who had returned from Africa were still taking additional leave and we were reinforced by an influx of about one hundred men from the Lancashire Fusiliers. All our new recruits received basic training, albeit without tanks, as the few Shermans available were being used for initial waterproofing training in A Squadron. We knew by now that, as part of 8th Armoured Brigade, we would be taking part in the initial assault of the invasion of Europe and that time for training was limited. Nonetheless, new crew members were given both individual training to make them totally assured in the exercise of their particular jobs and troop training to teach them to operate together and work tactically. The success of any tank battle depended on quick, accurate fire and for this clear wireless communication between the crew and with other tanks and headquarters was essential.

My own crew of four plus myself contained three desert veterans. Corporal Doug Footitt, the gunner, had already had two tanks shot away from under him in North Africa. He was a steady, common-sense type who hailed from Nottingham, as did Sam Kirman, the wireless operator, who was tough and uncompromising and had also baled out from two tanks in the desert. Then there was Arthur Reddish, the machine-gunner and co-driver, who came from Wigan. He was a good sportsman who enjoyed rugby, cricket and boxing and yet another whose tank had been knocked out in the desert. Only Geoff Storey, the driver, was a new reinforcement. He was from Leeds and he quickly showed himself to be calm and disciplined, a good driver with a nice sense of humour too. Footitt and Kirman were both twenty-five. Reddish was twenty-three and Storey twenty-four. What they must have thought about having a nineteen-year-old novice as their Tank Commander can only be guessed at, but I like to think that I gradually won their respect as together we survived the pressures of training. I had two other tanks in my troop, under Sergeants 'Sid' Sidaway and Kirby Tribe, both of them also desert veterans, so they too had to learn my capabilities the hard way, and I know there were a few giggles here and there behind my back. The only evidence I can present in my defence is what Arthur Reddish later wrote about me à propos the eve of D-Day: 'Lieutenant Stuart Hills was straight from Sandhurst and would be facing his baptism of fire, but we had no worries on that score. He had shown enough during the training period to convince us desert veterans that we had a good tank commander. He was quietly confident and fearless but tolerant and a good sportsman.'

Soon news came through that C Squadron, of which I was part, and B Squadron would undergo some special tank training for the invasion. There appeared to be considerable secrecy and mystery surrounding this training, which suggested that it might not be too savoury. Each squadron consisted of four HQ tanks and four troops each of three tanks, of which mine, No. 4 Troop, was one. The Squadron Leader was Major Stephen Mitchell, MC, and the second-in-command Captain Bill Enderby, who had seen action in Italy with 11th Hussars. Our destination for this training turned out to be the sea-front at Great Yarmouth, where we took over a row of boarding houses. Here we learned to our considerable surprise that we were to train on tanks which would swim – a somewhat alarming prospect as we tried to imagine tanks being launched thousands of yards from the shore and waddling in like so many overgrown ducks to attack the beaches of Europe in support of the infantry.

The concept was officially called the 'DD (Duplex Drive) tank'. It was a remarkable invention and had supposedly been conceived by the refugee scientist Nicholas Straussler, who had come up with a way of enabling an ordinary fighting tank to travel under its own power in the sea. The tank hull had a deck built round its middle on which was fitted a collapsible canvas screen that encircled the entire vehicle and, when inflated with compressed air, enabled the tank to float. Since the screen supported some thirty tons of tank, a less seaworthy craft can hardly be imagined. Driving power came from two propellers attached to the rear of the tank and turned by the main drive shaft. These propellers steered and powered the tank at a speed in the water of four knots, effectively making it a boat. Once on shore, the driver could change from propellers to tracks by firing an electrical charge which discarded the canvas screen and floating apparatus, and hey presto, it became a normal tank again. In the water, the tank commander had to stand on a kind of deck at the back of the tank, rather like a captain on a bridge, to give himself the clear vision he could not get in the tank turret, which was completely hidden by the canvas screen. The tank itself was mostly submerged in the water, which meant that the crew in the driving and fighting compartments were some eleven feet below sea level, and even though, like submariners, they were equipped with the Davis Escape Apparatus to allow them to escape if the tank were to sink, they found this a very unnerving experience. Needless to say we had our doubts, perhaps stemming from the old military maxim that, if you could not surprise the enemy, it was better to surprise your own side than no one at all.

For our initial training we travelled in three-ton lorries down to Frinton-on-Sea, where there was a suitable lake on which we could try the system out. The training tank was a Valentine as the Shermans were not yet ready. In anything other than in calm conditions, the Valentine would ship water alarmingly and its bilge pump could barely cope. Fortunately, we never had to take it to sea, but inevitably there were accidents. Once, a driver misheard an order to form line abreast as one to deflate. The tank sank in the middle of the lake, although all the crew escaped. Unsurprisingly, there were many grumbles from men who thought that 'being a bloody sailor in a bloody tank' was taking patriotism too far, but requests for danger pay, which was enjoyed by numerous navy personnel, was turned down by an unsympathetic War Office. I perched precariously on my bridge at the back of the tank, which was certainly better than sitting inside it, and peered over the canvas screen. I realised fairly quickly that the screen might protect me from the salt spray, but not from a German bullet or shell.

The part of the training we most dreaded was learning to use the Davis Escape Apparatus. This involved descending by ladder into a specially constructed hundred-foot water tank at the bottom of which rested the hull of a Sherman. We would take up our positions in the Sherman, wearing the apparatus, and then the water tank would be filled. Our ears thumped with the pressure and it was pitch-dark, so that I had to tap each man on the shoulder to tell him it was time to

swim to the surface. Some men found the whole business very disconcerting, especially the non-swimmers, and several flatly refused to enter
the tank in spite of direct orders and threats of all kinds.

Eventually 'Black Mike' Laycock was sent for. He addressed the
'mutineers' in his usual robust way, appealing to their sense of duty.
He turned to one of the men and said, 'I remember when you first joined
the Regiment and could not ride a horse, but you persevered and succeeded in the end.' 'Yes, sir,' came the reply, 'but horses don't go under
the bloody water.' Laycock went on to say that this behaviour was dis-
graceful and not in the traditions of the Regiment. Then he tried to
point out the simplicity of the operation by doing it himself. All went
well until he surfaced and, in his enthusiasm to prove the doubters
wrong, removed the apparatus in the incorrect sequence, which caused
him to choke and splutter. There were plenty of smirks concealed behind
hands. My own driver, Geoff Storey, had only joined my crew because
his predecessor was one of those who had refused to use this apparatus, something he found highly stressful.

We duly moved south to the so-called forts at Gosport on the Solent.
We were now given Shermans, which were bigger and heavier than the
Valentine, and we were going to launch into the sea. I had never particularly liked the sea and was more than a little afraid of water, so that
it had taken me some time to learn to swim. I was therefore very apprehensive about going to sea in a tank. We loaded from the quay on to
an LCT and a few hundred yards from the shore the ramp lowered, the
screen inflated and the tank moved down the ramp into the water. The
driver could tell when the tank was sea-borne because on his dash panel
there was a white tube, similar to a condom, which inflated with the
pressure of the water. Once afloat, he engaged third gear and we headed
for the beach, which was generally the Isle of Wight. The freeboard on
the Sherman was higher than on the Valentine, but this did not prevent
us from shipping a good deal of water when the sea was choppy. In
heavy swells the tank wallowed alarmingly and seemed liable to founder

at any minute. It certainly took me a little time to gain sufficient confidence in the whole exercise.

Our final training area was Fawley, where we were given brand-new Shermans which then had to be water-proofed and prepared for battle. For about three weeks we were briefed with code-named maps, photographs of beaches and sand-table models of coastlines – all of which were very comprehensive but gave no clue to our destination, which remained secret. More exercises followed, some of them when the weather was bad and the tides were indifferent. Tim Olphert became stuck on a sand-bar, and Monty Horley, another desert veteran, fired a round which landed very close to where an old lady lived, scaring the life out of her. We were given 'pep' tablets to keep us awake, a seven-day survival pack and tins of self-heating soup, which could be miraculously heated up with the tip of a lighted cigarette. We also had a rum ration, which was certainly welcome.

Our launches to the various beaches were usually made from between 4,000 and 7,000 yards out, so that at four knots it took a long time to reach the shore, especially if the sea was rough. On one occasion I received orders from the Squadron Leader by radio to launch in conditions I deemed suicidal. My own crew and troop were even more emphatically of the same opinion, but as an inexperienced and nervous young subaltern I was very concerned at the consequences of disobeying an order from a senior officer. My concern for the fate of my troop, however, caused me to press the case and eventually he agreed that conditions were too dangerous. Although one statistic records that during the training period some 30,000 DD launchings were made with just one fatality, I have read elsewhere that on Exercise Smash 1 on April 4 six tanks of the 4th/7th RDG 'drowned' with the loss of 6 men in a very heavy swell off Poole. We remained anxious, however, about what the state of the weather and the sea would be like on the great day, because the DD tank was far easier to operate in calmer waters.

By the end of May our training had been completed and it was quite clear that D-Day could not be far off. Throughout this whole period the strictest security had been enforced, because the DD tank was highly secret and was meant to give the Germans a big surprise. We were now, along with B Squadron, at Calshot in our old World War One bell-tents ranged in precise rows. A Squadron, who had ordinary Shermans and would be landed directly on to the beach, joined us in Hampshire, but they were in a separate camp at Hursley. Consequently I never saw Denis Elmore or Dick Holman, both of whom were in A Squadron. Denis and Dick had joined the Regiment about two or three weeks later than I had, so we only had a fleeting reunion before I went off to my DD tank training at Yarmouth and elsewhere. Indeed, I did not see them again until we were in France: the camps were packed with troops and all kinds of equipment and they were wired in and heavily guarded, so that there could be no contact with the outside world.

For some reason Keith Douglas came over to Calshot at the end of May, even though he was in A Squadron and second-in-command to Stanley Christopherson. We went for a walk in the woods near the camp. Although I had not seen him since Chippenham, he had made a considerable impression on me when we had discussed our drawings. I suppose that I was somewhat in awe of him and his intellect, but perhaps he felt that, as someone who had been through the hard North African campaign, he owed it to a nervous newcomer to encourage him and to play down his own fears. For some reason the Quartermaster had become very generous in his issuing of kit as D-Day approached, and I had just acquired a fine pair of khaki drill trousers. Keith rather admired these and I told him I was sure he could get some too, but he seemed to think that the QM would not give them to him. I had a sense that he underestimated himself at this moment, and that he was both tense and nervous about events to come.

Keith does seem to have felt increasingly that he would not survive. Right at the start of the war, he had announced to a friend that he would join a cavalry regiment and 'bloody well make my mark in this war.

For I will not come back.' Edmund Blunden, the First World War poet and author of that classic memoir of trench warfare, *Undertones of War*, had been Douglas's tutor in English Literature at Merton College, Oxford. (Interestingly, Blunden was also an old boy of Christ's Hospital.) Douglas wrote to him just before D-Day: 'I've been fattened up for the slaughter and am simply waiting for it to start … I am not much perturbed at the thought of not seeing England again, because a country which can allow her army to be used to the last gasp and be paid like skivvies isn't worth fighting for.'

Then, on the Sunday before D-Day, much to the surprise of Leslie Skinner, the Regimental Padre, Douglas joined the congregation in the village church at Sway, and after the service they walked together in the New Forest. Skinner records Keith's conviction that he would not return from Europe, although 'he was not morbid about it'. He could talk of and make plans for the days when the war would be over, but then would come back again to the feeling that he was unlikely to survive. He was sure of this. 'We walked and talked together,' the Padre remembered, 'only separating as the dawn was breaking.'

All of us at that time had to contemplate what might happen. I was a little nervous, but I had the advantage of simply not knowing how awful war could be. In contrast, Keith Douglas had been seriously wounded and had lost many friends; he also had to confront ghastly recollections of burnt and maimed men on the battlefield. I believe that he was weary of war and felt that he had used up most of his luck in North Africa. This produced a mounting fatalism as he thought about the hard and dangerous campaign ahead.

So we waited in our camp, alone with our thoughts and fears, aware that battle was close at hand yet also conscious that a supreme moment of history was arriving in which we would play a central role. I sat down to write my final letters to my brother and sister, and one to my far-off parents, who could not possibly know in their prison camp what their elder son was about to embark on.

In his camp at Hursley, Stanley Christopherson wrote: 'The weather at the beginning of June was extremely cold and unpleasant, and we all kept wondering whether there would be a postponement. Sometimes I hoped there would be – a kind of urge to put off the evil hour – and at other times I had a longing to get cracking and to get the thing started.' The answer was not long in coming. In the afternoon of Sunday June 4, the word came and quickly swept round the camp. We gathered our possessions, loaded what petrol, ammunition and food we immediately needed on our tanks and consigned the rest to the lorries of B Echelon. Then we moved in column out of the gate and down to the quay, where the LCTs waited for us.

CHAPTER FOUR **D-DAY**

Conditions in the Channel were unpleasant. As dawn broke on June 5, the dark, stormy night turned to a grey, cold and blustery day. Clouds raced across the sky and the westerly wind whipped the white tops off the waves and into the faces of soldiers and sailors alike. Each LCT was commanded by a sub-lieutenant and midshipman of the RNVR. It resembled an empty shoe box: the rear quarter was filled with engines, galley and bridge, and then between that and the bow door there was a well-deck space for five or six tanks and about thirty men. The naval crew were sick, like most of our men, as the craft pitched and rolled in the heaving sea. The LCT's bow would rise over a breaker and then there would be a stomach-turning, jarring crash as its flat bottom smashed into a trough. I was lucky, however, in that I never really felt sick.

The tanks themselves were securely fastened with steel hawsers and had chocks under them to prevent any movement which might have threatened them or indeed the ship. They were effectively ready for action when we came on board, so that we had little to do in the way of maintenance until we made ready to launch on D-Day itself. Despite the protective canvas canopy which covered the deck of the LCT, our blankets and our clothes were sodden from the rain and salt spray. I was wearing battle-dress, as we had not yet been given the tank overalls which we wore later in the campaign, and remained very wet because I had no change of clothing. The LCT itself was loaded in such a way that it was virtually impossible to move about. The best we could do was to put a tarpaulin over the space between one tank and the next, and try to settle down to cook, eat and sleep. But the deck was awash with vomit, so nobody felt much like eating, and sleep was virtually impossible in such a restricted area and uncomfortable conditions.

We felt that the sooner we commenced the operation, the better. My earlier training in the bleak Welsh mountains had helped to prepare me for the foul conditions, but at least I had then had my feet firmly on the ground. Now the roller-coaster bucketing of the craft made me long for dry land. In the middle of all this, Bill Enderby began to regale me with stories of the landing at Salerno, which did not provide much in the way of comfort; he, for sure, was aware of the dangers that lay ahead. All around us were the grey shapes of craft of different sizes as the armada of more than 5,000 ships slipped their anchors and gathered themselves for action, but radio silence meant there was no exchange of information. The Navy tried to issue us with a rum ration, although its indelible association with the smell of vomit has made it impossible for me to drink the stuff since.

Now that we were on board, we were allowed to open our sealed papers to find out where the landing was to be. The briefing took place in the Captain's cabin. Hitherto all place names at briefings had been in code, for only more senior officers had been let in on the Normandy secret. The Sherwood Rangers were part of 8th Armoured Brigade, one of eight independent armoured brigades put together before D-Day to support infantry formations with the firepower necessary to break through the German defences. We were to lend that support to many different formations during the coming campaign, but for D-Day itself we were to be in the van of the 50th (Northumbrian) Division assault on Gold Beach, on the western end of the British sector. 50th Division was to attack on a two-brigade front, 231 Brigade Group on the right as viewed by us and 69 Brigade on the left. The 4/7 Dragoon Guards supported 69 Brigade on what was known as 'King Red' beach in the Gold area, opposite La Rivière, and the Sherwood Rangers supported 231 Brigade on 'Jig' beach attacking Le Hamel. With the beach-heads secure, the Division was expected to push through and capture Bayeux by the end of D-Day.

The Sherwood Rangers were organised into three sabre squadrons, two equipped with DD Sherman tanks and one with ordinary Shermans. The role given to B Squadron was to swim in, supporting the 1st Hampshires on the west of 'Jig' beach, and C Squadron, of which I was part, was to swim in supporting the 1st Dorsets on the east. These two squadrons were to land at H-Hour minus five minutes, while the remaining one, A Squadron, would land as a reserve with ordinary Shermans straight from the LCT on to the beach a little later. As the tanks reached the beach, so they would drop their canvas screens and fan out along the shore, firing at every enemy position which might make life difficult for the infantry, who were just behind. That at any rate was the theory, but it was not hard to work out that the very task of swimming in from five miles out, taking at least an hour, would be fraught with difficulties caused by the rough sea, beach obstacles and enemy fire. The reserve infantry battalion of 231 Brigade was the 2nd Devons, who would land soon after the initial assault. The total complement of the Regiment amounted to about sixty heavy tanks, eleven light reconnaissance tanks and about a hundred supply vehicles – a command with formidable firepower.

Thus it was that a twenty-year-old military novice, less than two years out of school, found himself in the front rank of the sea-borne assault on Hitler's vaunted Atlantic Wall. We would hit the beach first, closely followed by the Dorset and Hampshire infantrymen, and then by the other components of the assault teams – the Centaur close-support tanks of the Royal Marine Armoured Support Regiment, the flail tanks and assault vehicles of the Royal Engineers and the underwater obstacle clearance teams from the Engineers and the Royal Navy. If I had time to take in the enormity of all this, it certainly did not register. Those responsible for building up our spirit had done a wonderful job, and with the certainty and daring of youth, which admits little in the way of danger or imminent death, I had no doubts that we would succeed.

My own over-confidence even bordered on stupidity, for before launching I decided not to put on my Mae West inflatable life-jacket, thinking that even if we sank and the dinghy did not inflate, I would not only be capable of swimming to shore myself but would be able to support the only non-swimmer in my crew. But I was not even that strong a swimmer and, weighed down as I was by my sodden battle-dress, boots, gaiters and revolver, I would not have gone ten yards in the water on my own, let alone if I had been trying to help someone else. I can only explain this over-optimism by saying that my training had made me supremely fit, probably more so than I had ever been before or would ever be again, and supremely confident too, so that common sense and elementary standards of safety and self-preservation went right out of the window. Perhaps I felt a bit like the 600 horsemen of the Light Brigade as they charged the Russian guns down that narrow valley at Balaclava – 'theirs not to reason why, theirs but to do and die' – although it might have occurred to me that at least they were riding horses on dry land and not trying to drive tanks through thousands of yards of surging sea.

All through that day of June 5, the vast armada of ships began moving out into the Channel. Anchored as we were outside Southampton Water, we could not fail to notice the increasing build-up as it became clear that this was the real thing and there would be no further postponement. Craft of every size and description steamed out from the Solent, Southampton and Portsmouth, and from ports further west and east. Force G, of which we were part, came through the Needles channel, exposing themselves as they went to a still strong westerly wind which made progress difficult. The wind was Force Five, the sea moderate with a slight swell, but with all the craft so weighed down with men and equipment, conditions for the soldiers and the naval crews remained uncomfortable. Above us there was a very high overcast, below which squadrons of our fighter aircraft maintained a reassuring vigil: I remember in particular the American Lockheed Lightnings with their distinctive twin-boom tails. Later in the day, things improved as the wind abated and became more northerly, and the sea swell reduced. Towards evening, the sun even appeared and it turned into what one soldier described as a 'perfect summer's evening; the Isle of Wight lay green and friendly, and tantalisingly peaceful behind the tapestry of warships'. On the flagship, the battleship HMS *Rodney*, Admiral Sir Bertram Ramsay's signal 'Good Luck and Press On' seemed to presage the quickening of pulses. From some ships there rang out cheers, immediately answered from across the water, as the great fleet set sail for France.

The convoys of landing craft were protected by a screen of warships below and by the combined Allied air forces above. Force G made its rendezvous with its warships in Area Z, south-east of the Isle of Wight. As darkness fell, we moved steadily southwards into the lanes which had been swept free of mines. Most vessels kept up with the general pace of the fleet, though some began to drop behind. The sea was crammed with ships, moving slowly in long columns one behind the other and shepherded along by corvettes and destroyers who would dash up alongside and shout instructions over the loud-hailer. All these escorts were painted in blue and white camouflage, and with the signals flying from their mast-heads and the Divisional signs painted on their bridges, it was a surprisingly colourful scene.

Stanley Christopherson wondered if other invaders of bygone times had 'the same rats-in-the-stomach feeling which I had then and always experienced before going in to bat, or ride in a steeplechase'. As night came, we began to prepare for action, sorting out our sets of maps and trying to identify the various place names and objectives on them. We constantly checked our tanks and made sure that all our kit and personal possessions were securely stowed. We ran through our launching drill again and applied the final water-proofing and sealing. In the darkness we were vaguely aware of the shape of ships around us, the noise of the engines combining with the restless sound of the waves and the occasional sting of spray on our faces, although conditions were nothing like as bad as they had been the previous night.

We talked quietly among ourselves and tried to snatch a few moments of sleep, but the tension and growing sense of excitement and anticipation made this impossible. The night was cold and the sea still quite choppy as the flat-bottomed LCT lost any protection from the English coast and began to slide about on the surface of the waves in mid-Channel. Many of us still felt sea-sick, despite the pills we had been issued to counter this, and we had by now been so long at sea that our sense of disorientation had grown. Mugs of hot soup were passed around and these gave us a momentary warmth. All of us were looking forward to the moment when we could leave the ships and sea behind us and get back on to dry land. Indeed, that anticipation overcame any accompanying nervousness about the prospect of going into action.

At around midnight we became aware of a steady drone in the sky above us as the planes carrying the British 6th Airborne Division passed us on their way to the drop-zones around the bridges of the Orne. Although I was unaware of it, a cricketing friend from the year above me at Tonbridge, Sandy Smith, was in one of the Horsa gliders carrying the *coup de main* company of the Oxford and Bucks Light Infantry towards their dramatic seizure of the vital Pegasus bridge over the Orne – arguably one of the most brilliant feats of arms of June 6, and one for which Sandy won the Military Cross.

We were up and about well before first light, and before the French coast came into view. As the dawn broke at about 0430 hours, the picture which presented itself was an extraordinary one. As far as the eye could see, over the rough and grey sea, there were boats and ships. The troop-carrying ships of Force G began reaching their lowering positions at about half-past five. The bombarding force of the Eastern Task Force was moving into position ready to put down its fire on Gold beach and targets inland. The cruisers *Orion, Ajax, Argonaut* and *Emerald* were joined by the Dutch gunboat *Flores* and Fleet and Hunt class destroyers. Above, the squadrons of rocket-firing Typhoon fighters and Mitchell and Mosquito bombers swept over to add their weight to the bombardment that was now engulfing the German defences.

H-Hour on the British beaches was to be 0730 hours, with the armour leading in five minutes before. The DD tanks were meant to be first ashore, taking up positions at the water's edge to engage enemy pillboxes and strong-points. They were to be followed by various specialised tanks which would clear minefields, deal with obstacles and bridge craters, ditches or other barriers. All this, it was hoped, would help the infantry to get ashore, across the beach and inland past the German shore defences, opening up exits and roads for the huge weight of following men, armour and vehicles which still circled offshore. The timing was meant to be precise, each successive wave intended in some way to ease the path for the next one to follow, yet in the course of events such precision proved impossible to maintain.

As the minutes ticked by and the sky brightened a little, so we began to ready ourselves for action. The steel hawsers holding down the tanks were released and the chocks below them removed. The protective canopy along the length of the LCT was removed by the naval crew. Although it was not raining, the wind was still fresh and the sea rough and grey. My battle-dress was still damp, but I adjusted the beret, with its regimental cap-badge, more tightly on my head and felt the security of my revolver in its holster on my web-belt. (Steel helmets were generally not used because of the problem of fitting wireless headphones over them.) I gathered together what few personal possessions I had with me, and what I could not fit in my pockets, I stowed in the tent-like container behind the turret – my shaving kit, a spare pair of socks and underpants, cigarettes, whisky flask and my wallet with a little money and a photograph of my girlfriend in the Wrens. We checked that everything carried on the outside of the tank was tightly lashed down, and when we were happy that all was done here, the crew climbed into their positions inside the Sherman.

Down in the lowest part of the hull, the driver, Geoff Storey, settled behind his controls. Alongside him Arthur Reddish, the co-driver and machine-gunner, squatted behind his ball-mounted 7.62-millimetre machine-gun, which was loaded with tracer to guide his fire to the target. In the turret Sam Kirman, the radio-operator, sat on the left of the 75-millimetre gun, checking the pre-determined frequencies for three-way communication with the crew, the troop and the squadron, while Doug Footitt, the gunner, sat on the right, checking the breech was well-oiled but knowing he could do little until we hit the beach and he could douse the German strong-points. (To fire the gun in the water risked blasting away the canvas flotation screen.) I took up my position on the back of the tank, on my command bridge constructed behind the turret. With the extra height this gave me, I could see even more clearly the mêlée of ships as they approached their lowering and launching stations. Arthur had christened our tank 'Bardin Collos'; I am not sure of the exact meaning, but he later wrote rather obliquely that 'it was an Arabic term and suggested the tank would become a casualty sooner rather than later'. This, he was quick to assure me after the event, was humour rather than defeatism.

Our LCT and others began deploying into assault formation for the run-in to the beach. With action imminent, the knots in my stomach began to tighten. I tried to compose myself, to remember what I had to do, to keep a clear head as the excitement mounted. Around us could be heard the drumbeat of the shore bombardment as the cruisers and destroyers fired off their main guns and the aircraft roared in to their targets. We were now headed straight for the shore and already I could pick out one or two features on the French coast. Not only was our LCT in the van of the assault, but our tank's position at the front of the LCT made it seem as if we were leading a great steeplechase and gave us a feeling of immense vulnerability. Around us were other LCTs and assorted craft, breasting the considerable waves as the spray broke across their forward ramps. By now Geoff Storey had the tank's engine running and we could feel the throb of the 410-horsepower twin diesel. I gave the order for the canvas screen to be inflated to provide us with the flotation we would need in the water, and I checked communication through the headphones with my crew and the troop. Everything now was ready for the moment when we would launch and swim to the beach. This is what we had trained for; this is what the whole country had been waiting for through four long years as we had hauled ourselves back from the depths of disaster.

The sea could certainly have been described as rough, but not for a moment did I believe that we would not make it to the shore. We had encountered similar conditions in training and there was no reason to suppose that 'Bardin Collos' would fail us. The record now suggests that the experience of the DD tanks varied enormously from sector o sector. On the American Utah beach the twenty-eight DD tanks available after one of the LCTs had hit a mine and sunk were all launched from about 3,000 yards out and swam in safely, although so slowly that they arrived a few minutes after the infantry they were supposed to be supporting. Yet on Omaha Beach the picture was very different. Here thirty-two DD tanks were launched about 6,000 yards out, and twenty-seven of these sank; another fifty-one were taken in to the beach by landing-craft.

In the British sector on Sword beach, thirty-four tanks of the 13th/18th Hussars launched from various distances. En route two were rammed and sank, four were disabled by enemy fire on the beach, five more were swamped by breakers and five were taken into the beach by landing-craft. (The tanks were low in the water and difficult to see in their olive-green battle colours.) In the Canadian sector on Juno beach, the majority of the DDs of the 6th and 10th Canadian Armoured Regiments arrived on the beach just behind the infantry, yet many of them were launched much closer to the shore than planned.

Since there were no obvious differences in the specifications of the DD tanks used by the British, Americans and Canadians and since the training of their crews had been broadly similar, it is fair to suppose that these variations were caused by fluctuating sea and tide conditions. The wind and tide were running strongly west to east, which gave greater protection to Utah at the base of the Cotentin peninsula and to the two more easterly British beaches. The distance at which the tanks were launched must also have been significant because at barely four knots they struggled to make headway through any kind of swell, and the heavier seas seemed to be further out. At Omaha, tank after tank went down their ramps, were swamped by waves and sank quickly; only those whose LCT commanders had the presence of mind to drive in close to the beach survived.

On Gold the intention was that the tanks of B and C Squadrons of the Sherwood Rangers Yeomanry would be launched at 7,000 yards, nearly four miles out. It quickly became clear to all of us that this would court disaster. The roughness of the sea, and the slow pace at which we would crawl through it, meant that we would simply be in the water for too long – and the longer we were there, the more chance there was of being struck by a wave that would swamp us, run down by another craft or even hit by German fire. (On Sword, a DD tank was run down by the LCT it had just left with the loss of most of its crew.) Furthermore, as we deployed towards the assault run, the planned discipline of the formation began to fragment. Through no fault of their own, some ships and craft began to lag behind, while others forced their way forward. To launch too far out risked not only sinking or being run down but also late arrival on the beach where the infantry so badly needed our protection.

I am not sure who made the decision to take us closer in, but it must have been agreed between the naval commanders of the LCTs and the tank squadron leaders. If Stephen Mitchell, C Squadron Leader, asked for my opinion, then I cannot recall making a contribution, although I do know that the tank commanders on my LCT strongly supported the delay. We were after all experienced in handling our tanks in the sea, even if we were now doing it in anger for the first time. We knew their capabilities and the last thing we wanted was to founder far out from shore before we had a chance to get into the action, with the added risk that we might not get picked up. So we drove further in.

I could now clearly see the shells from the naval bombardment falling on the shore and the fighter-bombers roaring in to their targets, and every now and then we observed huge puffs of smoke and flame as targets were hit. I began to search the shoreline for the objectives we were being sent in to knock out – the German pillboxes, artillery positions and machine-gun nests. The villas on the beach, many of them converted into strong-points, were clearly visible and many of them were on fire. The distance between us and the shore gradually narrowed until we were about 600 or 700 yards out. My headset began to crackle into life as orders came through. Gradually the LCT lowered the heavy ramp in the bows and I could see the narrow strip of beach and a house behind it: the maps and photographs we had been shown were now coming sharply to life. I instantly felt more vulnerable without the protection the ramp had given, and already I could see both spouts of water where the German shells were landing and the smaller indentations of machine-gun bullets.

As our own LCT came to a halt, so I became aware of others going past us. To our right the LCTs of B Squadron, under Major Hanson-Lawson, were up in line with us and I saw them drop their ramps too. I glimpsed Jimmie McWilliam, a Glaswegian with red hair and a quiet sense of humour who was a troop leader in B Squadron and had already been wounded in the desert. Others were clearly trying to get in closer, and the LCT carrying Tim Olphert and other C Squadron tanks went in to 200 yards out from the beach before disgorging its cargo. All those on his craft arrived safely on the beach and in advance of the 'funnies', the specialised tanks that were the brainchildren of General Sir Percy Hobart. The Crocodiles were flame-throwing tanks, modified Churchills towing a trailer filled with fuel which was discharged in a jet up to a distance of fifty yards: this was very effective against pillboxes and strongly held defensive positions. Then there were the Flails with a revolving chain in front of the tank to set off mines. Supplementing these were the Assault Vehicles Royal Engineers (AVREs), some carrying heavy dustbin-like explosive petard charges to destroy concrete obstacles, and others with bridge-laying, ditch-filling equipment or wooden and steel fascines to lay down over difficult or boggy ground.

Stephen Mitchell's craft, which Bill Enderby and I were watching, never did drop its ramp, and later we learned that it had collided with another craft in the night, damaging its bows, so that it had no alternative but to beach. Over the air I could hear some other station butting in, and Stephen's furious cries of 'Get off the mucking air, I'm trying to fight a battle'. Radio reception was extremely poor because of continual interference from other stations – hardly surprising considering the huge number of frequencies we had to use on D-Day.

The critical moment of launching was now upon us. I could see two AVRE Churchills brewing up on the beach – the tanks had been completely destroyed, and their crews killed, by 88-millimetre shells which had ignited the explosives they had been carrying to clear obstacles – and I wondered if this would not soon be our fate too. We were the front tank on the LCT, poised at the top of the ramp and clearly silhouetted, a perfect target for the German gunners. To make matters worse, the steel hawsers holding the ramp were not quite tight enough, and we would be in danger of tipping over when we launched, so we had to wait precious moments while this was rectified. In those few moments a shell slammed into the water just in front of us, then one on the side of the ramp and another on the starboard beam. Sergeant Sidaway was wounded and Bill Enderby too, in the arm, and it was surely only a matter of time before a shell hit us.

I gave the order, 'Go, go, go.' Geoff Storey moved into gear and we lumbered slowly down the ramp and flopped into the sea. Geoff engaged the propellers and we were on our way. I was still standing in my bridge position on the back of the tank, feeling terribly exposed and trying to peer over the canvas screen, while at the same time issuing orders to the driver and crew. The sea was rough and the struts holding the screen were hard pressed to do their job properly; possibly the screen itself had been damaged by one of the shells. At any rate, without it we would not be able to keep afloat for long. We had gone about fifty to seventy yards in the water towards the beach when it became clear that some-thing was seriously wrong and it certainly was not just the canvas screen. The tank was shipping water from the bottom. In the driver's com-partment, Geoff Storey was already knee-deep and he shouted, 'We're taking water fast.' Arthur Reddish slipped into the co-driver's com-partment and engaged the bilge pump; it worked, but the damage below must have been huge and soon the water was pouring from the driver's compartment on to the deck. It is my guess that one of the shells which had landed so close to us had damaged the plates beneath the tank. Here there was no real armour, and this part of the vehicle had been exposed while on the ramp. But whatever the cause, we were without doubt sinking, and sinking fast.

It was clear that we had no chance whatsoever of making it to the beach. I suppose on reflection that there was a certain irony, in that we had just left the protection of a naval ship only to find that we had been effectively torpedoed ourselves. The Sherman DD tank was about to become the Sherman submarine. I gave the order to bale out or abandon ship. Corporal Footitt had the presence of mind to pull the ripcord to inflate our yellow rubber dinghy, and Sam Kirman, our only non-swim-mer, put it over the side. The tank was now virtually awash and we did not have long. I frantically scrabbled about inside the turret to retrieve my map-case, but without success. Trying to work quickly and calmly in a sinking tank is hard at any time and, with shells dropping close by, it was harder still. Everything became tangled up, so I gave it up as a bad job, ripped off my earphones, jumped out of the turret and just fell into the dinghy. All our personal possessions went to the bottom of the sea.

Geoff Storey and Arthur Reddish came out through their hatches, no doubt relieved not to have to use the Davis Escape Apparatus, and they piled into the dinghy too, though not without Arthur going into the sea at one point. I, of course, was stupidly not wearing my Mae West life-preserver, so that it was fortunate that the dinghy had inflated correctly and not been punctured. The dinghy itself was not large, and we were very wet and cramped, but at least, temporarily anyway, we were safe. Seconds after we had all scrambled out, 'Bardin Collos' fulfilled the destiny of its name and disappeared beneath the waves. The two other tanks in my troop fared little better. Bill Enderby's did make it to the beach, but he himself had been wounded and had to be immediately evacuated. Sergeant-Major Robson's tank also sank, although he and his crew were saved, as were all the crew of my troop.

In all five tanks of C Squadron and three of B Squadron sank, along with five of the 4th/7th Royal Dragoon Guards. The rest made it, although many of them, like Tim Olphert's troop, had been driven in much closer to the beach by the Navy. Monty Horley, commanding a troop in B Squadron, was killed as he was landing his tank on the beach. His co-driver, Bert Jenkins, remembers that they had a shortish swim in. On arrival at the beach, while they were dropping the canvas screen, they were hit by heavy machine-gun fire, followed by a tremendous flash, which set the screen and spare fuel on fire. They all baled out in shallow water and Bert and two other crew members hid behind the tank. Monty Horley and his driver, Trooper Warboys, were not so lucky and were both fatally hit by machine-gun fire as they baled out. Snipers also wounded Colonel Anderson, who had to be evacuated to England and was never seen by us again. Michael Laycock duly took over command.

On Jack Holman's C Squadron LCT, they were first told that they would not have to swim in because of the state of the sea, so they deflated their swimming apparatus. Then this order was changed and they had to inflate again, but on Johnnie Mann's tank this was not possible because of an air leak, so his tank and all his crew's possessions were unceremoniously tipped off the front of the LCT to allow the others to launch. Jack managed to swim in but remembers the difficulty of navigating between the closely packed beach obstacles with mines on top of them: the tank commander had to stand on top of his turret, thus making him feel like an Aunt Sally at a fairground.

Jimmy McWilliam, the Glaswegian troop leader in B Squadron who later became a judge, believes that his tank swam in from about 1,000 yards. It reached the beach safely and, after he had dropped the screen, he put down a lot of covering fire for the infantry, who landed just behind him. He made his way to a fisherman's ramp 200 yards to his right, between Le Hamel and Arromanches, where a German gun emplacement was doing heavy damage to Horley and others. Some of the infantry were now piled on the back of his tank and he was approached by one of their officers, who pointed out a slit trench occupied by Germans. Jimmy moved towards the trench, threw in a couple of grenades and they surrendered. In the midst of all this a French policeman appeared on a bicycle, wanting to know what was going on. Major Hanson-Lawson, B Squadron Leader, now joined Jimmy and they pushed on

A Squadron, with Stanley Christopherson and Keith Douglas, Denis Elmore and Dick Holman, had crews mounted and tank engines running about a mile from land. They could hear the developing battle on their radios, with Stephen Mitchell's shouted oaths at least demonstrating that he was safe. They were to drive their tanks straight on to dry land about thirty minutes after H-Hour, but first their LCTs had to bring them in through the numerous underwater obstacles, attempting as they did so to avoid all the other craft manoeuvring in the vicinity. For a time Stanley's LCT was stuck on an iron stake, fortunately one without an explosive charge on it, until it managed to reverse and come in again. By this time they could see some B and C Squadron tanks on the beach engaging enemy positions. About 100 yards from the shore the LCT Commander gave the order 'full speed ahead' and drove his craft at the beach. When the bows touched, the ramp was released with a crash and each tank slowly made its way through a few feet of water to the shore. Here Stanley saw Bill Enderby, clutching his wounded arm in pain, making his way with other wounded on to a LCT which was reversing out to sea again. He waved to Bill, picked his way through the craters and debris of abandoned equipment and burnt-out tanks on the beach, and drove on inland.

The 1st Hampshires had met stiff opposition at Le Hamel and suffered comparatively heavy casualties, their commanding officer being severely wounded and their second-in-command killed; both they and the other infantry assault battalions on Gold were in no doubt about the value of the armour which accompanied them in. The enemy's appreciation had been that they would have no tanks thrown against them during the first five hours, yet even though Allied armour came ashore with the first waves of infantry, isolated German opposition persisted into the afternoon. Nevertheless, by 1100 hours seven lanes had been opened on Gold, and infantry and armour were pouring inland. Sherwood Ranger casualties on D-Day itself amounted to one officer and eight other ranks killed; certainly the overall figures were much lower than anticipated.

Two days after the landings General Montgomery wrote to his friend and colleague, General Simpson: 'Generally it can be said that the DD tanks proved their value, and casualties were high where they could not be used.' And the Supreme Commander, General Eisenhower, wrote: 'Apart from the factor of tactical surprise, the comparatively light casualties we sustained on all beaches, except Omaha, were in large measure due to the success of the novel mechanical contrivances which we employed and to the staggering moral and material effect of the mass of armour landed in the leading waves of the assault. It is doubtful if the assault forces could have firmly established themselves without the assistance of these weapons.'

Such assessments, even had they been divulged to my crew and me at the time, would not have been much comfort. We were still bouncing about on the waves in our little dinghy, increasingly aware that a battle was going on around us and that we were not particularly well placed either to participate in it or to protect ourselves from it. I was annoyed that I was not only out of the action and bobbing about in this wretched boat but had also lost all my kit, including my identity card, money, map-case and field-glasses. I think I laughed at our comical plight, although my crew might well have interpreted this as mere arrogance. I was certainly very wet and very uncomfortable too. The tidal current was still extremely strong and, flowing as it was from west to east, it was pushing us towards the La Rivière sector of Gold beach.

We were about 500 yards offshore and various options were open to us. We only had our hands with which to paddle, so we had no proper means of propelling or steering the dinghy, and the cross-current was too strong for us to do anything other than drift with it. Anyway, even if we had been able to paddle ashore, we should have been useless as a fighting unit and would probably have become casualties very quickly. As it was, we would sooner or later have been crippled by excruciating cramp from the cold conditions and, if we had simply allowed ourselves to drift, we could have ended up coming ashore anywhere or being carried out to sea. The best bet was to try to hail a ship. How long we drifted for, I am not sure, although the discomfort probably made it seem longer than it really was.

We could see the four other tanks from our LCT struggling to make it ashore; two were low in the water and did not make it. We could also see signs of fighting on the shore, where the infantry had now arrived in strength, supported in some places by DD and other tanks. We could see shells landing on the beach and could make out some rows of wounded being attended to. Two LCTs were on fire and foundering. More landing craft were nosing their way into the beach to disgorge more men and tanks. Every now and again there would be a bigger explosion on land as an ammunition dump or strong-point was hit. The naval bombardment had lifted from the beach and was being directed further inland: already there must have been forward observers ashore to direct our gunners. Overhead, aircraft were still coming in low, seeking out targets for themselves.

Then suddenly we heard the noise of an approaching shell. It exploded a few yards ahead of us, and moments later another landed the same distance behind. We had clearly been bracketed by a shore battery, and the next shell would probably have obliterated us. Just then a LCG (landing craft fitted with guns) spotted our plight. The captain brought it in to us at speed, pulled the five of us out of the dinghy and up on to the deck in a moment and roared off. A shell exploded just behind the boat's stern. We were taken below deck by two ratings, who gave us some much-needed whisky and chocolate bars and wrapped us in blankets to warm us up. We even found ourselves listening to the announcement of D-Day over the radio.

After a while we went back on deck to see what was happening. The LCG was patrolling the shore, and every now and again there would be a crack as its main gun was fired, followed by a burst from the twin machine-guns. A company of infantry appeared to be pinned down behind a sea wall by enemy fire coming from the large building they seemed to be attacking. A tank landing craft with 25-pounder guns opened up on the building from close range, as did a Churchill and two Shermans. Fire from the building ceased.

We saw more landing craft coming in to disembark men and vehicles directly on the beach, followed by some Churchills and self-propelled guns. Then we thought we saw our own A Squadron coming in, and the reserve infantry battalion in this sector, the 2nd Devons. Their job was now to push inland as fast as possible. I imagined that Denis and Dick must be there, and Stanley Christopherson and Keith Douglas. I silently wished them all luck.

All that day we remained at sea. As evening came, there were one or two sporadic bombing attacks but no damage to ships as far as I could see. Smoke and haze still hung over Gold beach, yet through it we could see all types of landing craft which had been driven on to the beach and were now stranded on obstacles and unable to get off. The odd body was floating with the tide. The battle itself may have moved further inland, but plenty of evidence remained as to the intensity of the struggle for the beach. We managed to get down some more food and then snatched some sleep, because by then we were dog-tired.

As morning came on D+1, the beach itself was silent of the noises of battle, except for the odd shell, but it was a hive of activity and there was a constant hum of motors and machinery as endless rows of ships moved in to land their cargoes of men and materials. Above us the skies were busy as fighter aircraft patrolled overhead, and further out to sea we were still aware of the presence of the big ships firing their main armament inland. The weight and complexity of the build-up gave us confidence that things must be going well. We wondered where the Sherwood Rangers were now and what casualties they might have taken.

And what was to become of us? The LCG was returning to England shortly and the idea of us going with it was not unattractive, but we were now very much in the hands of the Navy and in the end they made the decision for us. Perhaps feeling that we had outstayed our welcome, in the afternoon of D+1 they fished an abandoned dinghy out of the water, held it for us while we clambered in and wished us luck. We hardly had time to utter our thanks for their hospitality before they were gone into the distance. All that we could do was to take hold of the paddle and make for the shore, which took about half an hour. Between us we had one tin hat, my revolver and the clothes we stood up in. The Beachmaster, a jovial old captain, watched this rather ignominious and sheepish invasion force coming ashore and said: 'This will swing the balance in Montgomery's favour; there'll be consternation in Berlin.' We were about to rejoin the war.

CHAPTER FIVE **BATTLE**

That night of D+1 we spent huddled under tarpaulins on Gold beach. The beach area was flat and studded with boulders, rising gently to houses and villas dotted along the edge of the shore. Debris from the attack could be seen everywhere – the burnt-out hulks of tanks, shattered slabs of concrete obstacles, pieces of individual soldiers' equipment and numerous shell-holes. To add to the sense of clutter, a stream of troop reinforcements and vehicles continued to land and pick their way carefully off the beach to the marked exits. There was very little bombing, although the sky was coloured by wasted tracers and desultory anti-aircraft fire. We felt as though we had arrived late for a party and all the other guests had moved on without us. Certainly we did not have a clue where the Regiment was or how we would find it. After scrounging breakfast on June 8 from a group of Engineers working on the beach, we set off inland. My crew were clearly looking to me for a lead, although I felt by no means confident about what might prove a lengthy search. Snipers were active, so we walked in irregular file along the lanes in the general direction of Bayeux, which I knew had been one of the D-Day objectives.

Eventually, more by luck than judgement, we located the Brigade's Forward Delivery Squadron, where the replacement tanks had been concentrated. To my amazement the first person I saw was Denis Elmore, who had come ashore on D-Day with A Squadron. He was even more amazed to see me, because I had been posted 'Missing' on D-Day and he thought that I must be dead. The Padre had recorded in his diary on June 7: 'No news of Lt Hills or his crew. No body or grave.'

We stayed for about three days at the FDS. The Regiment was fighting fiercely but our orders were to remain here and to re-equip ourselves. This we did by appropriating one of the brand-new Shermans which were lined up there, armed with a 75-millimetre gun and two machine-guns. The crew tested the vehicle and pronounced it ready for battle, and we acquired essential items of personal kit to replace those we had lost in the sea. But still we waited for orders.

Gradually we absorbed news of what the Regiment had been doing in our absence. On D-Day itself A Squadron had driven four miles inland, fighting with the Essex Regiment to capture the high ground just outside Bayeux. The town was duly attacked and captured on June 7 without any significant German resistance, and the population turned out in considerable force to welcome their liberators. On the next day, June 8, all the armoured regiments of 8th Armoured Brigade moved south in a column, and the Sherwood Rangers were ordered to occupy some high ground known as Point 103, overlooking the village of St Pierre. Here they took up fire positions in the trees above the village, which appeared to be deserted. St Pierre was typical of small Norman villages in the area, the houses at the centre surrounded by high hedges which bordered narrow roads and farming land.

As no infantry had yet arrived, Keith Douglas and his bosom friend, John Bethell-Fox, both in A Squadron, went down on foot to the village and made some sort of contact with civilians who had taken refuge in the cellars of the houses. Both of them spoke excellent French. Eventually they persuaded an old man to come out of hiding, and he told them there were Germans in the village and tanks in the vicinity. On their way back they ran into a German patrol, but the meeting was so unexpected that both sides ran in different directions, with Keith Douglas emptying his revolver fruitlessly in the general direction of the enemy.

So far regimental casualties had been very light. This was now to change as the Germans recovered from their initial surprise and resistance began to stiffen. On the morning of June 9, Point 103 became increasingly uncomfortable as German mortar and shellfire found the range of what was a very prominent landmark. Enemy tanks were now observed down in St Pierre, and although the trees gave some cover, it was impossible to find a hull-down position, so that every time our tanks came forward to engage the German tanks below, they became a sitting target on the sky-line. Three tanks were knocked out and Lieutenant Peter Pepler of B Squadron was killed by a piece of shrapnel when returning to his tank under fire.

During a lull in the shelling, Douglas and Bethell-Fox set off again on foot to go down into St Pierre. Quite what the purpose was of this little adventure remains a mystery, but they left their tanks untenanted and it was done without the orders, permission or knowledge of Stanley Christopherson, their Squadron Leader. John Bethell-Fox managed to get back safely, but Keith Douglas was caught by a mortar shell and killed while he was running along a ditch towards the safety of his tank.

Padre Skinner heard of Keith's death that evening at B Echelon and remembered their conversation as they had walked in the New Forest after church service just before D-Day. He asked permission to go forward to recover the body, but the acting CO, Michael Laycock, refused this request because the enemy were dug in with tank support and commanded the ground where Keith lay. The next day the Padre was able to make his way to the spot, where he was surprised to find the body quite unmarked. He could only think that Keith had been killed by the airburst of a shell close above his head whose explosive force had forced a tiny splinter into his body or just ruptured vital internal organs. It is idle to speculate whether there might be some connection between

Douglas's increasing fatalism in the period before D-Day and his early death in France. Perhaps he had just become used to taking risks, proving his courage under fire time and time again, and now he had simply taken one unnecessary risk too many.

The Padre buried Douglas himself, close beside the hedge where he had been killed, and, though under sporadic rifle fire, he read the brief order of service over the grave. He found himself deeply affected. He then made a rough sketch map of the site, recording where he had buried both Douglas and Pepler, and forwarded it to the Graves Registration Unit and to Mrs Myrtle Kellett, widow of the Colonel killed in North Africa, who acted as Regimental Welfare Officer from her home in London. He noted on the map: 'Buried in open. Certain to be reburied.' Keith Douglas now lies more permanently honoured in Tilly-sur-Seulles War Cemetery, among about a thousand other casualties of the heavy fighting in this vicinity. He was twenty-four years old.

Worse was to follow on June 11. By this time heavy fighting had erupted around Point 103 as a determined German counter-attack developed: it involved both infantry and tanks and caused particularly heavy losses to the 24th Lancers. The Sherwood Rangers had been withdrawn a couple of miles to rest on the afternoon of June 9, but the next day they were back on Point 103 and down in the village of St Pierre. On June 11 two squadrons moved out towards Tilly to co-operate with 7th Armoured Division, while B Squadron remained in St Pierre with Regimental Headquarters. A conference was being held with the infantry in a farmhouse on the outskirts of the village. As the conference ended, a group emerged from the farmhouse and paused briefly beside the nearby command tank (known as 'Robin Hood') parked near the door. At that moment a heavy 105-millimetre shell landed beside the tank. It killed outright the acting CO, Michael Laycock, the Adjutant, George Jones, and the Intelligence Officer, Lawrence Head. Three others in the group were wounded, including Patrick McCraith, Recce Troop Leader. It was a devastating blow to the Regiment at such a crucial time. The command tank was destroyed but fortunately the tanks of the second-in-command (known as 'Little John'), the Adjutant ('Friar Tuck') and the Signals Officer ('Maid Marian') were undamaged.

Michael Laycock had joined the Sherwood Rangers before the war and fought right through North Africa with them. Though satirised by Keith Douglas and occasionally abrupt, with a considerable temper, he was as brave as a lion and would never ask any man to do what he was not prepared to do himself. To command the Regiment like his father before him had been his life's ambition. George Jones had had a very different path in life. He was the younger son of the head woodsman of the Laycock estate at Wiseton and had originally joined as a trooper, rising up through the ranks to sergeant-major and then becoming an officer at the start of the North African campaign. He had received just an elementary village-school education but he was hugely efficient and highly respected. The somewhat feudal relationship between himself and Laycock reached a moving and appropriate ending as they were buried side by side in the nearby orchard at dusk on that day, amid a determined enemy counter-attack on St Pierre and Point 103 which resulted in Brigadier Cracroft and his Brigade Major, Lawrence Biddle, being wounded. Later Laycock and Jones were reburied in Tilly-sur-Seulles with Keith Douglas.

Without doubt one of the stalwarts of this difficult time was the Padre, Leslie Skinner. He was a short, dark man with a very pronounced Yorkshire accent who had completed his training as a Presbyterian Minister in 1941 and then volunteered as an Army Chaplain. In March 1944 he became the senior of the four chaplains in the 8th Armoured Brigade and attached himself to the Sherwood Rangers. He always exuded energy and good humour, and he introduced his first service in Normandy with the words: 'There are no atheists in a slit trench.' This remark recalled an incident the day before when he had been forced to take refuge in just such a trench during shelling with four other men, all of whom were busy praying. He had as difficult and stressful a job as anyone in the fighting units, and he himself never shirked danger. He believed it his duty personally to bury all fatal casualties, often under fire, and to hold a brief service for them. He was indefatigable in visiting the wounded, writing to next of kin, sorting out the personal effects of those killed and generally circulating around the Regiment to cheer people up and hold impromptu services. He also kept both a daily diary and a meticulous Casualty Book, in which he recorded and updated all those killed, wounded and missing.

Skinner's diary also bears graphic testimony to the gruesome job he took upon himself of removing dead bodies from burnt-out tanks. In a later entry for August 17 he was to write: 'Buried the three dead and tried to reach remaining dead in tanks still too hot and burning. Place absolute shambles. Infantry dead and some Germans lying around. Horrible mess. Fearful job picking up bits and pieces and re-assembling for identification and putting in blankets for burial. Squadron Leader offered to lend me some men to help. Refused. Less men who live and fight in tanks have to do with this side of things the better. They know it happens but to force it on their attention is not good. My job. This was more than normally sick-making. Really ill – vomiting.' He was a remarkable and much-loved man.

While all this was going on, I remained at the Forward Delivery Squadron, awaiting orders. Vague items of news filtered through, notably the death of Michael Laycock, but I cannot remember hearing about Keith Douglas until I rejoined the Regiment. Orders finally arrived on Tuesday June 13. We set out in our spanking new Sherman through roads and fields littered with the bloated corpses of dead cattle, besieged by flies and by now stinking to high heaven. Here and there were the unburied bodies of soldiers of both sides, grotesque waxwork figures which seemingly had no connection with reality, and in the narrow lanes we had to take care not to run over them. Apart from the general destruction on Gold Beach, this was the first time in my life I had actually encountered death in both human and animal form. It brought home to me with a trembling horror what I was now going to face and perhaps suffer. I knew then that more scenes of carnage would inevitably follow and to this day I have a detestation of scenes involving blood and wounds.

We found the Regiment resting in a little apple orchard just the other side of Bayeux, where, two days later, Stanley Christopherson succeeded Michael Laycock in command. Theoretically Stephen Mitchell was senior to him, but they were good friends and Stephen did not really want the job, believing with others that Stanley was the right man. (Stanley remained in command right through to the end of the war.) I returned to C Squadron, now led by Peter Selerie, and we had just a couple of days' grace before I found myself in my first land battle.

I attended an officers' conference – the first to be taken by Stanley Christopherson. He brought me up to date with the tactical position, explaining that 8th Armoured Brigade's responsibility was from the eastern bank of the River Seulles to the village of Cristot, with the Canadians on our left and 7th Armoured Division on our right. The main focus of the heavy fighting had been around St Pierre and Point 103 against strong elements of both Panzer Lehr and 12 SS Panzer, who constantly probed our positions. To the south-west, the attack of 7th Armoured Division on Villers-Bocage had stalled and it had been forced to disengage. 8th Armoured Brigade would now be switched from supporting 50th Division to the newly arrived 49th Division, specifically its 147 Brigade. This infantry brigade consisted of 11 Royal Scots Fusiliers and 6 and 7 Duke of Wellington's Regiment. We would be in action the next morning, June 17, in support of this brigade around Cristot.

I went back to brief my crew. Sam Kirman was relieved to find that our troop would not be leading the attack, but we were under no illusions about the dangers ahead: our opponents were from the celebrated Panzer Lehr, reputedly the strongest German armoured formation, and the countryside in which we were operating posed considerable difficulties.

Well before dawn, we rose, dressed, straightened our blankets and rolled them up, placing them under a tarpaulin on the back of the tank. Doug Footitt had prepared bacon and beans, which we enjoyed with tea and our first cigarette of the day. Then we got into our positions in the tank, warmed up the engines and off we went – in a line with the other fifteen Shermans of C Squadron. We arrived at the start-line just before 0430 hours, just as the artillery was shelling the enemy positions. It was not quite light and some drizzle was falling. The infantry moved in single file down the left-hand side of the road and the tanks down the centre. The improving light allowed us to pick out the high banks on either side of us and the hedgerows above them.

Just as a smell, a taste (à Proust, if you like) or a noise can invoke particular memories, so from time to time I find myself remembering what it was like and how I felt as I fought in a tank. Even now, as I sometimes drive along a road at dawn, the morning mist hanging on the tranquil air, I once again experience a haunting feeling of solitude and vulnerability, and a sharp expectancy of danger. I stare at the passing fields and woods with the practised gaze of the tank commander, head and shoulders just above the turret, eyes darting from right to left, scanning the dark shapes of the trees and the misty hollows of the fields, and I recall past thoughts and fears about the dangers which lurked there and I feel anew that gut-wrenching anxiety about what might lie ahead for me in the emerging day.

Our chatter inside the turret was perfunctory and tense; our minds were alert but coiled for whatever instant response might be required. Each crew member had his own thoughts and fears but recognised his dependence on the rest and the necessity of at least giving the appearance of being calm. For the commander this was doubly so, because the fate of my crew depended in large measure on the speed of my response and the clarity of my decision-making. Even at twenty years of age, I had grasped that simple truth. Wireless communication helped me greatly in this respect, because the composure and self-possession of other, generally older and more experienced voices in the messages flowing to and fro gave me a sense of confidence and self-reliance.

In rest and sleep we were safe, but the dewy freshness of each dawn, whatever the time of year, brought with it new fears. The noise of the tanks starting their engines, the acrid smell of the diesel fumes, the stench of decomposing bodies, animal and human, in the close vicinity – all these signalled that the night was now gone and the dangers of the day beckoned. Survival was the hope and prayer of all, but duty and the task ahead drew us on. Was that an explosion, a shot, a thump? Whatever: the day had started and we were on parade.

The stillness on the morning of June 17 did not last long. The infantry suddenly went to ground. Clearly they had heard the sound of an incoming shell which we could not hear through our headphones. It exploded just in front of our tank with a blinding flash, shattering the driver's periscope, and two or three of the infantry stayed down. Tension was building as more shells and mortars exploded nearby. We reached the outskirts of Cristot, where buildings were on fire and there was a lot of smoke. At a T-junction we turned left into the village as a crackle of news came over the radio that our leading troop had been fired on by anti-tank weapons. Infantry were milling around the houses and into the orchards behind. There was the occasional burst of small arms fire, then a longer burst from a Spandau machine-gun. Several dead lay about, and Geoff Storey had to steer around a dead German and then a mangled horse and cart. I led the troop rather cautiously, allowing the other troops to cover us and then covering them as they in turn moved forward. We were constantly wary of fire from anti-tank guns and the hand-held Panzerfausts, especially from a belt of trees just south of the village. We called on Captain Arthur Warburton, who commanded our Essex Yeomanry support battery of 25-pounder self-propelled guns mounted on Sherman chassis, to put down a barrage on the belt.

So far most of the action had been in front of us and we had not yet opened fire. Then an infantry officer frantically called to us to support him in a small apple orchard. His men were in a ditch at the edge of the orchard, held up by enemy infantry in a hedgerow a hundred yards to their front. Our three Shermans went in with all guns blazing. The Germans retreated to another hedgerow further back and our infantry moved forward. We withdrew and I went to report while the crew brewed up some tea and ate their rations. It seemed we had taken the village at some cost to the infantry but with no casualties ourselves. My baptism of fire had been successfully negotiated, but whereas I had come out of it apprehensive and unscathed, I was well aware that this had been a comparatively minor engagement and that my crew had shown no signs of distress or unease.

On the next day, Sunday June 18, we were in action again around Boislonde, sometimes known as Point 102. Le Parc de Boislonde was high ground of largely open cornfields bounded by hedgerows and some woodland. In my troop Sergeant Tribe was now my 1A with Corporal Greenwood my 1B. As we moved out of Cristot, the village resembled a charnel house. A handcart stood in the middle of the road, piled high with bodies, and the German soldier who had been pulling it was half-standing, dead in the shafts. Here and there too were the corpses of British soldiers, marked by inverted rifles stuck in the ground by the bayonet, meaning that the body had been checked and just remained to be buried. The road was not metalled and our column of tanks moved relatively silently. Almost immediately, we came under heavy mortar fire and Corporal Greenwood was wounded, so I jumped into his tank there and then and left Doug Footitt to take over mine temporarily. The mortar shells landing among us produced clouds of smoke, which made visibility very poor, and the infantry were taking a real hammering.

John Semken, who was leading A Squadron, recalled all this vividly: 'The Germans treated us to a spate of very unpleasant shelling. Being shelled among trees is no joke because it produces an air-burst effect, and your tank turret provides no real protection. Well, then it happened

– the infantry battalion from the Duke of Wellington's Regiment burst from the wood in front of us, every man Jack of them running for his life. Everything was abandoned, except here and there a Bren Gun Carrier or half-track driven at speed over the rough terrain with soldiers clinging on, begging to be picked up. We could get no sense from anyone; every passing group shouted to us that "they were coming" and that they themselves were "the last out". We just waited with our fingers on the trigger, and nothing happened. And we went on waiting – and no Germans came.'

The battalion from the Duke of Wellington's Regiment had been heavily mortared and shelled, and they simply panicked, believing they were being attacked by tanks. It was difficult to move for fear of running over them, so we just had to wait to see if any attack on us materialised. The battalion concerned was disbanded after a Court of Enquiry attended by Stephen Mitchell, our second-in-command. It was the only such sign of panic I ever saw in the infantry, which, considering the punishment they often took, was testimony to the steadfastness of the British soldier.

Following this incident heavy shelling began – and it came from our side. The infantry battalion had told their own artillery that a German attack was coming and they put down a barrage right on top of us. Some were not quick enough to batten down the turret flaps under this friendly fire and there were casualties. Among them was John Bethell-Fox, who had his jaw smashed, and Denis Elmore, who was wounded in the back by a shell splinter. Luckily this was not as serious as it sounded, but he was evacuated back to England. It seemed incredible that, although we had joined the same Regiment on the same day, we had barely had a week in each other's company in England or France since January. At any rate, I was extremely pleased to hear in due course from both Denis and his mother that his wound was not too serious and that he would be out of the danger zone for a time. I had been longing for the chance to have a good, long chat with him about D-Day and the time after, but we had just never seemed to get together for long enough.

Later that day we were ordered to move further forward on Point 102. Supported by fresh infantry, we did so, and the next morning we were withdrawn. We remained in the Boislonde–Point 103 area, but mainly in a holding role and there were no further excitements. This ended my first period of action, and we now had about a week to re-group and prepare for our next adventure, which was to be the attack on Fontenay and Rauray supporting 49th Division at the start of the Epsom operation around Caen.

By this time I had become more confident in commanding a Sherman in the battle zone. There were two main types of Sherman. Mine was an M4 with a crew of five and a 75-millimetre gun. The other type was the Firefly, which had a crew of four and mounted a 17-pounder gun that could pierce the armour of German tanks. The advantages of the M4 were that it had two machine-guns (there was just one on the Firefly) and a quicker general rate of fire, and that it was faster over the ground, therefore more effective in support of infantry. But if a German Panther or Tiger tank turned up, we just had to whistle up a Firefly.

The Sherman had its faults, and the most serious of these was a tendency to catch fire too easily, which explains why it came to be christened the 'Ronson Lighter'. At thirty-two tons to the Tiger's fifty-six, it was also deficient in weight of armour, and the M4's 75-millimetre gun could not penetrate a Tiger's armour, whereas the latter's 88-millimetre gun easily penetrated the Sherman. Both the Tiger and the two types of Panther were daunting and fearsome opponents. The Panthers' armament was intimidating: the Panther Mark V carried a 75-millimetre gun and two 7.92-millimetre machine-guns, and the Jagdpanther an 88-millimetre gun and one 7.92-millimetre machine-gun. The frontal armour of the German tanks was also much thicker – 80 millimetres in the Panthers and a massive 155 millimetres in the Tiger, compared to the Sherman's 50 millimetres. In Normandy the German tanks prospered because of the nature of the ground: they could be dug in as immovable defensive obstacles and so their lack of manoeuvrability counted for less. Once the pursuit began, however, the Sherman's greater speed and endurance came into its own and our tanks overwhelmed the German defences in a mobile battle.

When on the move, I sat or more often stood on the right inside the turret, below the flap there. When under heavy mortar or shellfire, I would close this flap and use the periscope situated just below it. The gunner sat on my left, with the sight just in front of him for both the main gun and the upper machine-gun. The gunner controlled the electrical system which swung the turret and fired the guns electrically by means of foot buttons. The wireless operator doubled as gun loader and sat left of the gunner and the breech. The shells were stored on the turret floor, under it and in racks in the turret itself. The Sherman carried about a hundred shells in all, a mixture of high-explosive, armour-piercing and smoke rounds, as well as about twenty-five boxes of belted ammunition for the Browning machine-guns.

The wireless for internal and external communication was behind the gun between the commander and the operator. In the front lower compartment of the tank below the turret, the driver sat on the left and the co-driver/lap gunner, who fired the lower machine-gun, on the right. Both had periscopes under their respective flaps. We all had to be constantly on the alert for signs of danger from any direction, although unlike the German tanks we were not under any real threat from the air. We also carried a huge first-aid box with bandages, burn dressings and morphine. Accidents from crushed feet or fingers as the turret turned or from the recoil of the gun were as much a hazard as enemy fire.

Since there were about forty-five rounds of 75-millimetre shells actually in the turret, it was pretty cramped and I had to be careful of the recoil of the gun when it fired. The empty shells were ejected from the turret, save for a few which could then be used for urinating into when it was dangerous to get out. In a Firefly the gun was much bigger, so there was even less room in the turret and the co-driver had to be dispensed with to make room for the ammunition. I liked to command with my head outside the turret because it was much more comfortable, but there was an obvious danger from snipers and I learned to squat in a crouched position, with my eyes just above turret level, when danger threatened. Under shellfire the turret and all the hatches were closed.

On a rail alongside the skirt of the tank above the tracks was fitted a tarpaulin which could either be folded over the top of the turret as camouflage or pulled out sideways, supported by sticks at the corners, to make a bivouac under which we could sleep. There was just room for five to lie side by side, the commander always at one end of the row so that he would be immediately available if called for. We always remained fully dressed except for our boots, although in freezing conditions we had to rely on our mutual body heat to keep us warm. We wore belted grey denim overalls, with plenty of pockets, and the black beret, and we only shaved when it was possible to do so. We could use the spare links of track we sometimes carried on the outside of the tank as an extra layer of armour, and we could camouflage the vehicle with the branches of trees or whatever came to hand.

As far as food was concerned, we were supplied with rations we could eat while in action: small cardboard boxes filled with biscuits, chocolate and oatmeal slabs, together with pills to keep us awake. We had a Primus stove we could use outside the tank when things were quieter and on which we heated up tins of meat and vegetables, bully beef, soup and so forth. If we needed to cook on something bigger, we would fill a large tin with earth and diesel oil, set light to it and use a frying pan. Drink was supplied in tins of tea, sugar and powdered milk all mixed together: you simply added boiling water. We also tried to live off the land when we could and in Normandy our chocolate and cigarettes could be bartered for eggs, butter, cheese, chickens and

Calvados. Not surprisingly, after days in action the stench inside the tank became almost unbearable, and the fact we often could not get out for long periods of time resulted in regular bouts of severe constipation: we all looked forward to the occasions when it was safe enough for us to stretch our legs and answer calls of nature. Living so close to each other, we tended to drop all formality and the crew called me by my Christian name, yet in action very strict discipline prevailed over the intercom and they answered every order immediately. Trust was a key commodity, because our very lives depended on our ability to work well together: tank crews which fell out with each other were much more likely to end up dead.

Noise tended to be muffled by our headphones, but we were aware of shells falling and small arms fire, which often rattled on the outside of the tank. We did not envy the infantry their vulnerability under mortar and machine-gun fire, but on the other hand we were a big and natural target for the German artillery pieces and the Panzerfausts, which had far greater penetrating power than the American bazooka. In close country such as Normandy the Panzerfaust was a very dangerous weapon because it could easily be operated by a single soldier hiding behind a hedge. Yet the German 88-millimetre gun was the most feared weapon because it was both accurate and could fire a high-velocity, armour-piercing shell on a flat trajectory which made a terrible mess of any tank in its path. As well as these weapons, the Germans also had the MG42 Spandau machine-gun, which was better than anything we possessed, and more and heavier mortars than we did, including the Nebelwerfer, a multi-barrelled projector which could fire sixty or seventy bombs virtually simultaneously. The German soldiers were certainly a match for us and gave as good as they got. The NCOs and ordinary soldiers seemed able to assume responsibility if their officers were killed, and their discipline and training must have been first-rate. I had tremendous admiration for the manner in which they stuck to their well-organised defensive positions under the heaviest fire we could throw at them from both ground and air. Even after the heaviest pounding, they continued to retaliate until they were finally overcome.

We would not by choice have ventured to fight in the countryside in which we now found ourselves. 'Bocage' is described in the dictionary as 'pleasantly shaded woodland'. We would certainly not have agreed with the adverb. The bocage stretches across Normandy from the base of the Cotentin peninsula to south-west of Caen. South of Caen lies the Falaise plain, which was much more suitable for armoured operations, and this explains why Montgomery desperately wanted to break out beyond Caen. The bocage was – and still is – broken country, with pieces of high ground descending into valleys and criss-crossed by numerous small rivers and streams. The main roads were few and far between, but there were many smaller roads and lanes which were usually sunk beneath high banks with thick, mostly impenetrable hedgerows on top. These hedgerows were the result of hundreds of years' growth; they both marked the boundaries of small fields and they kept in the cattle. To make matters worse, the hedges had often curled over the top of the lanes to form a canopy. To escape from these lanes into the fields beyond, you usually had to negotiate a small gateway through which you went at your peril. There were also clumps of trees, larger woods and many apple orchards which were now in full leaf. Villages were dotted here and there, usually clusters of small farms around the church and rarely consisting of more than a dozen or so houses, with lanes coming in from three or four directions. It was all ground ideal for defensive operations. On the number of occasions I have returned since to the area, I am still confounded by the difficulties and dangers of attacking in such terrain. The ground is now more open to cultivation and pasture than it was in 1944, with fewer hedges and ditches, but it would still present a formidable problem for any military commander wanting to operate and manoeuvre through it successfully.

The bocage could be turned into a veritable fortress, and indeed it was. By now, however, the Germans' defences had become thinly spread as they tried to contain the threat of the Americans further west, to say nothing of their wider commitments in Italy and Russia. They were also under almost continual threat from the Allied air forces, who made movement by day on the roads very hazardous. But they were determined to prevent any kind of breakout around Caen, and in this kind of defensive operation they were exceptionally skilled. The Allied tanks would have preferred to stick to the high ground and better roads, but the Germans held most of the high ground and had their 88-millimetre guns placed to cover the main roads with devastating fire. So tanks, in their key role of supporting the infantry, had to go with them into the narrow lanes. They were handicapped by a variety of factors: their vision was limited, as were their own weapons' fields of fire, and it was difficult to traverse the turret in such a confined space. If they did venture through the gaps into the fields, mortar fire would be brought down, while any hedge could have a German soldier behind it, waiting to hit them with a Panzerfaust. If a Sherman tried to go over a bank or through a hedge, it immediately exposed its unarmoured belly to enemy fire. This was no rigid defence either, as the Germans' system of slit-trenches and gun positions was infinitely flexible, and even when they vacated a position, they could immediately call down a hail of mortar and other artillery fire on the attackers as they moved back to take up another defensive position. Aircraft could do little to help unless enemy tanks and formations were caught out in the open.

In almost every instance of our tanks attacking, we went forward together with the infantry. Communication between the two arms was difficult, especially when our flaps were sealed under fire, although later some enterprising commanders put a telephone on the outside of the tank so that the infantry commander could speak directly to the tank commander inside. We needed the infantry to protect us from anti-tank weapons, and they needed our support to deal with the machine-guns and small arms fire which threatened their advance and killed so many of them. Only the massive firepower produced by our tanks, artillery and aircraft could spare the infantry what would have been a completely unacceptable level of casualties. Montgomery not only wanted to avoid the slaughter which he and his contemporaries, now commanding armies, had suffered on the Western front in 1916–17, but he also knew that the British Army was desperately short of reserve manpower. He therefore needed to husband his resources. As it was, casualties among the infantry in the Normandy campaign were very high.

How some of our desert veterans longed for the open spaces of Libya and Tunisia, where tanks could manoeuvre and fight an altogether different type of battle to this close-range slugging match of attrition in which they were now involved, but we had little option and had to endure in our turn. The main difference, apart from the ranges at which the respective battles were fought, was the nature of the ground. In rolling desert, where attacking or defending tanks remained hull-down and invisible in small depressions, there were advantages for both sides. Furthermore, tanks could move at speeds which made them difficult targets, and there was no danger of an infantryman with a hand-held Panzerfaust suddenly popping up from nowhere to fire at close quarters. The bocage therefore posed unfamiliar and disconcerting problems, even for the experienced crews.

Between June 19 and June 23 the Regiment remained in the line, supporting various infantry units in a passive role. The weather was awful, a consequence of the huge gale which had blown up in the Channel and severely damaged the Mulberry harbours. Unloading of supplies and reinforcements had to stop completely for over three days and this badly affected the build-up for the coming Epsom offensive west of Caen. The Germans also benefited because the bad weather meant that allied air activity virtually ceased, so they could move more tanks and infantry into their defensive line without harassment. The offensive itself had to be put back a few days.

The objective of Epsom was to enlarge the bridgehead west of Caen to beyond the Odon river and subsequently to push on beyond the Orne to the high ground north of Brettville-sur-Laize, from where the roads converging on Caen from the south could be controlled. The role of 8th Armoured Brigade was to support 49th Division in attempting to capture Juvigny, Fontenay le Pesnel and the Rauray spur on the western side of the assault area. The capture of the Rauray spur would help protect the main advance towards the Odon by the 15th Scottish Division. The role of the Sherwood Rangers in all this was to support 147 Brigade in its attack on Fontenay. Six new officers had joined in the previous few days and it had been a somewhat rushed process of getting them used to the Sherman and the difficulties of leading a troop. B Squadron was to support the Royal Scots Fusiliers and C Squadron the Duke of Wellington's Regiment, with A Squadron temporarily in reserve.

The barrage began at 0330 hours on Sunday June 25 and at 0430 hours the attack moved downhill behind the barrage. Halfway down into the valley we encountered a heavy ground mist, which thickened the further we went and eventually reduced visibility to a few feet. Tanks and infantry lost contact and everything became confused. Meanwhile the enemy opened up with machine-guns, mortars, the lot, which gave the infantry a particularly hard time. Padre Skinner, who was helping to bring in casualties to the Regimental Aid Post, was himself wounded by shrapnel across his forehead and knocked out. He was evacuated to England and did not return until the end of July. The fighting in Fontenay was fierce and confused, with enemy tanks of 12 SS Panzer dug in defensively to the east of the town, and we did not have enough infantry to take the village. At about four o'clock in the afternoon the attack had clearly run out of steam, infantry losses had been heavy and we withdrew back to the heights of Point 102 above Fontenay to replenish our stocks of ammunition, refuel and have something to eat.

We thought that was it for the day, but at about seven o'clock that evening I was summoned to a conference. We had to go into Fontenay again as soon as it was dark, supporting a battalion of infantry in a silent attack. Worse still, my troop would be in the lead and my tank in front. My crew were not exactly overjoyed at this news, pointing out that a squadron of tanks and a battalion of infantry were being asked to do a job that a force three times larger had failed to do earlier. Fontenay had already proved something of a death-trap and now we were going to be the first in.

We made ourselves ready. Doug Footitt and Arthur Reddish put extra tracer bullets into the machine-gun belts: at night the inside of a tank was pitch-dark and the gunner's sights were useless, but the tracer would help the main gun find its targets. We would have to be careful of our own infantry straying into our line of fire, and Arthur kept some grenades handy in case we were attacked. It was clearly going to be tough, and I was by no means certain that we would be coming back.

About nine o'clock we climbed into our Sherman, warming the engines and marshalling into line. Fifteen minutes later we moved off into the night, over the crest of Point 102 and down towards Fontenay, which was another small Norman village of scattered houses, narrow streets and high hedges. The infantry was in single file on our right, the wrong side for our turret-mounted machine-gun. They were moving cautiously, alert to strange noises and trying to pick out landmarks in the darkness. We passed all the ground we had crossed earlier in the day and still there was no response from the enemy. Perhaps we had taken him by surprise. Then suddenly a machine-gun opened up, the infantry scattered and bullets hit the tank like the rat-a-tat-tat of a hammer. I ordered the tank to slew right and Doug Footitt opened up with his machine-gun on the enemy position and then fired two high-explosive shells which set the two-storey building alight.

Gradually we worked our way through the town. Resistance was unexpectedly light and the infantry was in and out of the houses. I then received orders to accompany a Churchill tank to blast a nearby German headquarters in a château which we duly destroyed. We moved off, with Arthur half outside his hatch and holding a Sten gun to deal with

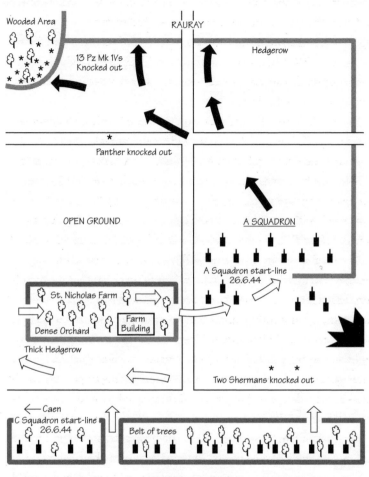

FONTENAY LE PESNEL

any Panzerfausts. By midnight Fontenay had been captured and the road to Caen cut. We stopped and tried to snatch some sleep while we could. It had been a very long day and a tough assignment. My crew were perhaps not quite as undisturbed and relaxed as they had been after Cristot. The strain was beginning to tell; it was showing in their eyes and in their slightly nervous movements as they reached for their

cigarettes or cups of tea. I knew that I had to appear relatively uncon-
cerned, whatever I was feeling inside, and do what I could to raise spirits and lift confidence.

At 0400 hours the next morning, June 25, we awoke, downed a
mug of tea and a bacon sandwich and then moved off again. C Squadron
was lined up along the road to Caen under the cover of a belt of trees.
Our objective was St Nicholas farm, south-east of Fontenay towards
Rauray. It was another murky day with light rain falling and visibility of
about a hundred yards. First the infantry tried to capture the farm on
their own, but were bloodily repulsed by automatic fire. I consulted
my map to try to work out where the main fire was coming from and
deduced that it must be from the farm's apple orchard and hedgerows.
Peter Selerie, C Squadron Leader, decided to take the armour in on their
own. Half of the squadron was on the left of the Rauray road, the other
half on the right. Our Sherman was in the middle of the left-hand group.
Suddenly the attack halted as two tanks on our right burst into flames.
The whole of Ian Greenaway's troop was knocked out. Ian himself was
badly wounded but won the MC for this action. Sergeant Rennie was
killed, and Sergeant Stock, who was now leading 3rd Troop, was
knocked out and very badly burnt. Almost immediately, I nearly suffered heart failure as our tank engine stalled halfway across an open
field. Then the recoil of the gun, which had been just fired, broke the
connection under the wireless set, so this also gave up and we were left
with no internal or external communications. I frantically seized a
screwdriver and, using every swear word I knew, mended the wire while
shouting at the operator to start the auxiliary motor to charge the batteries. For what seemed like an eternity we were a sitting duck, expecting the fatal shot at any moment and only too aware of what had just
happened to Ian and his troop.

Suddenly the engine roared into life and we were off again with the
others. We paused a moment to try to work out where the fire was
coming from, then swung left to come round the farm from behind.

We were now in front and burst through the hedgerow into the orchard, firing as we went. The grass was long and the foliage on the apple trees very dense: the enemy could have been hidden anywhere. We and the other Shermans hosed down the hedgerows and the farmhouse without having to worry about hitting our own infantry. It seemed to work, though, as we thrust out of the orchard and across the Rauray road into a paddock.

We paused a few minutes, wiped the sweat from our faces and checked the machine-gun belts. As we moved on through the paddock, Geoff Storey had to avoid about twenty dead cattle. We moved to the far hedgerow and were just able to see Rauray in the distance. A wooded area jutted out to our left, and suddenly Arthur spotted a Panzer Mark IV. 'Enemy hornet,' I heard through the intercom. Remembering my training at Lulworth, I ordered: 'Eleven o'clock. Two thousand five hundred yards. Gunner, traverse left, steady, on. Enemy tank. Armour piercing (AP). Fire when ready.' The first shot bounced once before hitting the Panzer. There was a plume of blue smoke from its exhaust as it lurched into reverse and stalled. It started to move again and a second shot hit it as it disappeared into the wood. The shots would not have penetrated but they might have damaged a track. This was my first tank-to-tank engagement and it had not been as conclusive as I might have wished.

Meanwhile A Squadron had begun moving up from Fontenay, the plan being that they would come through us and thrust towards Rauray. John Semken was Squadron Leader and he had already heard from C Squadron that there were tanks about, so his gun loader put an AP shell up the spout, just in case. As they cleared Fontenay, they were suddenly confronted by an enormous tank coming round the bend in front. It was hard to know who was more surprised, but John shrieked, 'Fire, it's a Hun', and they loosed off about ten rounds into the smoke. As this cleared away, it was observed that the crew were baling out as small flames came from inside the tank. It was a Tiger of 12th SS Panzer, the first Tiger to be captured in Normandy, and made an impressive sight at close quarters as both its size and the thickness of its armour became apparent. Although the range had been only sixty yards, not one Sherman shell had penetrated that armour. The fire in the Tiger, we discovered, had instead been caused by a shot hitting the side of the driver's observation visor and showering white-hot splinters into the tank. The driver had screamed that he had been hit and the commander had obligingly ordered his crew out.

A Squadron squeezed past the Tiger and into a field on the right where they deployed. During the next two hours they systematically shot up every hedgerow as they advanced. Some of John Semken's tanks were Sherman Fireflies, and they started knocking out one German tank after another. Sergeant Dring claimed no less than four himself, and a Panther was shot up by the whole squadron as it drove across our front, its crew baling out as it was still moving. The German infantry started to surrender, leaping out of the ground under the noses of the tanks, while our own infantry came up to finish things off. It had been a great day. Thirteen Panzer Mark IVs had been knocked out, along with a Tiger and a Panther. The enemy tank force defending Rauray had been eliminated and their infantry overrun. Aggressive tactics had paid off, and at relatively small cost to ourselves. C Squadron had lost two tanks, with two dead and two wounded. I felt encouraged by the way each squadron had performed and this was reflected in the general morale of my troop, in spite of the casualties. We had won a tank battle against significant opposition, and this gave our confidence an important boost.

The next day, June 27, it was B Squadron's turn to take the lead. They sent out two troops to investigate the situation in Rauray but ran into several Panthers which must have been brought up during the night. Three Shermans were destroyed, and Troop Leader Ray Scott and the experienced Sergeants Biddell and Green were killed. By midday Rauray had been cleared and in it were found about eight German tanks, all damaged to some extent, and one Tiger, which seemed to be in perfect working order. We tried to incorporate it into our ranks, but unfortunately High Command wanted it to be taken back to England. Later that afternoon B Squadron ran into more trouble around Rauray, and by the end of the day only had seven tanks still serviceable out of their usual sixteen. John Hanson-Lawson, Squadron Leader, was badly burnt when his tank was hit, and Sergeant Crookes, his signal sergeant, later died of his wounds. He had been with the Regiment since before the war.

The fighting over these three days had been heavy and unpleasant, something to which the steadily mounting casualty toll bore witness. The quality of German resistance had been predictably good: these were troops from crack Panzer Divisions who had already gained much experience in Russia. We had also been handicapped by low cloud, which had prevented our usual close air support from flying. We stayed in the area for some days as the main action developed to the east of us, but we had to withstand determined enemy counter-attacks on the Rauray spur. Our role was mostly defensive and we were able to call down naval gunfire on at least one occasion to break up an impending attack. At one time my tank became bogged down at an awkward moment and had to be towed out, but otherwise there were no further alarms.

Eventually on July 4 we were withdrawn and the whole Regiment moved back to rest in a delightful orchard near Chouain, together with our B Echelon. Dick Holman and I even managed to escape to an Army rest camp back on the coast, where we swam and generally relaxed, with good food and drink, away from the rigours of war. Mail was beginning to come through too and I took the opportunity to write home. Only a month had gone by since D-Day, but I felt that I had grown up rather more than that. I had gained in confidence from handling my tank in action and become more hardened to the sudden shocks and ghastly sights of war. I had known fear but also the comradeship of shared experience and the sheer exhilaration of living on the edge. I knew there would be tough times ahead, but I was now a professional among other professionals and we all knew what had to be done.

Epsom had not achieved all its objectives by any means and losses had been high in both infantry and tanks. But enemy tank losses had also been high and they could not so easily be replaced. Rommel had hoped to put together an armoured force sufficiently strong to break into the British bridgehead, but Epsom had forced him to commit too many of his tanks in defensive roles and it had become clear that the German forces were spread too thinly across the whole Allied bridgehead to contain it for long.

It was the first time I felt things were going our way – a dangerous feeling perhaps when I knew nothing of what lay ahead. But it was incontestable that we had made substantial inroads into France and were now unlikely to be driven out. The Normandy bridgehead was expanding as new supplies and reinforcements poured in and, although the pace of the advance was slower than we might have wished, we had no concern that the tide of battle would turn against us. The Germans were able to mount the odd local counter-attack, but their inability to do more showed that they were under real pressure, not least because they entirely lacked air cover. Although German resistance was to remain strong for another month or more, we felt that sooner or later the enemy would break somewhere along his extended line.

CHAPTER SIX **BREAK-OUT**

Our few days of rest at Chouain were a time for refreshment and reorganisation. It was the first occasion since the landing that the whole Regiment had been together. There were two new Squadron Leaders: Geoffrey Makins, a young major from the Royals, took over A Squadron, and Michael Gold returned from attachment with the 23rd Hussars to take over B Squadron. Michael was a pre-war Regimental officer who had served in North Africa but had then been taken away back in February to give the benefit of his battle experience to the Hussars. It is rumoured that, when he heard of the losses to his old B Squadron, he simply told his Colonel that he was leaving. No one higher up knew of the change until later.

He found a squadron which had been severely mauled and depleted in recent days. He wrote of this experience and his words were later included in Stanley Christopherson's *War Diary*: 'When I resumed command of my old squadron in the Sherwood Rangers, I found that many of my old friends had become casualties. I miss them all and, in particular, I would like to pay tribute to the memory of four sergeants, three of whom were killed in action during June and one who died of wounds received on the beaches. They are Sergeants Green, Biddell, Crookes and Digby. They were great friends these four and were largely instrumental in creating within the squadron an exceptional spirit of friendship and loyalty. They were as proud of the squadron as we are of them. To say they did their duty is an understatement; they were leaders and magnificent examples to us all.'

Dick Holman and I returned from our rest camp to find that the short break from action was coming to an end. Dick had been with me through training at Bovington and Sandhurst, and Denis Elmore and I had struck up quite a friendship with him as we were all much the same age. He came from a well-to-do family of mining machinery manufacturers in Cornwall, joining in the Regiment his elder brother Jack, who later commanded C Squadron. Dick was quieter and less effervescent than his brother and answered to the nickname 'Spam' among the troops. (This may have been because Jack, who had a penchant for bully beef, was known as 'Bully'.) They had both been at Sherborne and were good rugby players. Dick joined the Regiment about a month after me at the start of the year, along with Denis, and both had been posted to A Squadron. Consequently our paths had diverged during the training period as I went off for DD tank training, and we had only caught up again fleetingly in Normandy. Dick was a good troop leader who later won the MC, but I saw little of him in the Normandy battle because the different squadrons operated independently. He benefited greatly from having Sergeant Dring, who was probably the most successful tank commander in the Regiment, as his senior sergeant, but he was always in the thick of the action himself.

The usual conferences and order groups began to take place at Brigade HQ as we prepared again to go into the front line. Things were beginning to go well. The Americans had taken Cherbourg and were girding up their forces for the planned break-out on the western flank. Montgomery was preparing to have another go at Caen, and a new offensive to the east of the city, Goodwood, was in the offing. The Sherwood Rangers were now ordered to support the 50th Division, whom we had last seen on D-Day, in an attack in the Hottot area, to the west of Rauray and Fontenay. One of the crosses which the independent armoured brigades had to bear was to be moved around between different Divisions. Just as you became used to co-operating with a particular battalion or brigade, you were moved somewhere else, but that was the way it was and we just had to go where we were told.

There was a change too in my own role and the organisation of my crew. For the coming action I was to be Liaison Officer between the Regiment and the 50th Division. Frankly this did not involve very much and I was not kept particularly busy over the next few days, but it gave me some insight into the ways of command and improved my map-reading skills. I had to tell my crew that I would not be with them, and I introduced them to Lieutenant Frank Galvin, who would command the tank and the troop in my absence. Doug Footitt would not be with them either, because he had been given command of his own Sherman.

The losses among tank commanders meant that the Colonel was always on the lookout for suitable NCOs to be given their own tanks. I tried to persuade both Arthur Reddish and Sam Kirman to allow their names to be put forward, but to no avail. Both were very happy in their current specialist roles and believed that they were in a good crew. That was enough for them. Sam was an excellent radio operator who could always be relied upon to keep open the line between the Squadron and RHQ. He was punctilious in the way he would check his equipment regularly and, when he had his set 'on net', he locked it and was invariably spot on. Similarly Arthur, as a former infantryman himself, seemed to know exactly what kind of support the infantry needed, and his skills with the front machine-gun saved many a life. Both of them could double up as any member of the crew, and I knew that I was very lucky to have them, so I was not too disappointed when they turned down the chance of command. To replace Doug Footit came a new gunner, Dick Dexter, who had served through North Africa and was also something of a soccer star, playing on the wing for the Regiment.

On July 10 the Regiment moved to a concentration area near Folliot. The previous day Caen had fallen and the British and Canadian divisions involved had pushed up to the line of the River Odon. 12th Panzer Division had suffered particularly heavy losses. Further west, the need was to continue pushing out the bridgehead and to keep the German Panzer Divisions fully engaged in order to distract attention from preparations for Goodwood further east. Over the past couple of weeks Hottot had proved difficult to take, but 50th Division was determined to do so. From July 11 to 13 all three squadrons of the Sherwood Rangers were involved in heavy fighting in very difficult bocage country until Hottot was finally captured.

I could only glean details of the battle from afar as I moved about in my liaison duties. My own tank was very much involved and all its periscopes were smashed by mortar fire. Frank Galvin acquitted himself well, but the infantry again suffered heavy casualties. The CO of the 1st Hampshires was killed and his counterpart in the 2nd Devons wounded. Sadly the Sherwood Rangers also had losses, and one of them was my old tank gunner, Doug Footitt, who was killed in action the first time that he commanded his own tank. Arthur remembers shaking hands with him just before the action as they wished each other luck. 'I'm not looking forward to this lot, Red,' Doug had said. He was buried in Bayeux War Cemetery, and his death made the decision of Sam and Arthur to stay put all the easier to understand.

Five other tank commanders were killed or wounded in this action, bringing to forty the number lost since D-Day. Among those wounded were Lieutenants Ronnie Grellis and Michael Howden, but the biggest loss was Geoffrey Makins, who had only recently arrived to take over command of A Squadron. He was badly wounded by shrapnel while observing from his tank and taken to the Casualty Clearing Station, where he was visited by the Colonel a few days later. Stanley Christopherson thought he looked very ill, although the doctors believed he had a good chance of pulling through. Geoffrey died on September 4 and was buried in his home village of Rotherfield Greys in Oxford-shire, aged twenty-eight.

All this had taken place in a battle which we had been told before-hand would be easy. We had knocked out seven enemy tanks but had lost four ourselves as well as seven valuable crew commanders. The infantry had suffered even worse casualties. On July 14 we pulled out of the line, but we only had three days to train some replacement tank commanders, mainly recruited from the ranks, before we were back in the thick of it again. The Brigadier was becoming seriously alarmed at the rate of attrition and wanted the Regiment withdrawn for longer to allow replacements to be properly trained, but it could not be. He also added that the Brigade had seen more fighting than any comparable unit and that 'the Sherwood Rangers was the best trained regiment in this theatre of the war'. We might happily have traded the compliment for a longer respite.

Our new destination was even further west to the outer limit of the British sector. Around Caumont we relieved the 67th US Armored Battalion. Their commander, Colonel Wynn, had helped train the reg-iment in Palestine on the Honey reconnaissance tank, and all the Amer-ican troops in the area were friendly and hospitable. They wore helmets throughout the day, so we were ordered to do the same. They made excellent coffee and they had the local inhabitants well trained in sup-plying eggs, cream and cider. The line was close to the enemy and there was a lot of shelling, but we escaped without serious casualties. Cer-tainly it was a quieter sector than we had been used to. The reason for our presence was to allow the Americans to re-group their forces for the break-out, but at this time the main action was being fought east of Caen, where the Goodwood offensive began on July 18. The armoured formations involved in this ran into heavy enemy resistance, making only limited progress, and in retrospect I think we were well out of that one.

I used the opportunity of our rest to write some letters and I still have one I wrote to the Emtages in Dorking. It gives a good insight into my feelings at the time, although I no doubt toned down some of the descriptions. After thanking the Emtages for some parcels, I went on: 'I believe I last wrote to you at a rest camp where I had a pretty good time ... I was then sent as a liaison officer to Divisional HQ, which was most interesting and pretty comfortable. I actually only fought one day in the battle, which was pretty lucky. We had three more officer casualties (total now twenty-four) and my dear old gunner was killed – the first time he had been out of my tank since the start, so it was really very sad as we had become good pals and somehow he was not at all happy when he left my crew to command a tank of his own ... If I have learned nothing else about dodging Jerry weapons and bombs so far, I do know that you don't want to sit out in the open and ask for it. I always have that excited, rather contracted feeling when I'm under fire and keep telling myself to keep calm, which at times is rather difficult. When things do get really to such a pitch (as it has done twice to me so far) and you know that the next one is going to get you ... an icy calmness seems to pervade one's mind; it's extraordinary how little you seem to care and we all smile at one another as though we were drinking in some quiet pub. It's only before battle (or after it) that the turmoil takes place and one has to conquer that all-important emotion of fear, which every single man inevitably experiences. Battle is pretty grim, but it's the after-effects and the realisation of losses and dangers encountered that is the other half of it.'

There were two difficulties involved in writing home. The first was censorship, though officers were allowed to sign their own envelopes to register that the letter contained no strategic or secret information. (Other ranks had to present their letters to their troop officer in open envelopes so that they could be read. I cannot say that I was too assiduous in performing this task: more often than not, I just sealed the envelope and signed it, feeling that there was really very little information the men could impart which would break the rules.) The second difficulty was that I felt honour-bound not to worry unnecessarily the recipients of my letters. I knew that they would have some idea of the dangers of fighting a war, but they did not need to be made overwrought and alarmed by hair-raising accounts of what I was actually experiencing and seeing. That did not seem to be fair.

Meanwhile important changes had taken place within the Brigade. The 24th Lancers, formed only during the war, were disbanded in order to provide reinforcements for other armoured regiments. In their place to 8th Armoured Brigade came the 13th/18th Hussars, a regular mechanised cavalry unit. There came too a new Brigadier, Errol Prior-Palmer, who was to show great drive and initiative in the months ahead.

During our rests, particularly in sunny weather, we could not only relax but also wash ourselves and our clothes. We could barter our rations with the local inhabitants for fresh produce, and we could clean our guns, scour the crew compartment and undertake general maintenance tasks on the tank itself. We all joined in this spring-cleaning and it was done in a spirit of boyish humour as we relished the time spent out of danger. Yet our rest in the Caumont area proved all too brief. High Command wanted to continue putting pressure on the Germans in the Caen sector to allow American preparations further west to go ahead unhindered. This breakout, code-named Cobra, began on July 25 in the area of St Lô, but the British and Canadian forces had to keep attacking in order to prevent the Panzer Divisions disengaging and deploying to counter the American threat. So what was happening around Caen was very much part of the 'Battle of the Break-out', even though the Americans stole most of the glory. On July 30 Avranches was taken and Patton's tanks were poised to fan out into Brittany and to sweep round in a vast right hook which would render untenable the whole German position in France. But there was still much tough fighting ahead before this could be achieved.

We prepared for action again. I was now reunited with my former crew and really glad to see them again as liaison duties had not suited me. As a general dog's-body, I felt it a drudge and not entirely productive when compared with what my troop was doing elsewhere. Our Chaplain, Leslie Skinner, returned too on July 25, after his recovery from his wound and recuperation in England. He had had one or two problems with the Army Chaplain's Department before his posting back to us was confirmed. He wrote in his Diary on Wednesday July 26: 'Borrowed motor cycle and went forward to B Echelon. Saw most of men and lunched with the Doctor. Seemingly big attack imminent. Afternoon to 50 Div. HQ to beg Communion Set and linen. Saw Senior Chaplain (Warner) who had not heard that I was back ... Corps Chaplain wanted to know where I had come from and how. Evasive answers and grumble about Army's inability to keep up with paperwork.'

On the next day Leslie reported to Regimental HQ and received details of all casualties incurred since his departure. He wrote: 'There had been a total of ninety-three casualties. Sixty wounded. Twenty-two Killed in Action. Six died of wounds and Missing. Among those wounded at Rauray was Captain Ronnie Grellis of A Squadron, who had proved a good friend to me when I first came to the Regiment at Chippenham Park ... his wounds were severe and extensive. Most of his jaw was shot away and one hand badly damaged ... In following weeks and months I wrote to him from time to time, and more than once the Ward Sister replied on his behalf adding the private comments as to his continual cheerfulness and courage in spite of considerable suffering.' Ronnie was to recover and rejoin the Regiment at Hanover at the end of the war. But how pleased were all of us to have our Chaplain back with us as we prepared to face the fire again. He was just one of those people universally recognised as a 'good man'.

We had a new formation to support – the 43rd Wessex Division, often known as the Wyverns. We would be seeing a great deal of them over the months ahead. The Divisional Commander was Major-General Ivor Thomas, nicknamed 'von Thoma' after the German general of that name. He was a wiry little man with piercing eyes and a long nose protecting a bristling moustache, and he was almost entirely devoid of a sense of humour. He seemed to be one of those soldiers who positively enjoyed danger and discomfort, and he drove his troops pretty hard. The plan, known as Operation Bluecoat, was to punch a hole in the enemy line at Bricquessard, just to the south-east of where we had been at Caumont. Then we would seize the high ground south and south-west of Jurcques, and finally swing east to capture the high ground at Ondefontaine. Little did I know what we were preparing for.

We began Bluecoat on Sunday July 30, the Regiment in support of 130 Brigade, with each squadron helping one battalion. C Squadron's companion was to be the 7th Hampshires. We moved forward and waited for the bombers. Then came the growing roar of aero engines as hundreds of Lancasters came over searching for their targets. We could see the bomb doors open and seconds later we felt the earth shake with the percussion of the bombs exploding. Huge clouds of dust and smoke rose lazily from the target area and we could only imagine what it was like to be underneath it all. We advanced on a one-road front, A Squadron leading the attack on Briquessard, with B following and then us in reserve for the time being. It was thick bocage, heavily wooded and with hills, valleys, small rivers, narrow winding lanes – good ambush country and laced with minefields both on the road and in the fields, for the Germans had been able to prepare their defences.

In this sort of country, the infantry proceeded along the sides of the roads in advance of the tanks, as this lessened the chance of tanks being hit by Panzerfausts. If Spandau fire opened up on the infantry, they immediately went to ground in adjoining ditches and it was then that the tanks had to move forward to take retaliatory action with their own machine-guns or 75-millimetre HE shells. This might involve moving through gaps into the fields beyond the lanes, but we were wary of getting too far ahead of our infantry and they liked us around to give them shelter and protection.

Where the country was more open, the infantry would move ahead and, if fired upon, the tanks would respond with smoke shells to provide initial protection. The tanks would then advance, but the biggest danger was the possible presence of enemy tanks. We could also call up our own supporting artillery from the Essex Yeomanry who would put down additional covering fire. The infantry were obviously unable to advance if enemy tanks were in the vicinity and they could give us no protection from those tanks or self-propelled guns – which were usually the dreaded 88-millimetres – so we would use smoke to give ourselves cover. If we had an RAF forward observer with us, he could call up aircraft, but if we were on our own, we had to get on to Brigade over the wireless to secure help from a spotter plane and then call down the ubiquitous Typhoons.

When we entered a town or village, tanks did the softening-up first by destroying all possible positions where enemy infantry might be lurking. We simply hosed down the buildings with shells and machine-guns, and then called through our own infantry for systematic house-to-house clearance. There was always the danger of Panzerfausts in such an environment, just one infantryman who might be hiding behind a wall or doorway waiting to attack us from virtually any possible direction.

On this particular Sunday, our tanks quickly discovered that the road along which we were attacking was mined. The Teller plate mines were there to stop tanks and vehicles, while the smaller anti-personnel Schu mines were scattered in the fields to catch the infantry as they deployed. We constantly had to watch for Panzerfausts, and David Render in A Squadron picked one up from beside some now dead Germans, who had recently been firing it at him, and handed it in for examination. Next day, July 31, it was B Squadron's turn to lead the advance. The objective was Cahagnes, where the terrain was difficult, soggy and laced with mines, but the objective was finally taken on the next day. We slept inside our tank so that we were ready to move at a moment's notice, but this was a perfunctory arrangement and generally uncomfortable. Cahagnes was a terrible mess, like every other Normandy village we fought our way through: it had been bombed and then smashed up by the guns of the tanks. If any civilians were still there, they would have been hiding deep in their cellars.

On August 2 the squadrons went their own way and our own role became more intense and dangerous. We started at dawn, with my tank about fourth from the front. The infantry of the 7th Hampshires were with us, walking alongside the tank and covering our flank. Then we arrived at a T-junction, which was mined, along with the fields around it. The column halted to allow the sappers to come up and clear the mines, when suddenly a Tiger tank emerged from cover and moved to the high ground overlooking the road. It opened fire at about 2,000 yards and hit a tank further back in the column. With both ends of the road now blocked, we were bottled up and the Tiger was out of our range.

I shouted: 'Gunner, traverse right. Steady on Tiger. Smoke. 1,750 yards. Fire when ready.' Our shot landed just in front of the Tiger and the smoke soon obscured it from view. We fired again, this time just to the left of the tank, aiming to keep plenty of smoke between us and it. Other tank commanders did the same, while the air officer accompanying us called up four Typhoon fighter-bombers off the cab-rank to fire their rockets at the Tiger. We fired some red smoke to identify the target, and then the planes came in, very low and with a tremendous roar. The second plane scored a direct hit and, when the smoke cleared, we could see the Tiger lying on its side minus its turret and with no sign of any survivors. It was an awesome display of firepower and demonstrated only too clearly how important control of the skies was to our ultimate success.

The advance continued, but we came under heavy shellfire and it became too dangerous to leave the tank. The high ground of Mont Pincon and Ondefontaine dominated the area and, until we could capture these positions, enemy observers could bring down accurate artillery and mortar fire on us. Our Squadron Leader, Peter Selerie, was severely wounded in the left shoulder, back and right hand, and his driver, Trooper Howie, was killed. Peter was a great character and possessed of a somewhat exaggerated old world courtesy and charm. His portly figure, protruding blue eyes and bristling fair moustache were positively Pickwickian, and he could be maddeningly pedantic of speech, occasionally coming over the radio to say things like: 'I can without question discern three moving objects in yonder wood to my left front, which give me the impression of resembling three Tigers. It is my immediate intention to engage.' It could be infuriating but yet in a funny way also communicated calm in the heat of battle. Peter was evacuated to England, but returned to us in the autumn, only to be wounded again in Germany.

Jack Holman, Dick's brother, was now to take over C Squadron. Just as I had come to the Sherwood Rangers mainly because of my father's links, so Dick came because of Jack. He was a few years older than me, which to a twenty-year-old seemed a vast gulf of maturity. He was nearly always smiling and good-humoured, and tended to address everyone as 'old boy' in a rather public school sort of way. He was short and stocky, with the low-slung build of the very good rugby centre three-quarter that he was, and he also had both the eye and wrist of a an excellent squash player. (He had starred for Sherborne at rugby when they played Tonbridge in 1938.) His private means were considerable and his family's vast house in Cornwall had its own squash court, which helped explain his skill at the game. When he took over C Squadron after Peter Selerie had been wounded, his completely unflappable manner was a great help, and he had the habit of making even the most dangerous situation into something of a joke. He smoked copious cigarettes through a holder, and every time I joined his order group, he would say, 'Hullo, old boy, how's it going?' For some reason he also had a habit of referring to me as 'my dear old fruit' in a manner not unlike Henry Blofeld on *Test Match Special*. But he was possessed of great courage and was always up close in support of his forward troops.

We continued on through the afternoon of August 2, heading towards Jurcques. There was increasingly stiff opposition, with several more Tigers being spotted, and even the Regimental Aid Post was badly shelled. I had to be constantly on the alert for any sign of trouble and was careful not to present too much of myself above the rim of the turret, even though I had to know what the Hampshire infantrymen were doing. My driver, Geoff Storey, was invaluable. To be the driver of a tank in action is an unenviable task; quite unable to see anything beyond the field of his narrow slit or to hit back, Geoff had to listen to the thud of explosions and the noise of battle around him and calmly try to carry out my orders coming through the intercom: 'Drive advance full speed. Drive halt. Drive right or reverse.' Buried deep within the tank, he had the least chance of getting out if it was hit and so he inevitably brooded over potential dangers.

Right through that night we continued our advance with the infantry-men riding at times on the back of our tanks. There was the odd skirmish and dawn was breaking as we reached Jurcques. Dropping the infantry just outside the town, we entered at speed with our tank leading. The place had earlier been bombed, and there was a lot of dust and smoke still hanging about on the damp morning air. Some buildings were on fire, but we roared on without being fired upon. Then we found the road to La Bigne and, after successfully crossing the Odon, we were ordered to halt and leaguer in an orchard as the enemy mortar shells started to rain down.

Behind us the rear troops of tanks were not so lucky. There was a pair of enemy 88-millimetres covering the La Bigne road, where there was little cover. Two of our tanks were knocked out, one of them com-manded by a fellow twenty-year-old subaltern and friend, Jock Camp-bell, who was from Stamford Hill in London. The La Bigne road itself was heavy with our traffic, tanks and infantry carriers virtually head to tail for about half a mile. Suddenly two German self-propelled guns (SPs) were spotted on the high ground and Lieutenant Alan Birkett and his troop was sent off to engage them. They hit and damaged one SP, but Alan's tank was then hit by the other and set on fire. The tank was on a slope at the time and it began to run back down towards a bunch of infantry carriers and vehicles at the bottom, ammunition exploding all the time inside the burning tank. Then Sergeant Guy Sanders, MM, leaped aboard and steered the tank into a ditch, thus avoiding a major catastrophe. Alan Birkett, who came from Middlesborough, was killed and what remained of him and his crew inside the burnt-out tank was buried by the infantry of the Dorsets.

Padre Skinner tried the next day to recover the bodies of both Birkett and Campbell and their crews. He found that the Dorsets had already attended to the former, but in Campbell's tank three bodies were still inside, partially burnt and firmly welded together. He managed with difficulty to identify Campbell but was unable to remove the bodies.

Meanwhile we stayed in our orchard, awaiting orders and casually chatting. Our hatches remained down, for mortar bombs were still falling. Suddenly there was shouting outside and banging on the side of our tank. It was Jack 'Busty' Mitchell, a radio operator in the troop and a very colourful character. He had been a Territorial in the Sherwood Rangers before the war and had served right through the desert campaign. 'What's wrong with everyone?' he cried. 'Come outside. Bugger the mortars. I'm not scared of the bastards.' At this point I was called to a meeting by Jack Holman and, as I left the tank, I advised Mitchell to return to his. 'Not me,' he replied. 'They don't get me down.'

I continued my walk to the order group, and in the middle of it a mortar bomb landed very close to us, slightly wounding Sergeant Sanders, who was sitting on my right. The meeting ended and I walked back with my orders. There, lying just beside his tank, was Busty Mitchell, quite dead from a mortar fragment and with his cigarette still in his mouth. I could not wait for the Padre to come up, and there was too much mortar fire around to make it safe for him to come, so I returned to my own tank, picked up a shovel and buried Mitchell myself under the trees beside the River Odon, along with the body of Trooper Howie, Peter Selerie's driver. I said a short prayer over the graves, marked them for future identification and then returned to my tank for the continuing advance. This burial was in fact a unique occasion as I had no assistance. Arthur Reddish, who knew both Mitchell and Howie, admitted later: 'I wasn't up to burial just then. Neither were the other members of the crew.' But later on, whenever the Padre was unavailable there were usually sufficient willing hands for the grisly task – which was just as well, for it was a physically and emotionally draining experience on one's own.

By this time we were all very tired and the news that the advance would continue indefinitely did nothing to raise our spirits. Heavy shells were still falling intermittently and one landed very close to Arthur Reddish as he was talking to a friend, shaking him up severely. I called together my tank commanders in the troop for a last-minute conference, which was all the more important as we were to be the leading troop in the squadron. We took it in turns between the three of us to be the lead tank, and this time it was to be my turn. To be the leading tank of the leading troop of the leading squadron of the leading regiment, with the axis of advance along a narrow lane into a village known to be held by enemy armour and infantry, was, to put it mildly, bloody dangerous. It almost invariably resulted in your being brewed up by an anti-tank weapon. It was just as unpleasant for the infantry, but at least they could dive into the nearest ditch, whereas a Sherman could barely rotate its turret, let alone hide.

We were by now all too familiar with that fearful sense of anticipation whenever we turned a corner or crested a hill. We almost expected the crash of an anti-tank gun or a Tiger's 88-millimetre, that virtually simultaneous explosion of a shell hitting the tank, followed by a moment's pause to recover from the shock, and then the order to bale out. If we were lucky, we would scramble from the tank, trying to avoid the inevitable Spandau bullets or the arrival of a second shell, before we dashed to the nearest ditch and covered our heads. I had seen this happen to others and I was under no illusions about my own invulnerability. And now I had to lead again. My attitude at such times was one of anger and resentment, which was self-defeating if allowed to go too far. It was difficult to hide such vexation from the crew, who perhaps felt I should do more to protect them, but I never felt any bitterness towards me. On the other hand, the generals came under heavy fire from me, with some extremely rude things being said about their parentage and other matters.

We moved out from our orchard and into La Bigne, hosing down the houses as we went, systematically working our way through with the infantry. Once or twice the infantry were pinned down by machine-guns and we moved in to support, all the time apprehensive of that Panzerfaust in a doorway or upstairs window. It was again a bottle-neck with no room to manoeuvre: the weather was dull with low, circling clouds overhead and we anticipated meeting both enemy tanks and anti-tank guns. But resistance was not unduly strong and, after the village was cleared, the infantry dug in about a mile beyond and we passed through on our way to Ondefontaine.

It was now nearly dark, but still General Thomas wanted to push on. We were lined up on a new start-line when the mortars rained down and the infantry was forced to scatter, snuffing out the attack until a fresh battalion could be brought up. We stood to all through the night in our tank, which was now stinking to high heaven after about seventy hours without a break. Preparing meals in the tank only added to the stench, and although we were all worn out, we still had to be ready to move again at dawn.

Sporadic fighting had gone on in the area all through the night and losses were mounting. A Squadron was held up near St Pierre-du-Fresne by a Jagdpanther with an 88-millimetre gun but eventually broke through. Sergeant George Dring, that inveterate destroyer of tanks, stalked a Tiger on foot and then directed his own tank in to kill it. Two other Tigers, heavily bogged down in the wet ground, were captured intact.

The attack on Ondefontaine went in at dawn, our tank in the lead. As the light improved, we could see the small village perched on top of a ridge. The access road ran up its right-hand side and was heavily wooded and narrow. Enemy fire was much lighter than expected and we came out of the wood into relatively open ground. We moved cautiously to the churchyard at the edge of the village, then past the church to a T-junction. Tension rose as a platoon of infantry slipped past us and hid behind a stone house. Geoff Storey edged the nose of the tank past a protecting church wall. Swish, swish – two anti-tank tracer shells whistled past. 'Reverse,' I shouted and Geoff promptly complied. They had tried to lure us into a trap.

I got on the radio to Jack Holman. 'Is there another way into the village?' he asked. I suggested that we try to get around the church-yard. In our troop we now had Sergeant Guy Sanders and Sergeant-Major Robson and so were an experienced team, yet we could still not move in that direction without being fired on. The infantry commander tried to push us in closer to protect his men, but we did not want to commit suicide. Then Jack Holman came up and the three of us had a conference. I suggested that we pull back a little and the infantry commander agreed; he had just been informed that strong enemy tank and infantry elements were in the main street and at the far end of the village. I then asked for an artillery stonk on the place from the 25-pounder guns of the Essex Yeomanry and Jack Holman withdrew to lay this on.

My crew looked pleased with me as I came back and we pulled out of the village. They knew the danger we would have been in if we had had to advance further. The infantry came with us to take cover. One of their officers pointed out the church steeple, where he had seen a German observer operating a radio who might have been responsible for their very accurate mortar fire during the previous few hours. Our new gunner Dick Dexter's second shot went right through the steeple and a later patrol confirmed the presence of the dead German observer. Dexter was an experienced gunner from desert days and a quiet and reserved but pleasant character. He was also a good friend of Sam Kirman's, something for which I was grateful as it helped to weld the crew together. This was not always easy if the newcomer was a stranger and an unknown quantity.

The concentrated artillery barrage duly began, destroying entire houses with its stupendous power. We prepared to follow it in, force our way through to the far end of the village and dig in to repel any counter-attack. We moved forward again, passing the church and spraying the houses with machine-gun fire. The tanks of Sanders and Robson followed, the infantry of the Hampshires in close support. There was no opposition as we moved right through to the far end. The enemy had withdrawn, leaving some of their dead and some broken weaponry. One dead German I saw was an officer of the 10th Panzer Division. We continued on beyond the village, all the time expecting trouble, but none came. Finally we had traversed the whole plateau of high ground with just one shot being fired at us. Ondefontaine was ours.

We stopped and the transport came up with rations, fuel and ammunition. The regimental doctor came too and was horrified at our condition as we climbed out of our tanks for virtually the first time in three days. We were red-eyed and utterly exhausted, and the Doctor firmly told Brigade that we had to rest. Plans for the following day were cancelled and we ordered to get some sleep. Next morning I cooked the breakfast with Sergeant Sleep while we listened to the birds sing. Further ahead, elements of the Regiment, but more particularly the 13th/18th

The author - fifty years on. (*Author's collection*)

The author, *left,* and Denis Elmore at Lord's, July 1942, playing for Tonbridge School against Clifton College. (*Author's collection*)

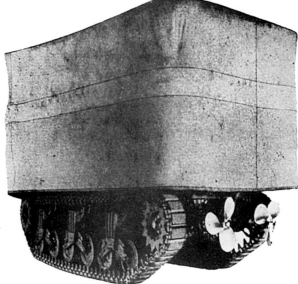

The DD (Duplex Drive) Sherman tank, *above* with the screen completely lowered and *below* with the screen raised ready for the sea. (*Imperial War Museum*)

The Reverend Leslie Skinner RA ChB, Chaplain, 8th (Independent) Armoured Brigade, attached to the Sherwood Rangers Yeomanry. (*Author's collection*)

A German Panther tank captured intact at St Nicholas Farm, near Rauray. A dead German soldier lies in the foreground. (*Imperial War Museum*)

Above, a knocked-out British Cromwell tank in the ruined streets of Villers-Bocage, Normandy. (*Imperial War Museum*)

Opposite, a German King Tiger knocked out at Le Plessis Grimoult. (*Imperial War Museum*)

Above, Units of II Armoured Division near St Charles de Percy. The tanks are of 3rd R.T.R. The infantry are of 4th Bn Kings Shropshire Light Infantry. (*Imperial War Museum*)

Opposite above, the Calvary at the top of the Berjou ridge. (*Author's collection*)

Opposite below, Corporal Burnett and Sergeant Nesling, both armed with 17-pounder guns, enter Gheel, September 10 1944. The author's tank, armed with a 75mm gun, follows in the rear. (*Author's collection*)

Above, from left to right, the author, 'Chalky' White, Tom Trott and Arthur Hinitt, part of 'Robin Force', in Weeze, Holland, February 1945. (*Author's collection*)

Opposite above, Captain Jimmy McWilliam's knocked-out tank after it had been moved behind the church in Gheel, September 11 1944. (*Author's collection*)

Opposite below, Konrad Köhne of the 2nd Battalion Fallschirmjager Regiment, who knocked out Jimmy McWilliam's tank with a panzerfaust. He also severely damaged the author's tank. (*Author's collection*)

Above, Investiture, Hoensbrook, Holland, November 30 1944. Top left in the photograph is Sergeant Doug Nelson (SRY). Below him, fourth from the left, is the author. On his left is Major Jack Holman (SRY), and third from the right, also in the middle row, is Major John Semken (SRY). In the front row, Lt Col Stanley Christopherson is second from the left, and on his left are Lt General Horrocks, Field Marshal Montgomery, Brigadier Prior-Palmer and Major General Thomas. The photograph is signed by Field Marshal Montgomery. *(Author's collection)*

Opposite above, from left to right, Capt Denis Markin (Signals Officer SRY), Major Derek Colls (12th/60th KRRC), Major Basil Ringrose (SRY), Major Chris Sedgewick (Essex Yeomanry), Lt Col Stanley Christopherson (SRY) - 'Robin Force', Weeze, Holland, February 1945. *(Author's collection)*

Opposite below, Trooper Arthur Hinitt. *(Author's collection)*

Above, Sergeant 'Nev' Hinitt. (*Author's collection*)

Right, Keith Douglas in the Western Desert.

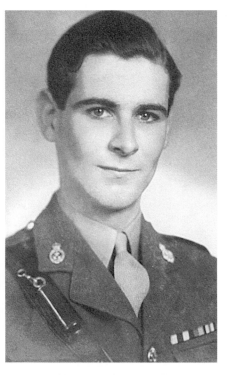

Above left, Lt Dick Holman. (*Author's collection*)

Above right, Major Jack Holman. (*Author's collection*)

Left, Major Tim Olphert. (*Author's collection*)

Left, the author in 1945. (*Author's collection*)

Right, Lt Denis Elmore. (*Author's collection*)

Hussars, were involved in the taking of Mont Pincon, a key feature in the area whose capture opened the door to further advances as the break-out gathered momentum.

Then, on Tuesday August 8, we were withdrawn from the line and retired five miles to another pleasant orchard at Beaumont, near Villers Bocage. As we settled down to rest, news came through that the Americans had taken Angers and Le Mans and were wheeling towards Paris. Padre Skinner still had work to do as he went back to recover and identify the bodies of Jock Campbell and his crew, whom he buried near the railway crossing at Jurcques. Jock now lies in Bayeux War Cemetery. Our casualties had been heavy; in C Squadron, apart from the two captains, Jack Holman and Johnnie Mann, the only other officer left apart from me was Frank Galvin.

It had been a tough spell and our casualties were beginning to bear down on my confidence. In the midst of my continual worry about my parents, I was now becoming more and more aware of the friends I was losing. Would my own luck hold – and what if it did not? I could visualise the distress my death would cause my family and friends. This was a somewhat negative line of thought, I admit, but one that was with me constantly.

On August 9 the Corps Commander, General (later Sir) Brian Horrocks, a tall, spare figure with greying hair, paid us a visit. During the fighting it was almost impossible to know how matters were developing elsewhere. I had faith that Montgomery's tactics round Caen would prove successful, but I had no idea how difficult things had become since D-Day. Horrocks addressed all officers and NCOs, making some very complimentary remarks about the Regiment. He reminded us that we had first fought under his command in 1942, when Rommel made a last desperate effort to reach Alexandria before the Battle of El Alamein, and that from then we had continually served under him, although he had been wounded at the end of the desert campaign. He produced a large map and showed us all the dispositions of both sides and how well he thought the battle was going. He radiated confidence and bonhomie and made it clear that the Germans were about to suffer a huge defeat. Then he showed us where we would be fighting next, crossing the River Noireau on a broad front. He even referred to the 43rd Division as 'dashing', whereupon a trooper told him that the infantry were more scared of their own General 'von Thoma' than they were of the enemy. Horrocks laughed out loud along with everyone else. It did us good to hear him and to realise what results all our efforts and sacrifice were producing.

There were other pleasures too in this rest period. A mobile bath unit arrived and so did clean clothes. Then came an ENSA concert party of mixed talents and the chance to play some football. We could visit Bayeux, catch up on lots of sleep, write some letters, enjoy plenty of local food and drink or simply soak up the sun as we lazed in the long grass with our cigarettes, our hopes and fears. This was what the Army called 'R and R' (Rest and Rehabilitation) and I daresay it served a useful purpose, although it never entirely freed the mind from thoughts of the dangers ahead. It was no more than a pleasant interlude and, rather like any holiday from school or work, it was over all too soon.

My own crew had a new member for the coming operation. Our gunner, Dick Dexter, was carted off in an ambulance. Nobody quite knew what had happened, but for some reason he would not come out of the tank. He slept in it, ate in it, refused the opportunity even of a game of football, which he loved. Sam speculated that he had become 'armour-conscious', needing to feel he had that security of being inside the tank all the time. Or perhaps he had drawn too deeply on his own particular well of endurance, had seen too many terrible sights, suffered too many vivid nightmares.

Throughout the close bocage of Normandy, the seemingly never-ending rain of mortars, particularly the multi-bomb Nebelwerfer, was very frightening. It was the unprotected infantry that suffered most, but not exclusively. The impact on a tank, which might resolve itself in physical concussion or, at worst, incineration, could lead to near panic and a shattering of morale. We cowered in our compartments under the intensity of these bombardments, knowing full well that there was no safer area to which we could try to move. Claustrophobia and the inability to escape from it were an added strain on our nerves – one felt literally hemmed in by the prospect of death or serious wounding and quite unable to end the onslaught. It was understandable, therefore, that such conditions led to some men becoming 'bomb-happy'.

Out of the stress of bombardment, however, humour could some-times emerge, and I am reminded of a celebrated occasion during the desert campaign when Michael Laycock saw a small puppy wriggling around pathetically amidst a hail of shells. 'Poor little thing,' he remarked, 'it wants his mummy.' 'So do I,' said Colonel Kellett.

At any rate, we now had a new gunner, Bill Cousins, another desert veteran and formerly gunner to Stephen Mitchell, who was now at RHQ. The others already knew Bill well and I came to know and value him very highly over the months ahead. He spoke in words of one syl-lable and nobody really knew his views on anything. 'I'll think about it', was his usual reply to questions or points made, but he was stolid and imperturbable and he saw me through some difficult times, in Belgium especially, before I took him off to be my driver when I became Intelli-gence Officer.

Our rest came to an end on Saturday August 12, as we returned to the line in Operation Blackwater, which was designed to maintain the pressure on the Germans around Caen, pushing them back to Condé and across the River Noireau. Once again we were with 130 Brigade, although C Squadron was in reserve for the start of the operation. 130 Brigade suffered a self-inflicted loss when General 'von Thoma' sacked their Brigadier for being too slow up to the start-line and then failing to make sufficiently rapid progress. Thomas had a reputation for sack-ing people, often unfairly, and he tended to interfere with the way subordinates ran their battles, with the result that nobody ever felt particularly secure. But this was probably his intention and it certainly produced results.

On August 13 and 14 we pushed on steadily, though the other two squadrons bore the brunt of it. St Denis-de-Mère was taken and Proussy. By the evening of August 15 we had come up to the River Noireau. In reality this was a gentle meandering stream with steep wooded heights on its far side, above which were the three fortified villages of Berjou, Le Canet and Le Hamel. The river was about twenty yards wide and three feet deep, and the way up the far side was a narrow winding track, overlooked by the enemy positions on the heights beyond. These heights were wreathed in smoke from the artillery fire, but we were under no illusions about what to expect from such a naturally strong defensive position. All the approaches to the river were under intense mortar and shellfire, carefully directed from the positions above. It did not look propitious.

That night the crossing was forced by the infantry. H Hour was at 6.00 p.m., with the 1 Worcesters making the initial attack which was then to be exploited by the 5th Duke of Cornwall's Light Infantry. The DCLI were commanded by Lieutenant-Colonel George Taylor and their Intelligence Officer was David Willcocks, later a musician of great distinction. Taylor and Willcocks reconnoitred the river to find a suitable crossing place but found that the bridge had been blown and the approaches to the river mined. They heard that the Worcesters had crossed successfully and then led their own men to the river, now under mortar fire. They waded across and moved into the wood opposite, then up the steep slope, reaching the top half an hour later. By this time it was dark and the battle for the ridge was still going on: one could hear sharp bursts of machine-gun fire and see the shallow, curving trails of tracer bullets as they flicked across the night sky towards the sterner gloom ahead.

At least two enemy battalions were holding the ridge, and the infantry companies of the Worcesters and DCLI were isolated without artillery support. They dug in for the night, all the time harassed by mortars and machine-guns, and Taylor sent Willcocks back to Brigade to stress the urgent need for armoured support and anti-tank guns. However, although the infantry could easily cross the Noireau, no tanks or vehicles could get across until a bridge had been laid by the Engineers. This also necessitated a big mine-clearing operation on all the roads and approaches to the river. All through the night these preparations took place. Occasionally there would be the sound of an explosion as a vehicle hit a mine, and from time to time the crump of mortar shells split the darkness. Meanwhile the infantry dug in further and prepared to cling on to what they had gained against the inevitable German counter-attack, probably with armoured support, in the morning. Just before first light the battle renewed and a steady stream of casualties came back down the hill.

We had spent the night in an orchard. It had rained hard and caught us sleeping outside on the ground near our tanks, so we were sopping wet. Our orders were to cross the river as soon as possible, but we waited while 204th Field Company RE built a tank ford and three trestle bridges to allow us to do so – a task that cost them several casualties to mines and shellfire. The Germans were fighting a fierce rearguard action to prevent our infantry's success from being consolidated.

Then, when it was still dark and misty, we received the orders to move. C Squadron would be in the lead. The approach was through a gorge with wooded hillsides. The air was warm and muggy and light rain was still falling. The stench inside the tank from our sodden clothes was strong, but we could not keep the hatches open for long because we began to come under mortar fire as we approached the river. Arthur Reddish suffered a painful crushed finger when a nearby mortar round thrust the open hatch downwards on to him. We paused for a time just before the river, waiting for the dawn and trying to cat-nap without much success. We could just about make out the dark, foreboding heights opposite, from which regular bursts of small arms fire could be heard. The shelling of the crossing area was virtually constant. We were told that the infantry were hanging on but desperately needed our support.

At first light we made our final approach down to the river. A path through the mines had been flagged and the river itself posed no real obstacle now. Our tank was about the seventh to cross. The road up the other side to the ridge above was steep and winding and heavily wooded on both sides. It appeared that our infantry broadly held one side of the road and the enemy the other, and we were under constant small arms fire and on the alert for Panzerfausts. Relieved, we made the climb without mishap. Lieutenant-Colonel Taylor of the DCLI was to record how the German counter-attacks were taking a steady toll of his men and that the enemy were in a position to cut him off should he have to retreat, when 'just in time [there was] a welcome roar from behind as the leading tanks of the Sherwood Rangers arrived'. We went for the top, saturating the surrounding hedges and bushes with machine-gun fire.

At the top we reached an open field on the right of the track. Here the mortaring was intense and to get out of the tank invited certain death, but we waited there for further orders. In C Squadron there were just three subalterns – myself, Stan Perry and Frank Galvin, who had taken over my tank for that short time at Hottot. The orders came that the objective was Berjou village, towards which we would move together with the DCLI. Thank heavens, it was not my turn to lead.

Stan Perry was to go first, moving along the ridge to the left. From this higher ground he could cover the road leading directly into Berjou, along which Frank Galvin and his troop would force their way. Then our troop would move up and through to take the objective. Things went wrong from the start. Stan pushed up to the left as planned, but immediately one of his tanks was hit by a Panzerfaust, forcing the crew to bale out, and then he himself was sniped through the arm. Only

Corporal Brooks of his troop was left, precariously placed, with his infantry, on the higher ground to the left.

It was then decided that Frank Galvin would move to the left in a flanking move rather than going straight down the road to Berjou. This would support Brooks and was also necessary because the road was under heavy fire. Frank duly set off and we awaited results. Once he had made it up there successfully, I could come up with my troop and move on to Berjou. But we heard nothing, except Corporal Brooks cursing loudly over the wireless about the failure of support to arrive. We could not raise Frank on our radio and we did not know what had happened to him until much later. Frank must have missed the turn to the left and gone straight down the road to Berjou. On that road his tank

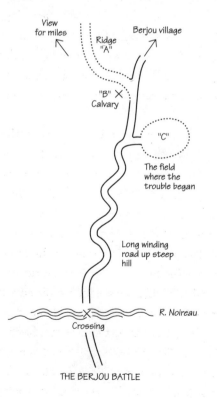

View for miles

Ridge "A"

Berjou village

"B" × Calvary

"C"

The field where the trouble began

Long winding road up steep hill

R. Noireau

Crossing

THE BERJOU BATTLE

took a direct hit from a Panzerfaust and the whole crew was killed. Padre Skinner recorded in his book: 'Five Sherwood Rangers KIA 16/8/44. Presumed to be Lt. Galvin, L/Cpl. Young, Tpr. Dixon, Tpr. Wright, Tpr. Brownlee. Unidentifiably burnt. Remains broken and scattered in the tank. Completely brewed up. No one known to have escaped. No personal effects.' It was a sombre epitaph and an end that we all secretly feared.

Meanwhile Corporal Brooks was still cursing at the lack of support he was getting and I decided to take my own troop up there. The plan to take Berjou was falling apart under pressure of events, but there was a clear need to extricate Brooks and the infantry with him. We moved without infantry support ourselves and so were constantly swivelling our periscopes for Panzerfausts. I made sure that I kept my head down as much as possible but occasionally had to sneak a look out. At one point, just as we made the turn left, I heard what sounded like the buzz of a bumble-bee very close to my head and I realised there must be snipers about. We could not fire much ourselves because our own infantry were around and we did not know quite where. I had the good fortune that day to have two very experienced commanders in my troop – Sergeant-Major Robson and Sergeant Nesling – who boosted my morale considerably. When we reached the higher ground where Brooks was, I found that he had wounded aboard from Stan Perry's tank, so I ordered him to go back to the field we had just left. I took up my position to the right of the track and waited for further infantry to arrive. The mortar and shellfire continued to be intense, and there seemed to be good observation posts for the enemy gunners in the woods opposite, so I asked the Essex Yeomanry to put down a barrage on them and we raked the posts with machine-gun fire.

Behind us there were all kinds of problems developing, the gist of which we picked up in bits and pieces over the radio. First came news of what had happened to Frank Galvin as his burning tank was found. Then his second tank commander, Sergeant Sleep, was drilled through the forehead by a sniper as he scanned the ground from an open hatch. Close by, the tank of Corporal Brooks was hit by a panzerfaust and he rolled off the tank wounded and down into the road, whereupon his close friend, Sergeant Guy Sanders, MM, who was following him, climbed down from his turret and ran to help him. Both of them were hit by the same panzerfaust and instantly killed. In a very short space of time C Squadron had lost six experienced tank commanders, four of them dead. It was a devastating blow.

I sat where I was as all this mayhem unfolded, fully aware that I was as vulnerable as anyone in such a forward position. My troop was effectively the only one left intact and had to conduct the advance alone. I now had not only my own infantry company from the DCLI but also Frank Galvin's, which had just turned up. We moved forward along a high ridge open to fire from either flank. The country was a little like Box Hill in Surrey, although more wooded, and at one stage I could see for about fifteen miles to the left – little copses, villages and even German columns. It was now a glorious summer's day, but everything was dulled by the task in hand and the extent of our casualties. To the front, the ground was rugged and bound by hedgerows, which still presented problems for us and the infantry.

I was now more or less in a battle on my own. There were no reinforcements forthcoming from the squadron and late in the afternoon I was ordered out on a further recce with a platoon of infantry. I had no idea what lay in front or what might happen. The fatal shot might come from anywhere and I was constantly expecting it. The platoon commander was an excellent fellow and I told him that, if he met any trouble, he was to halt and let me deal with it. The only opposition we expected to meet initially was enemy infantry, which would not be a problem. We duly encountered Spandau fire at the crest of a hill and then renewed mortaring. I moved forward and opened up because I could see the enemy quite clearly dug in under the hedgerows. We must have done some damage because shortly afterwards a trickle of prisoners began to come in. The infantry began to round them up and some of my crew helped. They looked young, lean and tough and came from the 3rd German Parachute Division, elite troops. We sat up under cover of the hill and I directed Arthur Warburton and his Essex Yeomanry 25-pounders on to possible enemy positions, especially those of his mortars, which continued to give us hell. One of Warburton's stonks must have hit an ammunition dump because there was a big explosion.

It was getting dark when Lieutenant-Colonel Taylor came up with the rest of his infantry. He wanted to put in another attack there and then, although it was hardly worth it because we already dominated the low ground ahead. I voiced my objections: I was losing touch with the squadron and the proposed attack would be at night, therefore difficult for tanks. Mine was also the only complete troop left in C Squadron and we would have had to make a long night march to put in the proposed attack. I said as much both to Lieutenant-Colonel Taylor and, over the radio, to Jack Holman and received permission to make my way back. We went down the hill again and leaguered for the night in a small orchard, where food, fuel and ammunition were brought to us, and then we flung ourselves on the ground and fell into blissful sleep.

Our part in the action was now over. On August 17 the other squadrons came forward to help the infantry to capture Berjou and the neighbouring village of Le Hamel. The whole Berjou Ridge above the Noireau was now in our hands, and as more senior officers came forward to view where the fighting had taken place, some astonishment was expressed that we had stormed such a formidable position so quickly. From up on the top it was possible to see clearly just why the Germans had given us such a hard time: the views down to the river and off to the east were stupendous. Every move we made must have been seen by the German artillery observers, who had been able to call down very accurate shell- and mortar fire.

Events were now moving fast elsewhere. The German forces in

Normandy were now virtually surrounded and trying desperately to escape through the only route open to them south-east of Falaise. 43 Division and 8th Armoured Brigade were on the north-west corner of the Falaise pocket, just to the east of Condé, and the bag in which the German Army was caught was rapidly collapsing. Terrible slaughter was going on inside the pocket through the constant Allied air attacks, but about half the Germans nevertheless managed to extricate themselves before the neck of the bag was closed finally around August 21. The Brigadier commanding 214 Brigade wrote to congratulate us on the work we had done around Berjou: 'No Brigade ever received better co-operation.' Our own Brigadier Prior-Palmer wrote in the same vein to Stanley Christopherson: 'Your chaps really did do a superhuman job up that ruddy mountain and I am sure some decorations were well-deserved.'

I, however, did not feel remotely euphoric. As the dawn broke on August 17, I stirred to the sound of birds singing and looked around me at the silent forms of my troop, who were still sleeping soundly. Only Arthur Reddish was up and about, because his swollen and painful finger had made sleep impossible. Gradually the events of the previous day began to come back and with them the realisation of what I had lost: Corporal Brooks trying to summon help and then being wiped out as he baled out; Sergeant Bill Sleep, seven years in the Army; and Sergeant Guy Sanders, MM, 35 years old and from Grimsby, whose loss was almost the hardest to take because he had been such a good soldier and seemingly indestructible. If he could be taken in an instant, gallantly trying to rescue his friend, what hope was there that the rest of us would survive? Then there was Frank Galvin, who had taken over my crew for a time and whom I had just started to befriend; now he and all his crew had perished almost as if they had never been. But there were the wounded too, and the knowledge that C Squadron had been decimated by the day's action. Six tank commanders had become casualties and I was the only officer troop leader left. To get all this into perspective was not easy, and it was not surprising that older heads noticed how low I was. I had come to rely on all these men, and we had shared much danger and discomfort since before D-Day. I sensed too an unreal atmosphere around the survivors, one of heavy disillusionment and disbelief. It was all too difficult and painful to grasp immediately: I still expected that at any minute the casualties would suddenly reappear as though nothing had happened. But gradually this dream faded into grim reality.

My own crew were sympathetic, although they had of course experienced bad times like this before in the desert. The Colonel came up in his brisk way to visit us and went straight to my tank. 'Ah Trooper Kirman,' he said to Sam, 'once again you kept open the lines of communication. Congratulations, and you'd better put up a stripe.'

'Thanks, Colonel,' Sam said, nodding, 'but one's no bloody good.'

'Then,' Stanley answered, 'you had better put up two.'

'Two's no bloody good either,' Sam said.

The Colonel knew his man. 'Then put three up – a signal sergeant.'

Sam's reply was instant. 'Now you're talking, Colonel.'

We all laughed, which was good for us, and we did not doubt that the redoubtable Sam would be a fine addition to the Sergeant's Mess. The episode also illustrated both the informality which sometimes characterised the Sherwood Rangers and why Stanley Christopherson was such a popular CO.

We received a visit from the Padre, who had been hard at work seeking out and burying those casualties he could find in one piece. On his own advance to Berjou he had been passing an orchard when he decided to step inside and help himself to a succulent red apple. But, as he approached the tree, two Germans suddenly rose up out of a hidden slit trench and surrendered themselves to him. The rest of his day had not been so amusing. Apart from having to try to get inside Frank Galvin's burning tank to see what might be left of the crew, he had also had to bury Sanders, Sleep and Brooks in a paddock behind a farm at the south-west end of Cambercourt. Not only that but he had also prepared for burial several German dead who had been lying around, before returning to his tent to record the casualty and burial returns, and to write to next of kin. He had had a quiet word with me, because he could see that I was upset, but by now I had begun to realise that all this was part of war and that I just had to get on and make the best of it.

Whenever we came out of action, as we did for a while after Berjou, there was a feeling of exuberance in spite of the casualties. We did not bubble like effervescent schoolboys but we knew that for a short spell the numbness would disappear from our minds and bodies and that, for a change, we could be human beings rather than automatons of destruction. We would spend a night in delicious sleep after a hard-fought battle and rise next morning when the sun was high in the sky. We would then indulge ourselves royally with a breakfast cooked from long-preserved rations which we had not had time to touch whilst in action. We would smoke our cigarettes, talk aimlessly among ourselves, replenish our tanks and do whatever maintenance jobs were necessary. We stripped naked in the warm sunshine and washed luxuriously in pails and dixies until we shone like marble. Then we would stretch out in the sun, read, sleep or attack our correspondence. Cooking, though, remained the main business of the day and, given the ready availability of the local produce, I do not think I have eaten better in my life.

Sometimes, when rest periods were more official, we of course had ENSA shows and organised baths. But, given good weather, what I liked most was to be left on my own. In those summer days the sun used to set very late and it was then that a good number of men used to get together for a sing-song. In my troop there was a splendid player of the accordion, Trooper Bennett. As the sun fell in the sky so we would sit around a fire, drinking our NAAFI beer ration laced with Calvados, and sing our hearts away. The songs ranged from the very bawdy to march and dance tunes, but there were soloists who could add a bit of class to proceedings. Occasionally I would be asked to perform and no one seemed to care how many mistakes I made or if I did not know all the words. Music is a fine thing for morale and these gatherings helped ours, as a sense of pride and well-being swelled in our chests. Many of the familiar faces had gone, but we were the men who had 'been and seen' and we were secretly proud of both the Regiment and ourselves.

It was only on late evenings such as these, when one was happy and contented, that the Army and the 'cause' meant anything to the ordinary soldier, for in battle or moments of stress, everything except concern for one's own safety was pushed into the background. And then, as darkness fell, we would slip away to our separate tanks, which stood there like huge black stones, and kip down by them, smoke our last cigarettes and sleep.

Sometimes this routine would go on for several days, but then the word would come round to pack up and we would be on our way. We became used to this, swearing a lot and grumbling as we busily stowed our kit and readied ourselves for the off. By this time some of the old faces would already have been replaced by new recruits, who had to be absorbed and educated into our way of doing things before they then became old faces themselves.

It was such a rest after Berjou and with it came a delightful walk with Terry Leinster, who was now Adjutant. We picked our way across the wooded and hilly countryside we had so recently assaulted. How the Germans must have rubbed their hands with glee as they watched us making that ascent. The ridge around Berjou commanded a magnificent view of the low-lying ground to the north and east and, if the enemy had been stronger on the ground to counter our attack, I cannot see how we could have succeeded. But such thoughts did not intrude too far on our walk, as Terry and I talked of more pleasant things.

We also received mail from home which, apart from leave, was the most beneficial tonic a fighting soldier could receive. I remember many times seeing men in tears of joy or sorrow as they opened their precious letters from home. Church services were organised and always well attended. Most of the congregation would not have been regular church-goers in civilian life, but they relished praying in such adverse circumstances and were undoubtedly sincere as they did so. Whatever denomination was recorded in their Pay Books, they knew something about love and fear, and they mostly accepted the existence of God.

We moved on. The whole Regiment was going to St Honorine de Chardonne, a few miles further on, a village which had not suffered any severe war damage and where civilians were starting to return to their homes. There we rested for a day or two, and on Sunday August 20 a Regimental church service was held to the chime of church bells. There were hymns and lessons and communion, and the Padre gave the 250 of us there a short but inspiring address. The battle for Normandy was over and we could now leave the bocage behind us to pursue the enemy in more open country.

CHAPTER SEVEN **PURSUIT**

O ur rest at St Honorine was short-lived. The German army was now in full retreat eastwards and Montgomery's orders were to 'destroy all enemy forces in north-east France'. But there were problems in promptly deploying all the Allied forces, which had to make a smart left wheel as they advanced out of Normandy. Consequently 11th Armoured Division went first and our Brigade then followed, on through the Falaise pocket via Chambois to L' Aigle.

The scenes in the Falaise pocket, where Allied air power had wreaked such destruction, were horrendous. The various German divisions had taken a terrible pounding in the Normandy battle; Panzer Lehr, for instance, had lost all its tanks and infantry units, while about 50,000 of the enemy had been killed and some 200,000 taken prisoner. Thousands still lay unburied within the pocket: the roads and fields were littered with German dead in various stages of decomposition. Then there were the carcasses of cows and horses, the smashed vehicles and abandoned carts laden with loot. Many of the human and animal bodies had swelled grotesquely in the summer sun, and the stench was awful. 'Who in God's name will do what about this lot?' asked Padre Skinner. It was a fair question.

At L' Aigle we paused for about three days. We had now been joined by a new second-in-command, Major The Lord Leigh. He was the replacement for Stephen Mitchell, who was returning to England, and a very engaging fellow. Popularly known as 'The Baron', Robin Leigh was small, tubby and had a very red face. He spoke little but, when he did, revealed a delightful sense of humour with a lovely giggle which shook the whole of his frame. He enjoyed his comforts and smoked a fine-looking pipe with rich tobacco. He came to us from the Gloucestershire Hussars, then in England, because he wanted some action, and he certainly fitted in well with the men of Nottinghamshire.

During the advance through the Falaise pocket, the Regiment had to pause for maintenance in an area of foul-smelling carnage. 'A bit of a mess,' Robin Leigh said to me. 'Is it generally as bad as this?' Press and news photographers certainly recorded the grisly scene, although I myself have never seen the results of their efforts: I can only surmise that the sheer horror of it all may have placed constraints on the publication of such material. For this was strong medicine, even for those of us who were more accustomed than those at home to the hideous visions of war. For my part, I was simply dazed and dumbfounded at what I witnessed. If it had all not been there before my eyes, I would have felt it to be utterly unreal.

Our stay at L' Aigle was in the rather more pleasant and sweet-smelling surroundings of a pear orchard. Here we were joined by the supporting element of soft vehicles, known as B Echelon. It is easy to forget, when describing the exploits of the fighting tanks of the Sherwood Rangers, how dependent we were on B Echelon. It was commanded by Major Roger Sutton-Nelthorpe, MBE, who was somewhat unfairly described by Keith Douglas as having 'sprung, miraculously enlarged, but otherwise unaltered, from an inky bench in a private preparatory school. He looks as if he had white rats in his pocket.' Roger did a sterling job in providing the back-up for the fighting part of the Regiment, and without this we simply could not have operated. He controlled the spare parts for tanks, towing equipment, maintenance crews and mechanical engineers, and all our supplies, from food to clerical stores.

Part of his command was known as A Echelon, which was looked after by Captain Ronnie Hutton, MC. Ronnie was about thirty-eight years old, a charming, completely unflappable Irishman with a great sense of humour and a strong compassion for others. Apart from the Padre, Ronnie had about the most disagreeable and dangerous job in the Regiment. He and his fleet of three-ton and fifteen-hundredweight lorries had to bring up supplies of fuel (both diesel and petrol), ammunition and food to the tanks when they leaguered for the night. This was often done under shell and mortar fire, which posed enormous dangers for his soft-skinned vehicles with their particular loads, but Ronnie never failed in his task, always had a joke up his sleeve and was a great source of strength, especially to young officers like myself. He and his men had done tremendously good work in the Berjou battle. One of my fellow subalterns, David Render, particularly remembers Ronnie's somewhat lax implementation of discipline, yet said that all those who served under him knew what was required and followed him without hesitation. His soft Irish brogue commanded respect without your being aware of it. Later in the campaign Ronnie requested a transfer to a fighting squadron and commanded A Squadron for a time, where his calm demeanour in action once again helped less experienced soldiers enormously.

We lazed on in the sun in our pear orchard at L' Aigle. We even played a game of cricket on a bumpy and interesting pitch which we improvised among the trees of the orchard. It was officers against the men and we were almost properly equipped too, for Roger Nelthorpe had the foresight to pack two pairs of pads, a bat and a cricket ball in one of his vehicles. Never let it be said that we invaded the Continent unprepared. I cannot remember how many I scored, but I think I did better than some fellow Old Tonbridgians languishing in a German POW camp: they were bowled out for 23 by a team of Old Cliftonians, who then replied with just 18. The wickets in France were clearly better than those in Germany.

Then on Sunday August 27 we received orders to move at very short notice. Certainly the notice was too short for Michael Gold, who had just driven off in a Jeep with his Squadron sergeant-major and clerk, supposedly to pay a visit to friends in his old regiment. He did not catch up with us for a couple of days, mainly because his visit had turned into a jaunt to see friends in the recently liberated Paris. He had driven straight to The Ritz, where he and his bemused companions, three of the first Englishmen in the city, were frequently toasted with the best champagne. By the time he rejoined us, his hangovers were only just wearing off.

Within an hour of receiving the order to move, the Regiment was heading out of its orchard towards the next main objective, the River Seine. The infantry of 43 Division were given the task of crossing the Seine at Vernon. This they achieved under fire and at some cost, and by the evening of August 26 they had established a bridgehead on the far side and some vehicles were being rafted across. The first tanks from 8th Armoured Brigade to cross were those of the 4th/7th Royal Dragoon Guards on August 27, and on the next day A and C Squadrons of the Sherwood Rangers crossed, along with other elements from the Brigade.

I had been joined in C Squadron by another subaltern, Ted Cooke, so we now had a full complement of officers in the two of us, Jack Holman, Jimmie McWilliam and Johnnie Mann. To reach the Seine, we had to cover over sixty miles, passing through towns such as Rugles, Conches, Évreux and Eure. At Eure my tank broke down and I spent a very pleasant evening with Dick Holman in the local hotel, where we had to fend off the gathering crowds of jubilant French inhabitants eager to buy us drinks and shower us with gifts. Then the next morning I had to leave my tank and crew in order to rejoin the Squadron at Vernon. Here I acquired another Sherman and was ferried across into the bridgehead on the far side to support the infantry battalion of the DCLI. It might have been the food I had eaten the previous night with Dick, but my stomach was in a frightful state all day and this did not make it any easier to fight in what was now a fast-moving battle as we advanced nearly thirty miles beyond the Seine.

Montgomery was urging all speed to drive the enemy from northern France, and the tanks of 8th Armoured Brigade found themselves in the vanguard of the advance in the general direction of Amiens. The country between the Seine and the Somme is open and rolling with wide fields, no hedges and good roads; apart from a few woods, the only trees are those surrounding villages. How different we found it from the closeness of the bocage, which had hindered us as much as it had helped the German defenders. Now all the advantage lay with the speedy Shermans, which could by-pass potential sources of trouble and rely on their mechanical efficiency to make ground very quickly. The Germans had of course covered the same stretch of country at comparable speeds in 1940 during their dash to the French coast. It was good tank country and now the success of their blitzkrieg tactics was easier to understand.

The Sherwood Rangers were able to adopt the old desert formation – one squadron in open formation in the lead, RHQ just behind, and the other two squadrons on either flank. We worked as an armoured regimental group, supported by a battery of guns from the Essex Yeomanry and a company of motorised infantry from the 12th/60th King's Royal Rifle Corps, under Derek Colls. The commanders of both these units travelled with our RHQ group, which allowed the best possible co-ordination of arms. To travel at top speed across hard, open country on a lovely morning, knowing that the Germans were on the run, was exhilarating to say the least, and everyone was in the best possible spirits. It was almost like taking part in a cross-country steeplechase or going on a pre-war motoring tour. In every village we passed we received terrific welcomes. Occasionally we would stop to receive the fruits of our success in the form of something to eat or drink, but usually we passed through in a cloud of dust, hardly able to see or hear the cheering groups of liberated French. No doubt we left them a little bewildered, wondering what on earth was happening after four long years of occupation and hardship, but we could only reflect that their lives were now about to change for the better and that they would soon catch up with events.

In the last three days of August we travelled a total of over a hundred miles. There was a short, sharp action at St Rémy, and then we moved on again towards the Somme and, beyond it, the even more open plains of Picardy. By now the local population was more clearly aware of what was happening. Church bells were rung and, if we paused for a time on the road, we could hear them in the next village. Men wearing FFI armbands and claiming to be the local Resistance warned of possible weapons sited ahead and handed over the odd German prisoner who might have been found lurking in the neighbourhood, though not without roughing him up first. In one village we picked up an American pilot who had been shot down over Caen and captured and had then escaped to join the local Resistance. Everywhere the French tricolour waved from windows and rooftops. The atmosphere was one of heady and delirious excitement which simply swept us along with it.

At night we would usually leaguer just outside a town or village. On August 30 we did so at Juvignes, five miles north of Beauvais, where we waited for B Echelon to come up. The pace of the pursuit posed real supply problems for Roger Sutton-Nelthorpe, Ronnie Hutton and their men. In one place five tanks of A Squadron became bogged down trying to cross a river and had to wait to be towed out. Then some of the tanks ran out of petrol and had to be left behind until the fuel truck caught up with them. Occasionally we needed to be resupplied with ammunition as we had to deal with pockets of the determined German rearguard, but for the most part the enemy columns were streaming back eastwards as fast as they could go, spurred on by the knowledge that they needed to escape the wrath of the local population even more than they did us.

Amiens itself was captured on August 31 by the tanks of 29th Armoured Brigade. We were a little further to the north and, on the next day, led the Brigade across the Somme at Longpré-les-Amiens and then headed north towards Doullens. It was a hard day's work, not only in terms of distance covered but also because we ran into significant German resistance for almost the first time since Normandy.

One casualty of this was Sergeant Cribben, MM, of the Recce Troop, who had also been recommended for the DCM for his sterling work in the crossing of the Noireau, when he had been with C Squadron. At Flesselles, a village just north of Amiens, a German Mark IV tank concealed in the railway station scored a direct hit on Cribben's tank, killing him and Trooper Sharp. Padre Skinner heard the news when on the road and at first was refused permission to investigate because of the continuing danger. At length he secured the services of a truck and driver and finally made his way into Flesselles on foot via a ditch and a farmyard. He could see Cribben's destroyed tank sitting near the churchyard and heard that the wounded had already been taken away by our men. The bodies of Cribben and Sharp had been washed and were beautifully laid out in the parsonage in white shrouds, and graves had already been dug in the churchyard under the noses of the Germans who were still there. Skinner recorded the two men's names, ranks and numbers, saw to the correct marking of the crosses and gave them to the village priest to place in position when the Germans had gone. Although no coffins were ready, a farmer produced some hessian and Skinner stitched the bodies up. Then he watched from the window as the priest led the funeral cortège down the street to the churchyard and conducted the service while the Germans watched thirty yards away from their tank without interference. Such were the courtesies of war. Skinner then slipped away to rejoin his driver, who was down in a ditch about ten yards from his truck, with a rifle in his hands and clearly apprehensive about where the good Padre had gone.

Meanwhile we had to fight a short action at Naours, and then a longer one at Doullens, which was strongly held by anti-tank guns and German infantry. We needed the services of our own motorised infantry from the 12/60th KRRC, eventually capturing 200 German prisoners and knocking out three tanks and three anti-tank guns. Sergeant Dring again distinguished himself, engaging a German horsed echelon only an hour or two after having to bale out of another tank after it was hit in the turret. Doullens also proved to be a flying-bomb launch site, so we inspected this and then motored on to Sus St Léger, where we spent the night. Altogether on September 1 we had crossed the Somme, travelled fifty miles and captured a large town, as well as taking many prisoners, so it all amounted to a good day's work.

It was a period of jostling and scrambling around in small units which were separated from one other by breakdowns, shortage of fuel and the tactical diversions necessary both to protect our flanks and to eliminate small but dangerous enemy pockets. We spent much time searching fields and farmhouses for signs of the enemy, although this usually proved to be a fruitless task. We could not exactly relax, but we were able to take stock more fully of the events of the past few breathless days and perhaps to begin to believe that we were now truly winning.

After a day's rest for maintenance, we pushed on again to and through Lille. My troop was dropped off with a battalion of the Durham Light Infantry to deal with the threat of a German column supposedly advancing from La Bassée, but although we waited for it all night, it never materialised. My temper was not improved by a young French boy who pestered me to spend the night with his singularly unattractive sister, and it took me several hours to catch up again with the Regiment beyond Lille.

On September 4 we crossed the border into Belgium, covering the left flank of 30 Corps. The border crossing was at Tournai, and we were given as enthusiastic a welcome in Belgium as we had been in France. The squadrons were by now widely split. A Squadron went to Oudenarde, B Squadron to the bridge at Kerkhof and C Squadron with RHQ to Renaix. Renaix was a delightful town, virtually unscathed by the war, and we were the first troops to arrive there. From the windows of virtually every house flew a Belgian flag and there were even some scattered Union Jacks and Stars and Stripes. Certain houses, apparently belonging to collaborators, had been burnt to the ground, and we saw some young women whose heads had been shaved because they had fraternised with the enemy. My troop had to guard a bridge: this only required one tank, so we could take it in turns and, in the meantime, enjoy the liberation festivities. We drank, sang and danced in the inn nearby and we all went mad. Finally a charming young girl took Bill Cousins and me to her house, where we were given five eggs each for our supper. Everyone had a similar story to tell.

On the next day C Squadron pushed even further north to the vicinity of Ghent, where we engaged an enemy column with some success, while elements of B Squadron under Bill Wharton patrolled just south of Renaix. Here Bill was informed by members of the local resistance that about 1,200 Germans were holding out in the nearby village of St Pierre. Bill went into the village under a white flag, but the German colonel refused to deal with anyone who was not of equal rank, and so Bill whistled up reinforcements. Stanley Christopherson, together with the rest of B Squadron and a company of the KRRC, now went to St Pierre, accompanied by Stephen Mitchell, who was still in the process of handing over to Lord Leigh as second-in-command and fortuitously spoke some German.

When they all arrived, Bill Wharton was in animated conversation with members of the Resistance, who claimed the Germans had recently shot four of their men and themselves wanted to shoot double that number of Germans. Eventually they produced a very old Renault to take Stanley into the town, on the grounds that the Germans would shoot at any military vehicle, and so this car, containing Stanley, Bill Wharton, Stephen Mitchell and the enormously fat village priest, then proceeded in very stop-start fashion into the village. The worthy priest balanced himself on the bonnet, waving a white flag in one hand and trying to hold on to his straw hat with the other.

Taken to the village inn, which was the German HQ, Stanley led his little group up the stairs to where the German colonel was holding a conference with twenty of his officers, who turned to look at the intruders with some disdain. 'I am Colonel Christopherson,' said Stanley imperiously. 'I presume you are commander of this garrison. If so, kindly clear the room so that we can discuss terms of surrender.'

The German colonel, a stout, dapper little man with a bull neck around which was hung the Iron Cross, bowed slightly, introduced himself and asked for five more minutes alone with his officers. Stanley granted this and retired to another room, where he found a German private guarding a Belgian major who told him that the garrison was strong in numbers and equipment and that the officers were determined to fight to the last round. He also said that they held four British prisoners, a crew from the Royal Tank Regiment.

Eventually they returned to the room where the Germans had been gathered. It now only contained the colonel and his adjutant, a tall and good-looking young man with a scarred face who resembled Raymond Massey. Stanley made it clear that the German position was hopeless but was disconcerted at the colonel's insistence that honour dictated he must fight on to delay the British advance. Negotiations then continued for some time, their progress possibly not helped by Stephen Mitchell's somewhat incomplete command of the German language. Whatever happened, we wanted to avoid a fight which we would obviously win over time but which would cause disruption to Brigade plans as well as both military and civilian casualties.

The crucial concern seemed to remain German honour, but eventually it was agreed that this had been satisfied and that the German garrison would surrender. The terms were that they would march out at seven o'clock that evening, with their arms, and formally surrender at a chosen rendezvous. Furthermore, no German soldier would be handed over to the Resistance. Stanley and his party then returned to the main body of their own troops, who had become desperately anxious about their fate in the intervening two hours. All duly moved to the appointed rendezvous, where it was agreed that Stanley and Derek Colls would take the formal surrender backed up by the squadron of tanks and the infantry.

At 7.30 p.m. there was still no sign of the German colonel and his men, but suddenly there was a burst of firing from the other side of the village. Immediately it was thought that the Germans were trying to break out, and Captain 'Hilda' Young, the Medical Officer, agreed to go into the village under a white flag both to treat the German wounded and find out what was going on. He came back to report that virtually all the Germans had gone, whereupon there was another sharp burst of firing, including some mortars. So Bill Wharton was now sent in again with a troop of tanks, only to find that the Germans had misunderstood the rendezvous and marched out to another crossroads the other side of the village. There they had encountered a battalion of Green Howards, who had no idea of what had transpired and simply opened fire.

Fortunately, only one German was killed before the Sherwood Rangers party arrived to explain everything. The mistake was explained to the German colonel and he then relayed it to his troops, whose discipline in this difficult situation was remarkable. The colonel addressed his men for about a quarter of an hour, explaining what had happened, telling them he had made an honourable surrender and bidding them farewell. When he had finished, he nodded to the unit's RSM, who gave the soldiers the order to break their arms by crashing their rifle-butts on the ground. Then each man raised his right hand and shouted 'Sieg

Heil!' three times. In its way, it was rather an impressive sight. Off they then all went into captivity, which greatly annoyed the Resistance, who still wanted to shoot eight Germans in revenge for the four men whom they had lost. I certainly would not have liked to have fallen into the hands of some of the Resistance we met. They were stern of feature, uncompromising in their demands and heavily armed.

On September 7 we left Renaix and the whole town came out to say goodbye. They seemed sorry to see us go, and the feeling was mutual as action soon beckoned again. General (later Sir) Miles Dempsey, Second Army Commander, called in to see us and declared that there was almost nothing left to oppose us once we reached Germany. Some believed this kind of guff from on high, but not many. We had seen how the German Army had defended France and Belgium, and it seemed most unlikely that their resistance would suddenly disintegrate when they were defending their own homeland.

We followed the Guards Armoured Division through Voorde and into Brussels, which had only just been liberated. Our progress through the city recalled the scenes of triumphant Romans parading through their own capital. The Colonel, concerned at the difficulty of taking an armoured regimental group, together with all its supply vehicles, through the Brussels streets, made the mistake of despatching Michael Gold on a recce. But Michael, fresh from the liberation of Paris, was not a man to rush a moment like this. He clearly felt that we all needed to savour the heady brew of liberation and took us right through the centre of the city. It seemed the whole population was out on the streets. We sat on top of our tanks and tried to catch the copious quantities of food, flowers and wine thrown at us by the delirious crowds. We waved until our arms were sore, returned their cheers and grabbed at any girl who came close enough. Never have I seen such a spontaneous outburst of sheer joy, and our own smiles were as broad as the ocean. All the same, our delirium was not of quite the same order as that of those we had liberated. For them the war was truly over, whereas for us that was still in the future. We were all light-headed and content to share the ecstatic and frenzied welcome, but we were not entirely devoid of anxieties: my own remained centred on my parents' plight in Hong Kong and on the destruction being wrought on our families at home by the V1 and V2 attacks.

Our progress through Brussels was very slow and evening was falling as we moved out the other side and on towards Louvain. We spent the night at Herschot, a few miles north of Brussels, having covered the best part of sixty miles that day. Two days of rest and maintenance followed. These were badly needed: some of the tanks which had landed on D-Day had covered about 2,000 miles. We now had the opportunity to return to Brussels and most of us took it. I went back with Jack Holman and Ted Cooke and we had a terrific time. Every restaurant we entered contained people desperate to buy us a drink or a meal. Beautiful girls implored us to dance and to give them the insignia off our battledresses as souvenirs. I like to think that we extracted suitable forfeits for our generosity, but all I can say is that this was probably the only time in my life when I might reasonably have asked for a harem and had my wish granted. Quite how we found our way back to the Regiment, I do not know, but I have always had a soft spot for the Belgian capital ever since.

Beyond Brussels, however, German resistance was stiffening and we were about to get into some of the most bitter fighting the Regiment endured during the whole war. For C Squadron, it was certainly worse than Berjou. My own crew was also about to change. Since Arthur Reddish had retired to England with his damaged finger after Normandy, I was left with a smaller crew of four for the chase through France – Bill Cousins (gunner), Geoff Storey (driver) and Sam Kirman (wireless operator). Now Geoff and Sam, both of whom had been with me through training to D-Day and beyond, were to go. Geoff was moved to another, less experienced crew, while Sam, so recently promoted sergeant, went to RHQ to operate for the Regimental second-in-command. In their place came Bob Ingall as my driver and Corporal Jim Darrington as wireless operator. Together with Bill Cousins, they made a formidable bunch, although we were still short of manpower and so didn't have a co-driver/lap-gunner, something of a disadvantage in close fighting.

Our progress through Brussels and the festive spirit of our stay in the area had made us a little blasé about the continuing threat posed by the war. I certainly felt that I had by now become something of a veteran and that I could deal with any situation which presented itself. For a mere stripling of twenty, these were dangerous thoughts, and I ought to have known enough about the German Army from my time in Normandy to realise that wounded and cornered tigers have to be treated with the greatest caution and respect. This lesson I was soon to learn at Gheel.

CHAPTER EIGHT **GHEEL**

On September 6 the Guards Armoured Division, leading XXX Corps, were ordered to capture two bridges over the Albert Canal on the road to Arnhem. This was a preliminary to Operation Comet, which in its turn became Operation Market Garden. One bridge had been destroyed but the other, at Beeringen, was still usable by infantry and a small bridgehead was established on September 7. Gradually the bridgehead was enlarged and Royal Engineers built a Bailey bridge to take tanks. German resistance in the area was very stiff: a miscellaneous collection of retreating troops had been formed into a battle group with the precise intention of defending the line of the Albert Canal, and as the Germans began to appreciate the importance of the line, so they brought down reinforcements from the north to strengthen their defences still further.

It was imperative that this defence line be destroyed because of the imminence of Market Garden at Arnhem. In addition, 11th Armoured Division had been having great difficulty in breaking out of the Antwerp area just to the west, so the Commander XXX Corps, General Horrocks, ordered 50th Northumbrian Division to capture another bridgehead over the Albert Canal at Gheel. Early on September 8, the 69th Brigade of this division attacked across the canal and began the building of a bridge. On the next day 151 Brigade passed through and captured the village of Oostham on the way to Gheel, but they found themselves under heavy German counter-attack from tanks and infantry. Thus it was that early in the morning of September 10, Stanley Christopherson received orders to take the Sherwood Rangers into the bridgehead to support 151 Brigade and drive through to capture Gheel, a largish town a few miles beyond the Albert Canal.

The insecurity of the whole situation was shown vividly when Stanley reached 151 Brigade HQ. The Brigadier had crossed the canal and established his HQ within the small perimeter, confident enough to bring his caravan with him. As Stanley was discussing with him the plan for bringing the Regiment up, the Brigadier's Intelligence Officer approached and said: 'I think I should tell you, sir, that there are two enemy tanks in a sunken lane 300 yards to our left flank. If you look carefully, you can see them and it is quite easy to hear them.'

'For God's sake,' exclaimed the Brigadier, 'bring your tanks up quickly.' Whereupon he barked out some rapid orders and both his HQ and his caravan hurtled back over the Albert Canal, pursued by machine-gun bullets from the German tanks.

It was mid-morning on September 10 when we first set off from our position south of the Albert Canal. Visibility was good but the weather was sultry with the threat of thunder. Lack of information about the enemy made our crossing seem uneventful and tolerably pleasant, but then ignorance is bliss. C Squadron was to support the 6th Battalion Durham Light Infantry; all the battalions of 151 Brigade came from the DLI. We linked up with them to the south-west of Gheel and at 1400 hours, after a preliminary artillery barrage, we started off towards the town, the infantry just ahead of our tanks. The approach was across flat pastureland, devoid of the sort of dangers we had faced in Normandy. But we were aware that carefree swanning through the countryside was at an end and we remained watchful. The atmosphere was tense.

The company I was supporting seemed abnormally small, since I never saw more than about thirty men, and after we had gone about a hundred yards, the inevitable Spandaus opened up. The infantry had a rotten time and I could see them falling to the left and right of me. One of their officers was virtually cut in half as he received a belt of bullets all to himself. They then went to ground in whatever cover they could find and frantically waved at us to take the lead. It was one of those days when I thanked my lucky stars that I had not volunteered to join the infantry.

My own troop that day consisted of myself, Sergeant Nesling and Corporal Burnett. Both of their tanks were Fireflies fitted with the 17-pounder gun, which was much more suited to a tank-killing role, while my own tank's 75-millimetre was an ideal weapon for infantry support because of its higher rate of fire. But the Fireflies lacked a second machine-gun and, as I did not have a co-driver/lap-gunner, my own tank was also effectively operating with just one machine-gun. So the firepower in my troop was more limited than would have seemed wise in the circumstances.

Nonetheless we advanced beyond the infantry cowering in whatever holes they could scrape out of the ground, and we put down the heaviest fire we could with both our machine-guns and main guns. The Germans remained in their slit trenches firing back but lacked the capacity to do us much harm. At one stage I moved so close to their trenches that I had to reverse my tank in order to depress the gun sufficiently to fire high explosive point-blank. All this had the desired effect. The enemy simply could not cope with the weight of fire we put down, and we just ran the trenches over so that the infantry following behind us could poke the Germans out at the point of the bayonet. From time to time a white flag would appear in some positions, but we could not get out to take the surrender for fear of being sniped at from elsewhere, and so we just by-passed these groups and left them to the infantry. In fact, the surrendering Germans were loth to emerge into the open themselves because of the very real danger that they would be shot by their own side. The fanaticism of the defenders in this particular sector was very marked; they seemed to be relatively young and, when night fell, we could hear them shouting in English: 'We are prepared to die for Hitler. We intend to die for Hitler.'

B Squadron, following closely behind us and then fanning out into the south-west corner of the bridgehead in support of the 9th DLI, also experienced some intense fighting. That afternoon they were violently counter-attacked and, although they withstood it, Michael Gold was wounded in the head, subsequently losing an eye. He retired to hospital in Brussels, where he benefited from the attention of recently met Belgian friends who brought him so much champagne that a continuous stream of the stuff seemed to be foaming from his empty eye socket.

Meanwhile my troop joined the road that ran into Gheel from the west. I told the nearest platoon commander, the only other officer I could see, that if he followed closely behind me, I would put a shell into every house on either side of the street: this would reduce the danger from the Spandau fire that was always such a nightmare for the infantry. As we moved into the town outskirts, we knocked out an 88-millimetre sited near a farmhouse and then steadily made our way towards the centre. Our progress was accompanied by the almost con-stant pinging of Spandau bullets on the armour of the tank. I directed our fire into every house we passed, and we then approached a T-junc-tion where another 88-millimetre and an ammunition lorry were burn-ing. Germans were now surrendering in ever increasing numbers. Civilians also began to come out of their houses and wave Belgian flags at us, so I really had the feeling that another town had been suc-cessfully liberated. I calculated that in our passage through the town we had fired about sixty shells: we were beginning to run short of ammu-nition, and so I left the infantry to look after the prisoners and headed straight into the main square of Gheel to cover the northern and east-ern approaches. Corporal Burnett, just behind me, brewed up a German staff car and three officers who had been in it ran for their lives, and we also destroyed four light anti-aircraft guns. We had encountered only moderate resistance and had not yet seen any German tanks or serviceable anti-tank weapons apart from the one 88-millimetre we had shot up.

At the centre of Gheel, where I was now firmly planted with my troop, all seemed quiet, so much so that I called up Jack Holman on the radio to tell him the way was clear. He roared up about ten minutes later in his scout car, by which time I had positioned my troop of tanks and the infantry to cover the main approaches from north and east. The rest of C Squadron had reached Gheel and were either somewhere in the town or on the outskirts. Jack himself made his HQ with us in the main square, and we assumed that the position would soon be consolidated by the arrival of further support.

As the day wore on, however, it became clear that all was not well. There appeared to be fierce fighting going on in other parts of the bridgehead this side of the Albert Canal and, when I switched over to the radio frequencies of other squadrons, the presence of German tanks was mentioned several times. Just before dark, disturbing reports came through that a strong German counter-attack had been mounted on the bridgehead, and soon after news that the road back to the canal had been cut: we were effectively surrounded in Gheel. Even more ominously, the civilians began to take down the flags and bunting with which they had greeted us, no doubt anticipating that we might not be around for much longer. It was a rather eerie feeling to realise that they knew something we did not.

I let Sergeant Nesling go further up the road to the north off the square towards the railway, and I then made a recce on foot myself. On the level crossing stood a self-propelled gun and there were clear signs that other Germans were in the vicinity. We retreated back to our previous positions in the square to await events. Soon, around dusk, the sound of firing erupted not very far away. I later learned that the whole of Ted Cooke's troop had been knocked out and Ted himself killed. I had become quite friendly with him since he had joined us after Berjou, and we had spent a good day together in Brussels. He came from Gloucestershire, looked like Gary Cooper, had recently been married and was just twenty-one years old.

The enemy were now very close to us in the square. Suddenly a German self-propelled gun appeared down the road I was watching, but I saw him before he saw us and shot him up. The problem was that it was impossible to watch all the approaches satisfactorily with just three tanks and half a company of infantry. Jack called up the Colonel to ask for more tank support but was told that this was impossible before morning. We were now very short of ammunition, but Sergeant Stanton made a bold dash with the ammunition truck through the German cordon to reach us – an act of considerable heroism.

As darkness fell, we became increasingly nervous. The Germans opposing us were very determined. Their infantry kept penetrating within our lines and then used flares to illuminate our tanks, making them an easy target for their own tanks as they crept up. Our own infantry was so thin on the ground that it was virtually impossible to stop this infiltration. Between Gheel and the canal were a lot of sunken lanes and orchards, which gave plenty of cover to the attackers. Johnnie Mann was hit in the head by a sniper as he stood in his turret and then his tank was set on fire, engulfing the whole crew. Johnnie was one of the most experienced officers left in the Regiment, having been with it since North Africa.

We remained on the alert throughout the night, which was the worst I have ever spent anywhere. The infantry kept sending us deeply pessimistic reports and then asking us to go out and perform some impossible task, such as dealing with an enemy patrol they had supposedly seen to their front. The Germans kept pushing tanks and SP guns forward. Just before midnight we heard what sounded like a Jagdpanther, but for a long time we could not see where it was. Then Corporal

Burnett spotted it creeping down a side street, waited for it around a corner and sent an armour-piercing shot from his 17-pounder into its fighting compartment at just ten yards' range. I felt the blast a good hundred yards away and of course waited in even greater trepidation for the next infiltration by the enemy. Tank battles at such short range were not likely to lead to a very long life, I thought to myself, and I am sure everyone else there was thinking exactly the same. Sadly, Corporal Burnett was killed by a sniper the next day and my troop lost a very skilled and brave tank commander.

At dawn we heard still more German tanks milling around and they began to shell us in earnest. My own tank was covered in bricks, plaster and glass. There was dust everywhere, even inside the tank. All my crew were tired and apprehensive, as I was too, but I thanked my lucky stars that I had men as steadfast as Bob Ingall, Jim Darrington and Bill Cousins with me. The infantry with us from the DLI were nothing like so steadfast; they were clearly demoralised and battle-weary, having been in the van of the advance since D-Day. They abandoned some of their positions and even some of the anti-tank guns which they had brought into Gheel, so I had to go and remove the firing-pins to prevent the guns being of use to the enemy.

When morning came, we realised that we had no infantry left in front of us to protect us from Panzerfausts. Just in front of us a Bren Gun Carrier was brewed up, and shells were falling all around. The Germans must have felt confident that we were finished because at about mid-day, when things seemed quieter, their infantry started marching up the road towards us in line. This was a golden opportunity and we made the most of it, firing our machine-guns at close range into their formation. Then, a little later, I had a message from Jack to join him in the square on foot: he had decided to withdraw to prepared positions to the south and he wanted to inform Jimmy McWilliam and me how he proposed to effect this really rather difficult and dangerous manoeuvre. Jack was aware that our position in the centre of Gheel was precarious, to say the least. Only six tanks of the squadron were still intact and it could only be a matter of time before we were over-run. Furthermore B Squadron, in trying to reinforce us, had lost seven tanks themselves; Michael Gold and Colin Thompson had been wounded, and Dick Holman in A Squadron had been very lucky to escape almost unscathed when his tank was hit and one of his crew killed. In the event, he had to retire from action for a while with burst eardrums.

Jimmy and I made our way back to our tanks, which had been stand-

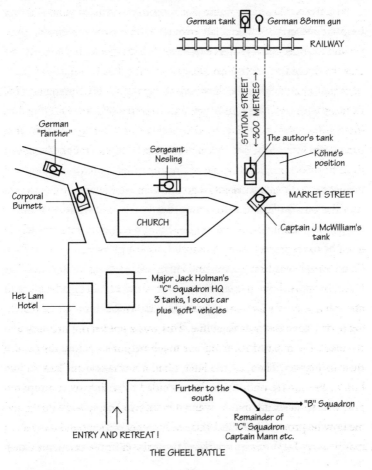

THE GHEEL BATTLE

ing virtually back-to-back while he watched one road and I another. Suddenly there was an almighty crash and Jimmy's tank burst into flames. He and all his crew tumbled out except for his driver, Corporal Higgins, whom we presumed (and hoped) had been killed outright. It was a wicked moment: I had no idea from where the shot had come or what kind of weapon had been used, and it was clear that Jimmy's crew were no wiser than us. I moved slightly forward, presuming Jimmy must have been hit by something coming down the street he had been watching, but in truth the shot could have come either from that direction or from one of any number of houses overlooking us. A single German infantryman with a Panzerfaust was the likeliest suspect, either in a window or a doorway, but anyway I sent a message over the air that we were now another tank short.

My mind was full of horrors. I had seen at the closest possible range what had happened to Jimmy and now it was very likely that the same thing was going to happen to me. Here I was sitting in my Sherman with all its firepower, but I could not identify any target or even guess in what direction I should be looking. Sure enough, about two minutes later, there was a terrific sheet of flame and shower of sparks as we were hit. We fired the Browning machine-gun in what we thought was the direction of the shot and backed furiously if rather clumsily into the main square, thankful to be able to move at all. A piece of shrapnel had grazed my forehead and taken my beret with it, but that was the extent of the damage to any of us. My driver, Bob Ingall, said that he had seen a German infantryman a second before he fired his Panzerfaust at us and had felt the blast on his legs. I did not have the chance right then to look at the damage, but I later found that half a track plate had been shot away on our starboard side and that a hole had been punched right through the entire sprocket assembly into the differential. If we had had a co-driver that day, he would almost certainly have been killed or at least lost his legs. I could only thank God that the German had not fired directly at the turret, because the range could not have been more than ten yards. We were very fortunate still to be alive, let alone able to move.

The biggest fear of any tank crew was a direct hit. Most of us experienced one at some time or another, and it was largely a matter of luck whether you emerged alive. Much depended on what hit you and where on the tank the shot struck. The Sherman, and in particular the marks which were petrol- rather than diesel-fuelled, caught fire easily and, almost invariably, it did so the first time it was hit. The worst fear was to be hit by an armour-piercing high-velocity shell from another tank or a specialised anti-tank gun such as an 88-millimetre. The result of this was devastating, regardless of the point of impact. If the shot struck the turret, the driver and co-driver might be able to bale out unscathed before fire took hold; conversely, a shot in the driver's section might allow the turret crew to escape. If the shot lodged in the armour but did not penetrate, fragments from the inside of the armour could be detached like small projectiles through the interior of the tank, inflicting vicious wounds on the crew. If the shot penetrated the hull, then the shell's white-hot nose would ricochet about inside, burning and destroying whatever it touched. Any ammunition or fuel with which it came into contact would ignite and the tank would start burning fiercely. Those not killed outright by the initial impact had a second or two to escape through the turret or a hatch but, even if they succeeded in getting out, they would almost certainly suffer disfiguring burns or worse. Usually, however, there was little left to recover from a burning tank except a few bones and a heap of ashes.

For those watching, the sight of a burning tank was terrible to behold. Because the fire was contained within the armoured hull, flames and smoke were forced out of the turret with some strength and velocity. Then, if the shells stored inside were exploding, the smoke came out in puffs, assuming the form of symmetrical rings which possessed a baleful beauty all of their own. The first time I saw something like this was on D-day itself when I glimpsed two Churchills burning on the beach, but I had seen it many times since – at Fontenay, Ondefontaine, Berjou and now in Gheel. Sometimes it was impossible to know until later whether or not the crew had survived; you hoped for the best but feared the worst. I remember seeing Sergeant Stock at St Nicholas Farm, just beyond Fontenay, soon after he had baled out. He was very badly burnt but managed to recover, and quite by chance after the war I ran into him – he was easily recognisable by his scarred face – in a London night club of which he was the proprietor.

Luckily the shot which struck my tank in Gheel was from a Panzerfaust rather than an 88-millimetre. A Panzerfaust fired at relatively close range could penetrate the hull although not necessarily set it on fire. If my adversary had fired at the turret of my tank, I would have had it for sure, but luckily he aimed at the empty co-driver's compartment. As it was, the impact was considerable and, with the top of my head sticking out of the turret, I knew that I had done well to escape with just a grazed forehead. Jimmy's tank had been hit more solidly and in those circumstances a Panzerfaust shot could be deadly, as indeed it was for Corporal Higgins.

I jumped out of my tank in the main square and ran across to talk to Jack. Meanwhile Sergeant Nesling, who was commanding the remaining tank of my troop, still had to come back from his rather exposed forward position. He managed this at top speed and with his Browning blazing away at the area from which he believed the Panzerfaust shot had come. He was later awarded the DCM for his brave conduct. Jack and I were now the only two officers left from the Squadron. Jimmy McWilliam was sitting in a doorway. He appeared quite cheerful but had been badly burnt and one of his hands and a leg looked messy. It was the third time that he had been wounded and this particular occasion had tested his considerable sense of humour to the limit. But he was still able to joke and tell me what he intended to do when he got back to Glasgow, so I had the feeling that he would be all right.

We now had permission to withdraw and we completed this safely while there was still daylight. The order was pre-determined, with tanks going first and last and protecting the infantry, the fitters and the wounded in the middle. I cannot recall that we suffered any casualties in this manoeuvre, but I am certain that we would have been wiped out if we had stayed in Gheel any longer. We spent a day regrouping and then came up into the town again, this time accompanied by elements of the 15th Scottish Division. We were shelled on our approach but otherwise the town was much quieter. The Germans had forcibly removed all Belgian males between the ages of sixteen and sixty when they retreated, and the women of the town were crying uncontrollably. Gheel itself was a shambles, with hundreds of our own and German dead still lying around.

Padre Leslie Skinner recorded in his diary what he saw and did on September 12: 'After half an hour shelling died down and I managed to take the truck forward to Gheel. Took up bodies I had buried hurriedly last night, then cleared what was left of Johnnie Mann's tank and two others brewed up yesterday. Fearful job searching ash. Went on to clear two other tanks knocked out yesterday. Ghastly – two orderlies helping me had to give up. Buried ten across canal in extension of Stelen Parish Church grounds where infantry had already begun burials. In view of time factor in crossing and re-crossing canal decided to bury remaining casualties in Gheel. Collected several more and left them stitched in blankets etc behind churchyard wall while I went for others. When I returned found Belgian civilians had prepared a space for a mass grave for several civilians dead and had gathered up the Sherwood Rangers previously prepared for burial by me. Quite an argument ensued. At last agreed to have two services. I would bury my dead at one end and leave them to do the same with their own. As I read the service, shells flew over very close. When one actually hit the church, the Belgians fled, leaving me and my driver to finish the service. When the next shell hit the church wall above our heads, we both instinctively dived for cover. Only time in my life I have actually been in the grave during a service. At time did not seem at all odd – merely sensible. Few moments later service resumed and finished.'

Stanley Christopherson was well aware just how hard the fighting had been in Gheel: he had had a narrow escape himself. German infantry had infiltrated the previous night and attacked the reserve company positions just 300 yards from RHQ. The threat lasted all through that night and well into the next day, from tanks as well as infantry. On the afternoon of September 11 a corporal from a section close to Stanley's tank came across and pointed out a tank creeping down a lane about 300 yards to the front.

'I should just like you to confirm, sir,' the corporal said, 'that the tank over there is one of yours.'

Stanley wandered over to look and suddenly realised it was a German Panther. The HQ tanks were completely exposed and Stanley's own tank had only the wireless operator in it. Luckily the German tank commander was more worried at that moment about his rear and the turret was pointing the other way. Stanley did not want to give away his position by starting his own tank's engine, so he raced across to Dick Holman's A Squadron troop and enlisted the aid of Sergeant Charity, whose Sherman had a 17-pounder gun. Stanley stood on the back of this tank and directed it down a sunken lane to find a position from which it could engage the Panther. The first two shots missed, but they woke up the Panther, which began to traverse its gun ominously towards them. The third armour-piercing shot struck home into the Panther's turret and three more followed, destroying the German tank. It had been a very close call.

The fighting around Gheel had been the worst the Regiment had endured since D-Day. It was clear that these were experienced German troops with a fierce commitment to the cause, backed up by heavy armoured support and anti-tank weapons. The Sherwood Rangers suffered 46 casualties, half of whom (a very high proportion) were dead, and these included two officers killed and another three wounded. Another fatal casualty was my old driver, Geoff Storey, whose whole crew had gone. Eleven tanks had been knocked out and two damaged – the highest number in one engagement since seventeen had been lost in the desert at Wadi Zem Zem. Tanks were easily replaceable, but experienced crews were not and an awful lot of them were killed or wounded at Gheel. A shiver goes down my spine whenever I revisit the town, for I know that I was extremely lucky to come out of the place unscathed. Nevertheless it is an action on which I look back with some pride because I know that C Squadron fought a good fight, and that we were instrumental in ensuring that the bridgehead beyond the Albert Canal would not be driven in by the enemy. If this had happened, our drive towards the Rhine might well have been stalled.

Even now, I find it difficult to explain what battle is like. Many who have fought in the front line on land or sea or in the air have endeavoured to describe their feelings while in action, trying to convey the physical and mental sensations in a way that non-combatants can comprehend. In one sense I have been both lucky and unlucky in that over a period of fifty years I have had recurring dreams of being in action again. Each time within my dream I have told myself that I am really dreaming, only having to accept, within the vividness of my dream, that I am not. And in that instant the horror returns and I find myself in both despair and terror. Once I am awake, it is over and sublime relief returns. Unhappily, of course, there was no such relief at the time. To fall asleep after some horrendous and distressing action such as Berjou or Gheel was never a problem, as I was totally drained. The subsequent awakening, however, brought utter dejection: one felt a sense of hopelessness, gloom and depression as one realised that the strains and torment were about to continue. As a comparative youngster, certainly to begin with, I was paradoxically perhaps better able to cope than my seniors, who had been through more than I had, but quite what reserves and resources I called upon I do not know. All I am certain of is that I was fearful, and that I was glad to have good companions around me.

I often elected to guard alone for a lengthy period during the night. This gave me the opportunity to gaze at the stars and think great thoughts about life and the universe, which somehow gave me strength and resolve. I was as afraid of being badly wounded as of death itself, but I was also aware that fate was bound to play its hand in determining my destiny. It was not a lot of comfort, but at least it was a philosophy I could accept without having to worry further.

CHAPTER NINE **NIJMEGEN**

The fighting at Gheel was followed by a few days' rest at Leopolds-burg, about thirty miles or so east and close to Beeringen. It was attractive wooded countryside and we camped in some heather among the trees. The rest of the 8th Armoured Brigade was there too, cele-brating the first official stand-down that could be remembered since D-Day. A party was held for officers at Brigade HQ, and we also heard that at long last some decorations had come through for the Regiment. John Semken, A Squadron Commander, had won the MC, along with Ian Greenaway, who had lost a leg in Normandy, and Johnnie Mann, so recently killed at Gheel. There were also MMs for Sergeants Saunders, Nelson and Birch, while Sergeant Dring had won a bar to his MM. All of these were thoroughly deserved and gave a lift to the whole Regi-ment: our deeds had been both recorded and appreciated.

Two new officers joined C Squadron at Leopoldsburg. Captain Dick Radcliff, an Australian from Tasmania, came to us from the disbanded 24th Lancers, with whom he had landed in Normandy, and Second Lieutenant John Holmes arrived direct from Sandhurst. Jack Holman was very pleased to be promoted major and remained in command of the squadron. Change affected me too because Jim Darrington, my wireless operator, was taken away from me to command his own tank in my troop.

Our rest at Leopoldsburg was gradually overtaken by preparations for the next big push, and it was clear that this was something out of the ordinary. The Colonel attended a conference at XXX Corps HQ, where General Horrocks spoke of present dispositions and future plans. Stanley was a little put out that Horrocks showered tributes on 43 and 50 Divisions for their successes in recent weeks, and also congratulated 11th Armoured and Guards Armoured Divisions, but made little mention of our own 8th Armoured Brigade. This was felt to be a bit hard considering how much help we had given the two infantry divisions to get them this far. Within large formations, such as an Army Corps, teamwork is the essence of success and no single part can function properly without the support given by all kinds of different arms. It is therefore always inappropriate for a Corps Commander to single out anyone in public in such a fashion; all this can be left to the judgement of history. To be fair to Horrocks, however, he was later very complimentary indeed about the Regiment.

The other part of Horrocks's briefing concerned the coming Operation Market Garden. Much space in the military history books has been expended on Arnhem. It was Montgomery's idea, enthusiastically supported by Eisenhower, to use the Allied Airborne Army to capture vital bridges at Eindhoven, Grave, Nijmegen and finally Arnhem. XXX Corps would then advance as fast as possible along the airborne carpet laid down and drive northwards across the Lower Rhine and into Germany. If successful, the operation would cut off all the German forces in Holland, open up the port of Antwerp and put the British armour on the north German plain the far side of the Rhine with an open road to Berlin. But it was a massive gamble, one which involved Eisenhower holding back Patton in Lorraine to ensure that Market Garden had sufficient fuel. It also depended on perfect timing and some luck, neither of which materialised. Montgomery has been accused of negligence in ignoring the presence of strong German Panzer units in the Arnhem area, while the other main problem was the very narrow road along which the tanks of XXX Corps had to advance quickly enough to relieve the lightly armed airborne forces.

The lead for XXX Corps was to be taken by the Guards Armoured Division, who made good progress to start with. They joined up with the Americans at Eindhoven and then drove through to Nijmegen. Here they became part of the epic operation of the US 82nd Airborne to capture the Nijmegen bridge, so vividly portrayed in the film *A Bridge Too Far*. This involved an assault across the river by an American battalion to hit the bridge from the far side and prevent the Germans from blowing it. General Dempsey described the assault as one of the great feats of arms of the whole war, and it opened up the bridge and the road beyond to the British tanks, with Arnhem just nine miles away. For one reason or another, however, the tanks of Guards Armoured failed to press on, setting up defensive positions for the night just beyond Nijmegen while Colonel Frost and his beleaguered forces grimly held on at Arnhem Bridge. When the tanks finally moved out next morning, they were stopped about halfway to Arnhem by enemy forces and that afternoon the defenders of Arnhem were finally overwhelmed and the whole operation failed. Colonel Frost later put the blame firmly on the lack of drive by Guards Armoured, comparing their relatively light casualties with those suffered by the British 1st Airborne and US 82nd. Forty years later, he stood on the bridge at a reunion, shook his fist and roared a question into the air for the Guards: 'Do you call that fighting?' It may have been an unfair judgement born of frustration, but the arguments about who was to blame for Arnhem have reverberated loudly down the years.

Would 8th Armoured Brigade or the Sherwood Rangers have done any better? It's impossible to say. Certainly, for the next six months the front line in Holland hardly moved, condemning both us and the other British and American forces in the area to a largely static slogging match in miserable conditions. Arnhem was probably worth the gamble, but its failure took the momentum out of the Allied advance and it transformed the German Army from a dispirited, beaten force into one prepared to fight tenaciously in defence of its own homeland. And of this we were all to suffer the consequences.

The Sherwood Rangers were detached from the rest of 8th Armoured Brigade for this entire operation and given initially an independent picketing role. We were some way behind the spearhead of the advance, but reached Grave on the evening of September 20. There was not much opposition, although the enemy sporadically cut the road behind us. Eventually we moved on further to Brackenstein, just south of Nijmegen, where we came under the command of General Gavin and the US 82nd Airborne Division. Here we were to remain for some time to come, working with the Americans to widen the Nijmegen bridgehead to the east of the town.

The 82nd Airborne held a large area, dominated by the high ground around Dekkenswald and Groesbeek. The line passed through Nijmegen, Beek and Enbrock, and it actually ran over the German border about a mile or so from the Reichswald, a large, forested area which was to be the scene of heavy fighting over the next few weeks. The Americans did not entirely appreciate the difficulties of operating tanks in the Reichswald: their general suggested to us that we might like to clear a section of it without infantry support – a task that eventually involved many divisions. However Ian McKay did take his Recce Troop over the German frontier near Beek and they became the first British troops to cross into Germany. All this was enthusiastically written up by the British Press and announced on the BBC by Frank Gillard, so the Sherwood Rangers achieved some good publicity and received congratulatory letters from various sources including the Town Clerk of Newark. I was myself interviewed by Frank Gillard and, on the BBC the following morning, Denis Elmore's sister Sheila heard that I was also named as one of the first to cross the frontier.

The widening of the Nijmegen bridgehead involved two squadrons working each day while the third rested, and this went on for about three weeks during which C Squadron always seemed to get the difficult jobs. Every time my troop went out, we seemed to find trouble, although I greatly enjoyed working with the Americans, who were grand soldiers. General Horrocks later told me that the two American Airborne Divisions, the 82nd and the 101st, were the pick of the US Army. As events unfolded, I was to have ample grounds for endorsing Horrocks's opinion. The Americans' apparent brashness and their swashbuckling attitude towards danger seemed to verge on the reckless and likely to precipitate unnecessary risks. But I found that their cocky bearing gave us encouragement rather than cause for concern. The fact that the flamboyance of the Sherwood Rangers also appealed to them resulted in a happy and successful partnership.

On our first patrol with the 82nd we did a recce eastwards and met little opposition, but the second occasion was rather different. We went down the river towards Beek to put in an attack on some strongly held positions just inside the German border. Our axis of advance was along three roughly parallel dyke roads. I led my troop down the right-hand one, John Holmes took his down the left-hand one nearest the river, and the other three tanks went down the middle. It was raining and extremely dismal as we set off, and I was feeling anything but confident. We were not able to get off the roads because the fields beyond were flooded, and so were sitting ducks if fired on. The American infantry followed us up between the roads and we fired everything we had to give them good cover; indeed, I remember Bill Cousins, my gunner, claimed a pig and several chickens en route. There was no sign of the enemy until we neared a windmill, where they had been dug in along the side of the road. As we came along, they ran for it and we fired a few shots at their backsides, but as we drew closer to the windmill a certain amount of fire came from the orchard between me and it. A German with a Panzerfaust was spotted just in time by Bill Cousins, who shot first, and I moved my tank down a convenient path towards the orchard to deal with the threat from that direction. Jim Darrington, following close behind me in his tank, carried on towards the windmill and was almost immediately hit by a Panzerfaust. He managed to bale out with his crew before his tank was then hit by three shells from an 88-millimetre and started brewing up. The third member of my troop, Sergeant Nesling, saw what had happened and quickly cut down the path to join me in the orchard.

Meanwhile the other two troops had made better progress and it was left to me to try to extricate myself and my troop successfully. I sent Jim Darrington and his crew back, but since it was futile for me to try to get back on to the road again, I stayed where I was and was then joined by Sergeant Jones from the middle troop. This at least meant that I had three tanks, but the Germans knew exactly where we were and they started to shell us rather too accurately. The American infantry

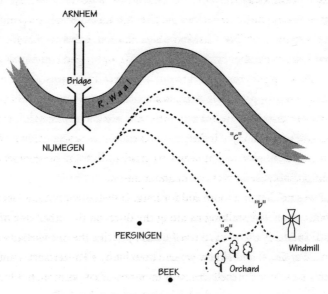

ACTION EAST OF NIJMEGEN

were still with us, out in the open in very shallow and vulnerable trenches, but their fortitude was remarkable. I decided to try to move forward to improve the situation and give the infantry more protection, but I only succeeded in driving into a hidden dyke. The tank heeled over on to its side and we were stuck fast, unable to move without assistance or to fire our guns. Our plight was compounded by the presence of enemy positions only 400 yards to our front. They must have felt that this was their lucky day and began firing 20-millimetre machine-guns at us. The bullets could not penetrate the turret but made a fearful racket and caused sparks to fly around inside, and there was some risk that shots would come straight through the turret flaps and into the tank. We felt like a very large duck in a fairground shooting gallery. I tried to remain calm inside the tank with my crew, but we were all sweating profusely and swearing volubly.

The Germans' fire also set alight some bedding on Sergeant Jones's tank, not far away from us. He climbed from the turret and put the flames out, no mean feat under the circumstances, then hauled himself back into his tank. He must have been in quite a temper, because the next shell he fired hit the machine-gun post and wiped it out. This only marginally improved my position: there were still plenty of Germans in close proximity and I had no means of shooting at them. All I could do was to give Jack Holman and the infantry colonel an idea of what was going on via my wireless. To make matters worse, Arthur Warburton was unable to put down an artillery barrage on the German positions because he was out of ammunition.

I was not left at a loose end for long. Unbeknown to us, a German infantryman was stalking us along the ditch on the other side of the road. Suddenly there was a terrific flash just like the one we had experienced at Gheel and I knew we had been hit by a Panzerfaust. I am not even sure where the shell struck us in our inverted position, but luckily it did not cause any damage beyond the initial shock. We managed to bale out quickly and ran for the nearest ditch. Sergeant Nesling let fly with his 17-pounder at the offending German and his Panzerfaust and destroyed both. I saw no purpose now in hanging around and, along with my crew, dashed swiftly from ditch to ditch. Every time a machine-gun opened up, we sprawled headlong into the dirt before moving on again as it swung away. There was also considerable danger from shell-fire, yet we eventually made it to where Jack and Squadron HQ were positioned further back along the road. I stayed with Jack until night fell and then made my way into Beek. We had had to leave all our kit in the tank when we baled out, so I scrounged around and managed to acquire some magnificent blankets from a house in Beek, where I kipped down for the night. I am slightly ashamed to admit that I also found a house obviously owned by an artist and I helped myself to some of his materials. Next day I returned to the Squadron and was fitted out with replacement kit and a brand-new tank. Two vivid accounts in the *Kent Messenger* and London *Evening Standard* reported the fact that we had been the first British tanks to enter Germany, and these accounts duly proved a talking point for relatives and friends in England.

Elsewhere, A Squadron had been operating further south of Beek in the area of Mook, where some Germans were still resisting, and they suffered another officer casualty when Lieutenant Harry Heenan was killed in a most unlucky way. David Render, who was his best friend, recounts how they were both about 700 yards apart, just north of Mook with their respective troops. A German 88-millimetre opened up on David and caused him to retreat rapidly. David then notified Harry of the gun's location and Harry, now on foot, guided one of his tanks to direct fire on it. The gun was duly destroyed. Harry was so elated by this that he rushed back to his tank and, as he jumped into the turret with his Sten gun, he dropped it, so that the base of the Sten hit the floor of the turret, setting off the firing mechanism and fatally wounding him in the thigh and stomach. Harry was just twenty-one years old, from Cottingham in Yorkshire, and he was buried in a new cemetery created by No. 3 Casualty Clearing Station in a wooded area known as Jonkerbos, about four kilometres from Nijmegen.

At various stages in later life I have retraced the route we took from the Normandy beaches into Germany, and visits to the Commonwealth war cemeteries in which Sherwood Rangers lie have been an important feature of each pilgrimage. The work of the Commonwealth War Graves Commission has been an inspiration not just to veterans like me, but to succeeding generations of schoolchildren who are now able to research their family histories on its computer web-site. I still cannot visit any of the cemeteries, whether from the First or Second War, without feeling the tears rise, not just at the thought of young lives known to me and so tragically cut short, but also at the sheer peacefulness and quiet beauty of each place. The nature of the fast-moving 1939–45 war means that there is nothing like the concentration of death that you find along the Somme or at Ypres, but I defy anyone to enter the British war cemeteries at Bayeux or at Tilly-sur-Seulles, where Keith Douglas and Michael Laycock lie, or at Arnhem without feeling a surge of pride and emotion.

During these operations in support of the Americans, Stanley Christopherson liaised closely with the CO of the American 325 Regiment, Colonel William C. Billingslea. One day two officers from the Guards Armoured visited the two colonels at the American HQ with the news that the Guards would relieve us in a few days' time. Stanley introduced them to Colonel Billingslea and his staff and then explained present dispositions and future plans. A small group then went further forward with Stanley to obtain a better view of the land and, as they crawled through some trees, they must have been spotted because quite heavy shelling started. When this died down and everyone surfaced from cover, it was found that the American adjutant had been killed and one of the Guards officers was missing. Later that evening the other officer returned to say that there was no trace of his companion, who had been the Regimental Intelligence Officer. So Stanley went back to where they had been shelled and could find nothing except a compass lying on the ground, which was duly identified as the Guards officer's. On closer inspection, Stanley discovered that the compass had been lying on the edge of the remains of a slit trench which had obviously received a direct hit from a very large shell. They dug down and found enough fragments to indicate that the Guards officer must have jumped into this trench when the shelling started, but had then been virtually obliterated. It was a sobering realisation that a shell could remove practically all evidence of a human being and even Stanley was badly shaken: he had been speaking to the man barely moments before and had discovered that he was just twenty-one and had only joined his regiment that day. Such are the vagaries of war.

Stanley had great respect for Colonel Billingslea, who was more than ready to accept the dangers of being in the front line. Several times they came under heavy shellfire together, and on one occasion near Mook all their accompanying party was wounded except themselves. As it happened, Mook was shortly to be the location of perhaps the most exciting operation I took part in, and it was the Americans with whom I was to be involved.

Each squadron worked two days and rested for one, and each time we operated it tended to be alternately in the Beek or Mook sectors. I had had my fun at Beek and now C Squadron was sent further south towards Mook. I was actually sitting in the town of Groesbeek, watching the eastern flank, when Jack came on the air and said that a party of Americans were in a jam just to the north-east of me in Den Heuvel woods. Would I go up with my troop and give them a hand?

I set off up the road from Groesbeek, closely followed by the tanks of Sergeants Robinson and Collis. As I turned off the road into a field just short of the American HQ, a couple of high-explosive shells burst near my tank and I realised that we must be under observation by the enemy. I moved the tanks out of sight behind some trees and made my way on foot to the American HQ to find out what they wanted us to do. A patrol of about thirty men had been trapped in Den Heuvel Wood, with a number of wounded, and they needed my tanks, along with a platoon of their own infantry, to get them out.

It seemed a hopeless task since I would not be able to fire my own guns for fear of hitting the American patrol and I would be under enemy observation and fire the whole time. However, it was no time to argue, so I said that I would be back in ten minutes with my tanks. As I walked back, a series of emotions overtook me and I was not far from tears. It appeared to be as close to a suicide mission as I could think of, but I had my orders and there was no question of being able to escape my obligation. I reported over the air to Jack what we were going to do, perhaps hoping that he would realise the absurdity of the demand and somehow extricate me, but he could only offer encouragement and good luck. I was certainly going to need it.

I reached my own tank, climbed in and explained to my crew what we were going to do. Not surprisingly, they were even less enthusiastic than I was, but we all realised we simply had to give it our best shot.

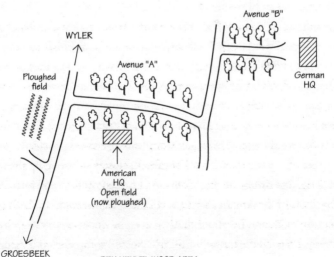

DEN HEUVEL WOOD AREA

It says something for the resilience and imperturbability of the British soldier that such situations were arising on the front all the time, and the
sense of duty almost always prevailed. I called up the other two tanks in
my troop, gave them orders to follow me closely and keep on the move
the whole time. We then roared down the avenue of trees to the American HQ, where we picked up the platoon who would accompany us. I
made it clear to the American lieutenant in command that we must
move quickly, so as not to present too juicy a target for the German
guns. He and his men were heavily armed and had an extremely determined look about them.

We moved off as fast as we could, turned left at a T-junction about
a hundred yards on, and then very soon right into another avenue of
trees which led to the wood. Behind the wood was the German HQ
and the volume of fire showed that we were under constant observation. At the end of the avenue, I placed myself in one corner of the
wood, with Sergeant Collis at the other corner, while Sergeant Robinson
went into the wood with the American platoon to pick up their men.
All three tanks blazed away with their 75-millimetres and machine-
guns in the direction of the enemy and this probably had the desired
effect because, although the German shelling and machine-gun fire was
both heavy and accurate, they did not send over any solid shot which
might have penetrated our tank armour. Most of the American wounded
were carefully placed on the back of Sergeant Robinson's tank, although
I also had some on mine, and we set off back as fast as we could. Other
members of the patrol rode on the tanks in order to hold the wounded
on, and there were also some German prisoners involved, although
unfortunately none of them reached our lines. When we reached the
safety of the American HQ, we unloaded the wounded and I found
that the only healthy man riding on my tank had been wounded too.
We were thanked profusely for our help, bade farewell and returned
to Groesbeek. I remember thinking that I had had quite enough excitement for one day.

We were relaxing near Groesbeek, thanking our lucky stars still to be alive and smoking a much-needed cigarette, when Jack came on the air and said very politely that the Americans again required our services and would I mind cutting up to their HQ for a second time. It all felt a bit like fagging at school and I gave him my views in no uncertain manner before resignedly turning the tank round and making my way forward, along with my troop, to find out what the Americans wanted this time. The news was that they were sending in a stronger force to capture Den Heuvel Wood and the German HQ, and they would appreciate the support of our tanks.

I briefed my crew and the other two tanks of my troop, indicating that we would go flat out into the wood firing all the time with whatever we had. The American infantry would try to protect us from anti-tank weapons. This time the shelling was even more intense, but I roared into the wood and fired on the German HQ, which was a big white house, until my gun jammed. Meanwhile the Americans were fighting hard in the wood, cleaning up the German positions, and they were helped by Sergeant Robinson, whom I called up to join me when my gun jammed. A similar request to Sergeant Collis received no answer, but I continued calling him as, my job done, I made my way back through the wood. The reason for this silence became evident as I emerged into the avenue, where I saw the tank of Collis with smoke pouring from its turret and no sign of the crew. Enemy fire made it impossible to approach and I just hoped that they had got out safely. I could only guess that Collis had not kept moving fast enough in approaching the wood and had been caught by an armour-piercing round. Robinson and I decided not to risk the roads but to make our way back cross-country, so we bade farewell to the Americans and set off to run the gauntlet of enemy fire.

Halfway across a field my driver stalled the engine, but luckily we were not spotted and we managed to get going again. Suddenly we saw Sergeant Collis and his crew, whom we feared were still in their burning tank. They were severely shaken but otherwise unscathed. Apparently the tank had been hit by a shell which had not penetrated the Sherman but had nevertheless disabled it. They had therefore baled out. A few seconds later, an armour-piercing round had gone straight through the turret and brewed up the tank. We gave them a lift back to Groesbeek, where we reported the day's proceedings to Jack and then signed off for the day. It had certainly been a rather full one, and it had been so exciting partly because I had known from the outset that it was going to be extremely dangerous, something which was not often the case.

Later the Colonel received some appreciative letters from the Americans and others. The 82nd Divisional Commander, General James Gavin, wrote that 'we will always remember the Sherwood Rangers Yeomanry for its splendid fighting qualities' and General 'Boy' Browning, commanding the Airborne Corps, told us that 'the American Airborne Division expressed unstinted praise and admiration for the way in which your people have operated'. However, the best compliment came from the Americans with whom we had been most directly involved – Colonel Billingslea and the 325th Glider Infantry:

To: Officer Commanding, the Nottinghamshire Yeomanry (Sherwood Rangers).

1. It is desired to express to you on behalf of this Regiment our appreciation for the fine support given by your organisation throughout the period that it was with us. Particularly I wish to mention the extremely excellent work done by your unit during the attack across the flats near Mook.

2. Your entire command demonstrated a splendid spirit of co-operation in all its relations with this organisation.

3. The Regiment wishes you and all members of your unit the best of luck and the greatest success in all your future undertakings.

Signed,

C. Billingslea, Lieutenant-Colonel 325 Glider Infantry Commanding.

I can only say that the feeling of respect was mutual. They were the finest troops with whom we had the pleasure of co-operating, and I was pleased that my little part in these operations had contributed to the high standing we had with the Americans.

In fact, my days as a Troop Leader were numbered. On September 28 we were up near Beek again when the enemy counter-attacked strongly in the area. They did so before first light, not realising that C Squadron tanks had remained in position all night. When the dawn came, the German armour and infantry were unable to move back or forward across open flat ground. C Squadron had a field day, especially John Holmes, who was sitting on the road nearest the river. He knocked out three tanks himself and Sergeant Nesling another on the road near the windmill. One of John's victims was a Panther, which tried to back off into an empty house, but John's gunner kept pumping shells into it and the house itself collapsed in flames around the tank. The 82nd Infantry with us were also magnificent despite heavy enemy shelling. I remember one man gamely hanging on in a slit trench and continuing to fire his weapon with a leg and an arm blown off.

Then, on October 2, we attacked in support of the Americans near Mook again, towards Middleaar. It was an attack across open country which cost us two tanks, but we did push the line forward further towards the Reichswald. I remember the action particularly because my tank acted as an Observation Post for the artillery of the Essex Yeomanry, and we produced such an accurate barrage on the enemy positions that many prisoners came out. Bill Cousins, my own gunner, was superb that day, pouring shells into the enemy and inflicting many casualties. We were shelled in return quite heavily, and one projectile landed so close that it filled my turret with mud. In the afternoon we retired from the fray because the gun was not working properly, although at the time I had no idea this was to be my last day in action for a while.

We went back for a short rest to Winssen, three miles out of Nijmegen. There the Colonel approached me to ask if I would like to transfer to Regimental HQ as Intelligence Officer. I think he believed that I was becoming fatigued, since I had led my troop virtually continuously since D-Day and had recently taken two serious hits from Panzerfausts. For my part I was quite relieved, because I had been finding tank fighting an increasing strain and I felt that my reflexes were not as good as they had been. It is conceivable that I may even have become just a little 'bomb-happy', but there was no stigma in that and any good commander needed to recognise when someone was due for a rest, because failure to do so endangered not only the soldier himself but also his crew and possibly others.

It is probable that Stanley took advice in this from our Regimental Doctor, who kept a close eye on the welfare of all those in positions of responsibility, especially the youngest of us, and gave sage medical advice. Dr Charles Florence Young, MC, had been with the Regiment since just after El Alamein, and held the rank of Captain RAMC. He was universally known as 'Hilda', a nickname he had acquired before he joined us. He was a tall, middle-aged man with greying hair, a fair complexion, prominent front teeth and a pronounced stoop, so that, as he walked along in his army boots, his head always seemed to precede him. He was a man of independent means who had joined the Army at the outbreak of war and had earned the Military Cross with the British Expeditionary Force in France before being evacuated from Dunkirk. In peacetime he had a practice in Somerset and had deducted a number of years off his age in order to be allowed to join up. He looked younger than he really was.

Dr Young had distinguished himself with the Sherwood Rangers in North Africa, where he often had to use an unarmoured truck. Typically, when the shelling was bad, he would set off on foot across the battlefield, medical kit on his back. He had a mania for seeking out Teller and S Mines, which he would try to lift himself, walking in front of his truck to spare his driver any danger, and many times the Colonel had to warn him about his safety. This predilection might have been explained by the fact that he also had a degree in engineering, which led him often to give help and advice to the engine fitters. His practical skills also led him to invent a 'fly-proof' toilet which even the officers were ordered to use. He caught a fever in Africa which was nearly the end of him but recovered locally and stayed with the Regiment. On the voyage home he was conducting medical experiments into the efficacy of various drugs in counteracting loss of sleep, but after two days he fell asleep himself and nearly went overboard.

For the invasion of Europe Dr Young was better equipped than he had been in the desert. He had two armoured half-track vehicles and he filled them with enough equipment for a hospital. He even made private arrangements to be supplied with whole blood instead of the blood plasma ordinarily supplied in the field. However, when the loading lists arrived for D-Day, there was trouble. For the actual assault Hilda was to have only one half-track and the Padre was to travel with him.

'Absolutely not,' said Hilda and so resolutely dug in his heels that even Colonel Anderson could not resolve the problem. Once he had been taken aside, Hilda explained that he was concerned with the living and the Padre with the dead, and that he did not want to be held up by him in a fast-moving battle. So the Padre was fixed up with a motorcycle for his private transport and all was well.

During the fighting in Normandy Hilda had another clash with authority. The Regiment had been fighting unremittingly around the time of Ondefontaine for several days without sleep. Hilda drove to Brigade HQ, insisted on seeing the Brigadier in person and warned him that the Regiment was no longer fit to fight. His standing was such that the Brigadier cancelled the next day's operation.

He was always cheerful and would roar with laughter at jokes, especially his own, of which he alone would see the point. His laugh was raucous and infectious, causing his whole body to shake. He was also more than a little absent-minded, especially with names. He disdained personal comfort and would usually sleep on a stretcher in the open. He was immensely hard-working and conscientious, and often had to be restrained from dashing up to burning tanks to attend the wounded, rather than waiting for them to be brought to the Regimental Aid Post. He worked himself literally to exhaustion and continued with the Regiment to the end of the war, adding two mentions in despatches to his earlier MC.

Padre Skinner wrote of Dr Young: 'Hilda is infuriating. Whenever one gets mad at him, he is nearly always proved right. Under the ultra-prosaic matter-of-factness and scientific limitations of his thinking, he has an almost fey asceticism and a compassion that knows no bounds when it comes to helping people. He hated to show it and never knew it shone through the whole time.'

After the war he took a hospital post in charge of the accident section, where he was a great trial to the nursing staff, from whom he required an equal dedication to his own. He died unmarried and only a few years after his widowed mother, to whom he was devoted. He was a great source of comfort to me and often offered me wise advice, and he was certainly very conscious of and knowledgeable about the effects of battle on the human frame. Indeed, I can just picture him taking the Colonel aside and saying to him: 'I think young Hills may have had enough for the time being.'

I reported to RHQ on or about October 8, and I was allowed to take Bill Cousins with me as my Dingo driver because he needed a rest as much as anyone. The Dingo was a Humber scout car with four-wheel drive and could accommodate two comfortably. Bill had been almost continuously in action through North Africa and since D-Day but by a savage irony he was wounded our first night at RHQ. We were established in a watchtower at Winssen and at nightfall the Germans started to shell the area. The RHQ officers, myself included, happened to be entertaining a few Guards officers at dinner. As the shelling became worse, I began to wonder who would be the first to suggest that we moved to a safer area, but I suppose that neither we nor the Guards wanted to be the first to chicken out. Eventually a shell landed too close for anyone's comfort and we all sought shelter where we could – Terry Leinster and I in a room on the ground floor. We tried to sleep, thinking that the shelling was just random. But as it became heavier and more accurate, the windows above us started splintering and we moved our beds to the other side of the house.

We tried to sleep again, but the shelling was more and more on top of us, each shot landing within twenty yards of the house, so Terry and I just lay flat on the ground, hoping that there would not be a direct hit. I remember thinking that it would be just my luck to come out of troop action and then be taken out by a shell the first night I spent in a more cushy billet. Immediately one group of shells landed particularly close and we heard the cries and screams of the wounded and a shout for stretcher-bearers. Terry and I dashed round to the front, where I had parked the Dingo, to see if Bill was alright. We could see no sign of him and, as more shells landed close by, we raced down the steps into the cellar of the house, where the Colonel and other officers were. There he made me stay because of the severity of the shelling. Soon after Bill Cousins and some others were brought down wounded to the cellar, where Hilda Young ministered to them. Bill was the most serious case, with severe shrapnel wounds to his legs, and he had to be evacuated back to England. He had been caught sleeping out in the open near the Dingo, which had been badly damaged, three shells landing less than five yards away from it. The Colonel suspected that our HQ had been pinpointed by collaborators, of which there were quite a few in this region, and from this time on we evacuated civilians from forward areas.

There was an amusing aftermath to this incident. The RHQ clerical duo, Sergeants Clive Payne and Frank Holland (both of whom were subsequently awarded BEMs), had pitched their tent in the garden beside the tower. When we emerged from the cellar in the morning, there was the tent surrounded by shell craters. Both men were still sleeping peacefully under its tattered remains: they at least had decided to stand their ground.

For the rest of that month of October, the Sherwood Rangers operated in a static defence role, supporting either 43rd Division or the Americans. Two squadrons were in the line in rotation, but we took part in no pre-planned attacks. I settled in to my role as Intelligence Officer and tried to get to know better the various people at HQ. New officers arrived, many of them from the Gloucestershire Hussars, Robin Leigh's regiment. One of them, 'Frenchie' Houghton, took over as Adjutant, allowing Terry Leinster to return to a sabre squadron. Frenchie had been a lawyer before the war and was half French, hence his nickname. He had a quick brain and a delightful sense of humour, but I had trouble deciphering his writing, which was appalling, and his wayward sense of dress did not amuse the Brigadier.

Frenchie established RHQ in an inn near Mook, which was a stroke of genius. The wife of the inn-keeper was a one-time opera singer who one night entertained us to a concert. Her singing was formidable but it went on for over two and a half hours: Robin Leigh fell asleep and accompanied her with his snoring. The Colonel also acquired from a local policeman a dog which he named Beek. This animal accompanied him throughout the rest of the campaign but was considerably disliked by others at RHQ because of its shrill, high-pitched bark and its habit of snapping at anyone it thought the Colonel disliked.

Peter Selerie returned to us after being wounded in Normandy and immediately took over B Squadron. Another recruit from the Gloucestershire Hussars, Dick Coleman, became second-in-command of C Squadron. The weather was getting colder and we were being prepared for our coming assault on the Siegfried Line. The Colonel attended a demonstration of infantry working with flame-throwing tanks which showed how to attack the pillboxes, concrete emplacements and hedgehogs of this formidable position.

I spent much of my time driving around, visiting various Division and Brigade HQs, gleaning what information I could that would be of use. I also had to keep the Regimental War Diary each day and ensure that the maps being used were up to date. It was rather fun driving around in an open car after having been cooped up for so long in a tank. I was also able to take my sketchbook and try to record little scenes and places and people that I came across. It was an opportunity to forget about war and think about the more ordinary things of life, and there was also the chance to talk to those I met. It was a time during which my mind was refreshed and my spirit rejuvenated – rather like an exeat from school – and I relished being free from the strains and responsibilities of leadership, even if only temporarily.

On October 30 news came through that Jack Holman and I had been awarded the Military Cross, which thrilled me no end, although I tried to remain nonchalant. In my case the award was for my work during the crossing of the Noireau and the subsequent assault on the Berjou ridge back in August. It was often a source of wonder to front-line troops how the award of decorations was arrived at. Many served in the front line for six years, were wounded two or three times, yet came away with no award. Others, who took part in a single action and did little else of note, found themselves with a scarcely deserved medal. Men such as Jimmy McWilliam, Leslie Skinner, Tim Olphert and David Render received no awards, but those of us serving at the front knew that they were more deserving than some others who did.

I have always liked the words of that wise old bird Ecclesiasticus, who first enjoins us to 'praise famous men' but then goes on to extol those 'who have no memorial. For these were merciful men whose righteousness has not been forgotten; their bodies are buried in peace, but their name liveth for evermore.' So it certainly is in war, and indeed in peacetime too, when one is regularly left bemused by the inequities of the Honours' List. Many of us know of individuals who have provided years of devoted service without any recognition or reward, and yet they are all too often passed over in favour of those who do little more than work in secure and well-remunerated jobs.

I had a congratulatory letter from Brigadier Prior-Palmer about my own award, and on the last day of November the investiture took place at Hoensbrook, where the band of the Life Guards played and Field Marshal Montgomery was the investing officer, although he turned up late. Monty gave us a few words in his inimitable and rather squeaky voice and then pinned the medals on us. The Colonel received his DSO, MCs went to John Sempken, Jack Holman and myself, and Sergeant Nelson received the MM. We had our photos taken separately and as a group with Monty, who then signed them for us. Generals Horrocks and Thomas (43rd Division) were also there, so that I was surrounded by top brass for the first and only time in my life. I felt proud and elated, as surely any twenty-year-old would in such circumstances.

CHAPTER TEN **SIEGFRIED LINE**

The arrival of winter was a source of real discomfort. Although we were issued with effectively lined tank suits, the intake of air for the tank's engine came as a freezing blast through the turret hatch which further increased the chill, particularly for the commander. Sleeping outside became a problem, especially on snow-covered ground which had to be cleared before our tarpaulin cover could be pitched outside the tank – and if there was additional snow in the night, its weight caused this makeshift covering to droop. It was also necessary with vehicles at a standstill to keep their engines running to prevent them from freezing up. We were still better off than the infantry, of course, equipped as they were only with greatcoats and groundsheets.

The Allied forces were by now gearing themselves up for the assault on the Siegfried Line. Montgomery's directive to 21st Army Group was issued on November 2. The operations to open Antwerp and drive the enemy north of the Lower Maas in south-west Holland would be completed; then Second Army would drive the enemy east of the Meuse in the Venlo area. This required a re-grouping of forces in which the 1st Canadian Army would take over the front in the north from the sea to the Reichswald Forest. British 2nd Army would then extend its flank southwards to Geilenkirchen, taking over some of the Twelfth Army

Group front. Those American divisions such as the 82nd and 101st Airborne, which had been lent to 21st Army Group for the Arnhem operation and with which the Sherwood Rangers had been fighting through September and October, would be returned to the American Army.

We had been expecting to make our assault on the Siegfried Line through the Reichswald, but fortunately this plan was cancelled in the general reorganisation. As a result, we found ourselves moving south and, at very short notice on November 8, our tanks were loaded on to transporters and moved to the area of Sittard, just to the east of the Meuse and in the general area of Aachen. Aachen had been captured earlier by the Americans after a terrific battle and was the first big German town to be taken. Regimental HQ was established in the little Dutch village of Schinnen, where we came under the direct command of XXX Corps and General Horrocks. The weather was positively foul – extremely cold with intermittent snow and sleet, and increasingly difficult conditions under foot.

This move from Mook to Sittard was over a distance of some 140 miles and Stanley Christopherson had asked me to recce the route in advance. Moving sixty tanks and all the soft-skinned vehicles was no easy task, and it was important not to pile up in a cul-de-sac. I therefore left with Bert Crowhurst, my new Dingo driver, edging Eindhoven to Leopoldsburg and then in a south-easterly direction to Sittard. It was not as straightforward as it would be today, since there were no signposts and many of the direct roads were damaged, so we had to make numerous detours. From Mook to Leopoldsburg, however, was pretty clear cut, so I told Stanley that I would wait and lead onwards from there. But our recce the day before had left Bert and me extremely tired, and on arriving at Leopoldsburg we pulled well off the road and fell asleep.

We were woken by the angry voice of the Colonel shouting over the radio, 'Twenty-two (the Recce Troop code), we are well past

Leopoldsburg. Where the hell are you?' I was so startled and in such a panic that I could not think for the moment what to say, except that we were further ahead and that, if he continued along the road, he would soon catch us up. But how to get past him and all the vehicles in the convoy without being seen?

From my map I could see no road on which I could by-pass them, although there was a railway line running almost parallel. This was the option I took. Driving fast – and we had to be very fast – along railway lines and sleepers for about ten miles is not very comfortable. Bert and I had every bone in our bodies shaken to bits as the whole time we listened to a choleric and increasingly exasperated Colonel over the wireless. I kept telling him that we were just ahead and prayed. At last I found a turn-off from the railway line on to the road and, miraculously, I could see that the column was now behind us. We had four flat tyres and the whole chassis was groaning beneath us, but all I felt was profound relief as we led the column safely to Sittard.

General Horrocks had decided that 8th Armoured Brigade would support two different divisions in the coming assault. 4th/7th Dragoon Guards and 13th/18th Hussars would support the 43rd Division, while the Sherwood Rangers were allotted to a brand-new American division. The 84th US Infantry Division, the Railsplitters, were newly come from America and had not yet been committed to battle, so they needed an experienced armoured formation to help them on their baptism. Horrocks had plumped for us because of our previous happy co-operation with US units and because he personally had a high regard for the Sherwood Rangers. 'A new division will need someone to lead them,' he said, 'and you are the boys for the job.' He told the Americans, 'I am giving you my most experienced armoured regiment, the Sherwood Rangers.'

The Colonel went off for a conference at the American Divisional HQ, situated at Gulpen. The division consisted of three regiments, roughly equivalent to the British brigade, the 332, 333 and 334

Regiments. The Sherwood Rangers moved to Palenberg, a coal-mining town and very desolate place at that time because it had been devastated by shellfire and its roads were rivers of mud from the recent heavy rains and the constant movement of large vehicles. I accompanied Regimental HQ wherever it went and at Palenberg the destruction was such that we had to establish sleeping quarters in the cellars of what buildings remained, using ground floors as offices.

All of us at RHQ had to meet and get to know our American opposite numbers, who asked us a lot of questions about our battle experience. They were itching to get into the action and prove themselves, but the dreadful weather conditions did dampen enthusiasm somewhat and there was understandably some nervousness at the expected strength of the German defences. It was certainly not the best of circumstances in which to be taking an untried unit into battle. I spent my time assimilating intelligence information, especially map work, and then relaying it to the squadrons in the appropriate format, something which often entailed giving lectures about the general situation at the front. For this purpose I had to spend much of my time to-ing and fro-ing between Brigade HQ and the American HQ to find out whatever was available from air reconnaissance, wireless intercepts and intelligence summaries. At Brigade level and above, Intelligence Officers were properly trained staff officers who probably spoke German and included interrogation of prisoners in their list of duties. I was just a reasonably well-educated twenty-year-old who had to learn as he went along.

I had to update the maps, continue to write up the Regimental War Diary each night and take notes of any meetings attended by the Colonel at Brigade HQ or elsewhere. In this sense I suppose I was, in a sense, the Colonel's Personal Assistant, constantly at his beck and call. I also had the essential task of keeping A and B Echelons informed of where the sabre squadrons were so that these could be resupplied or any tank which had got bogged down could be recovered. Some of this could be done on the wireless, but I was also on the road in my Dingo for much of the day as I shuttled backwards and forwards. The job did not require particularly high intelligence, just an active dog's-body.

Much time and energy were devoted to planning and preparing for the coming operation. Mostly we were to operate with 334 Regiment, whose commander was nice enough but rather indecisive. He liked everyone to have their say in meetings and Stanley became increasingly frustrated. Not only had this American Division never worked with tanks before, but it had never fought a battle. Horrocks described the 84th as 'an impressive product of American training methods, composed of splendid, very brave, very tough young men'. But he was disturbed by the failure of American division and corps commanders and their staffs ever to visit the front lines and found that, in contrast to the British, the men were not getting hot meals brought up from the rear. He tried to tell these American commanders to get up front and see conditions for themselves, but on the whole such advice seems to have fallen on deaf ears, for combat veterans have recorded that only on the rarest occasions were American staff officers seen in the front line. It was all rather reminiscent of the behaviour of the British High Command at Passchendaele in 1917.

An added complication to the preparation for this battle was that we were having to operate with various funny tanks to breach the Siegfried Line. Flame-throwing Crocodiles, mine-clearing Flails and obstacle-clearing AVREs were part of the plan, and on November 17 all the armour carried out a dress rehearsal of the breaching part of the operation. The weather was very wet and much of the potential battle area a sea of mud, so tanks kept getting stuck.

The battle for us began on the next day, November 18. Two days previously the US 2nd Armoured Division attacked on our right, securing their objectives. Now we were to go in with 334 Regiment with the objective of securing the high ground east of Geilenkirchen and Prummern. Because of my particular job in writing up the Diary each night, I had a more objective and detailed view of this battle than any so far recorded, but I was also behind the main actions being fought, so my account may lack immediacy and excitement.

The battle essentially consisted of a six-day slogging match against carefully prepared concrete defensive positions. These defences consisted of numerous pillboxes, surrounded by wire and mines, and with walls so thick that the Shermans' 17-pounder guns could not penetrate them. Not since D-Day had we encountered such obstacles. The artillery barrage started at 0330 hours on November 18, and the attack commenced at 0500 hours in artificial moonlight created by very effective batteries of searchlights. By midday A and B Squadrons, leading the attack, had achieved their objectives, taking the high ground north-east of Geilenkirchen and the village of Prummern. Three hundred and fifty prisoners had been taken and about six pillboxes captured or knocked out. The Sherwood Rangers could justly claim to have been the first British troops to breach the Siegfried Line.

This had not been achieved without cost. The American infantry of the 84th Division made up for any lack of experience with outstanding courage, but their casualties were considerable. In A Squadron, Lieutenant Crosbie was killed outright by an armour-piercing round through the turret and there were several wounded. These included the redoubtable Sergeant Dring, who was attempting to repeat the tactics he had used in Normandy of stalking German tanks on foot – an approach which had already earned him the MM and Bar. He and his gunner had knocked out more German tanks than anyone else in the Regiment, and he had been continuously in the thick of the action since El Alamein. But this time he came across a Panther which he thought had been knocked out, only to find it was very much alive and shooting at him. A high-explosive shell landed very near him and he was lucky to escape with a badly wounded hand, which put him out of the war for good.

John Semken, leading A Squadron, was also fortunate. His tank drove over a cluster of four mines which exploded simultaneously, but there were no casualties. He was to have another two tanks destroyed by mines under him that day, and in the afternoon Padre Skinner, worried that he was missing, went forward to try to find him. Eventually he came across a small captured pillbox and found John inside reading poetry. He remained rather confused for some time by what was presumably some kind of delayed concussion, but by the evening had recovered 'his customary blasé good spirits and balance'.

The battle continued fiercely on November 19. The weather remained awful and the ground was a sea of liquid brown mud in which no wheeled vehicle could move. Most of the action was undertaken by B and C Squadrons as they cleared and consolidated areas captured the previous day and tried to move towards the village of Wurm. Peter Selerie, who had only recently returned after being wounded in Normandy to lead B Squadron, had his tank destroyed and was wounded again in the arm and thigh. John Holmes, who had distinguished himself at Beek the previous month, was hit in the head by shrapnel and died half an hour later. Corporal Whitfield, one of the most experienced fitters in the Regiment, was killed when he stepped on a mine while trying to recover a bogged-down tank. It was not until November 23 that the Padre could retrieve Whitfield's body and bury it. He wrote: 'Recovering bodies in minefields was always a nasty business. One seemed able to carry on, uncomfortably, for a time until fear began to take over. It would press in on one that it was walking about here that this poor chap got it. One began to shake from head to foot and became almost too afraid to move. Being all alone at this time did not help.'

It was not only in the fighting units that the true meaning of courage could be found. Padre Skinner was constantly at odds with the chaplain establishment. He believed that chaplains should serve with the forward troops, whereas not enough of them did and too many built their little empires further back at the Casualty Clearing Stations and hospitals. As he saw it: 'In the last resort it all boils down to what one considers a padre's job to be. Those who saw the role in what they called "spiritual" terms wanted padres further back, caring for the wounded and working in areas where "services" could be seen to be more suitably done. They usually described front-line padres as "playing at being soldiers" or as being "ecclesiastical undertakers".

'The book,' the Padre continued, 'said that for burials a chaplain could call on five men, but from where? In a forward area that meant asking for a whole tank crew, which was nonsense. To send to the echelon two or three miles back was impracticable. But for me, I always had the strong feeling that the less men fighting in tanks saw of what happened to a tank hit by armour-piercing shell, the better. The fact that at the back of their minds they all knew did not change my mind that I would sooner clear the tank on my own than accept tank crews as helpers if at all possible. In any case tanks were made to get into not to get out of. There was not much room for one man lifting a body out of the driving seat or tank turret, let alone more than one. Once a tank had been hit, and the wounded, if any, got away, other tanks of the troop knew that one or more of their comrades remained in that tank. They drew comfort from me, or anyone else, just going to look, even if the actual removal for burial had to wait till later. The morale and spiritual needs of the men actually doing the fighting seemed to me to be paramount. One of the finest things that happened to me in my time with the Sherwood Rangers was a letter that John Sempken wrote to me as he left the Regiment to go back to England: "Your presence among us was something we always took for granted, and for which we never spoke our thanks in any proper way, yet by being there you helped to keep us sane in all the hell of what we had to do and might have become."'

On November 19 RHQ was shelled and Corporal Hewitt was killed in the house next to mine. Throughout this operation I was very busy moving, with difficulty, between the Regiment, Brigade and the US Division, swapping our news and dispositions for theirs. On one occasion I conversed for ten minutes with the Commander US 2nd Armored Division, thinking he was rather a well-informed private. When the

Colonel came in, I had to give him the dispositions of the various units on either side of us as well as our own. All the maps had to be constantly up-dated, and he had a habit of losing or damaging his, despite them being in short supply. I also had to negotiate my way round his dog, which was probably the more difficult of the two tasks.

Progress remained painfully slow. The enemy's defences were strong, and both the weather and conditions on the ground were terrible. Geilenkirchen itself fell, and then the focus turned towards Wurm and yet another Beek, but the going had become desperately difficult and it was with some relief that the Regiment was withdrawn on the evening of November 23, returning to Corps Reserve in the pleasant Dutch village of Schinnen, about six miles from the front. So ended six days of most unpleasant and costly fighting. There were sixty-three casualties, including three officers and twelve other ranks killed. Ten tanks had been destroyed and another ten seriously damaged, but we had broken through the Siegfried Line. Just before the battle ended, I picked up General Horrocks from a traffic jam and took him back in my Dingo to his HQ, where I had tea with him. He seemed a very charming man, easy to talk to, and I made a good contact with his Intelligence Officer. Later Horrocks visited the regiment in Schinnen to thank us for our part in the battle and told us that we had been chosen because 'we were one of the most experienced regiments in the western European theatre'. The only problem, of course, with receiving such accolades is that you get to fight too often.

The next month or so was to be relatively quiet. We had already spent time in Schinnen on our way to attack the Siegfried Line and now we returned to our old billets. The local inhabitants gave us a great welcome when we arrived, turning out in full force and wanting to know how we had fared. Some were even in tears when they found that those they had previously billeted had been killed or wounded. Regimental HQ was re-established at the local pub, where there were comfortable beds and, most importantly, a bath.

On our second night there, a concert was given in the village hall by the local brass band. They had not played together for five years yet they turned out in full uniform and gave us some stirring music. We sat in the front row, along with the Brigadier, who had been specially invited, and the music was so loud and enthusiastic that we were almost blown out of our seats. In the interval both the Mayor and the Colonel gave short speeches, and there was a general air of bonhomie and celebration.

Although two troops had to be at four hours' notice of action and the remainder of the Regiment at twenty-four hours', nothing of significance developed on our front. Some new officers joined: they had to be absorbed into our ways and included Lieutenant Gaiger, who had been a close friend in training of John Holmes. Padre Skinner took him to see John's grave at the Prummern cross-roads.

After the investiture had been held at Brigade on November 30, I had the chance to visit Brussels twice. The Brigade had a rest camp at Louvain, but we tended to spend our time at the Plaza Hotel in Brussels, which was comfortable and not too expensive. There was a bathroom with each bedroom, early morning tea, a shoe-cleaning and suit-pressing service and excellent food, all for 90 francs for 48 hours (a little less than ten shillings). My monthly allowance was about £30, and each visit to Brussels made a large hole in it. There was the opportunity to shop, eat mountains of rich food, drink more than was good for us and search out what entertainment we could find. I bought some Coty scent for the Emtages, and in the clubs and cabarets there were plenty of pretty girls to dance with. My usual companion was Dick Holman, but there were others too and we had a whale of a time. It is not difficult to picture young men just released from the tensions of war and now on the loose in a big city which was itself still celebrating its liberation. The mood was one of gay abandonment on all sides and nothing I have experienced in peacetime has come close to rivalling it.

It was also now possible for those who had been out six months to get UK leave. We decided that we would put all eligible names into a hat and hold the draw on Christmas Day. Our preparations for this were only mildly disturbed by the start of the German offensive in the Ardennes which began on December 18. This put us on alert and required us to man a defensive line to the east, but the fighting was to be confined to the American sector and, much to everyone's relief, our involvement was not required. The German attack did, however, have the effect of postponing a XXX Corps offensive in the Reichswald. We also heard that a German SS officer had been caught in a nearby village wearing American uniform and subsequently shot.

In early December I received my first letter from my father for three years. It had been written in May 1942 from Stanley Camp and taken two and a half years to reach me by I know not what route. It was addressed to my brother Peter and me, so I wasted no opportunity in copying it out in a letter to him in England. The letter was written in pencil in bold capital letters on thin rice paper and said this:

My dear Stuart and Peter,

This is the first opportunity of writing a letter and I hope it will reach you. Believe Mummy is nursing troops Kowloon. We cannot communicate and have been separated since December 8. Have not heard from you since last August except telegram October 25. Hope you are both well and happy. Our house shelled and destroyed by fire with contents. I am interned Stanley in large prison camp since December 25. Suffering rather badly from gout, otherwise well, but very much thinner. Hope somebody is looking after you as it is quite impossible for us to do anything at present. Helen is still at Sydney but have no news from her. We have two meals each day 11.30 and 5.30. Much love to you both and best of luck.

Daddy

(From H.S. Hills, Block 13, Room 49, British Internment Camp, Stanley)

To receive this out of the blue was both a shock and a blessing. Obviously I had thought a lot about my parents and what sort of a state they might be in, but the dangers and excitement of my own life had pushed this to the back of my mind. The brevity and deliberate understatement of my father's letter, and the fact that it was so out of date, made it difficult for me to come to terms with my parents' situation. The story would reach its conclusion, of course, but not before the end of the war, and it was likely that the war in Europe would finish before the one in the Far East. Clearly, I could not be certain that I would be alive to see that end and the same applied to my parents, so we all just had to hope and pray for the best.

We spent the last Christmas of the war in our friendly village of Schinnen. There was a Carol service on Christmas Eve and then a Communion service early on Christmas Day. This service was held in the same room where the men had lunch. It was a tradition that the officers served lunch to the men before having their own and this proved to be a memorable meal, consisting of fresh pork, tinned turkey, plum pudding and plenty to drink. Before we sat down to ours, there was a cocktail party and the giving of presents from the Christmas tree which were intended to raise a laugh. We also held our draw for leave, in which I came out sixth and received the first vacancy in February. Then, after lunch, we gave a party for the children of Schinnen, with Neville Fearn dressing up as Father Christmas and George Culley, from the Essex Yeomanry, as a clown. These two were towed on a sleigh through the village streets behind a Honey tank, finishing at the village hall, where chocolate, saved up by the men from their rations, was given out to the children. George Culley was a talented clown and acrobat. His thick moustache, of which he was very proud, fairly glistened in the cold, and the children's excitement warmed all our hearts.

After Christmas it was back to the war again and we spent New Year's Eve in the line at Schinveld. On the previous two nights the Germans had infiltrated into our positions and there were casualties, particularly to the infantry. Consequently we were rather edgy as 1945 dawned, but each squadron was able to drink in the New Year, albeit in conditions which were extremely cold because of the continual snow and frost. Eventually on New Year's Day itself we were relieved by the 4th/7th Royal Dragoons and moved back to another village called Schimmert, which was not quite as pleasant as Schinnen.

On January 5, Denis Elmore turned up at the Regiment again. He was accompanied on this draft by John Bethell-Fox, who, like Denis, had been wounded in Normandy. I had of course not seen Denis since June 1944, but I had heard in a letter from his mother that he had been recuperating mainly at his parents' home near Tonbridge. A Tonbridge contemporary of us both, Niel Hare, was also at home recovering from wounds and had spent a lot of time with Denis. They used to drink at the Rose and Crown in the High Street, visit the old Ritz Cinema and then go on to the Hilden Manor, which was then some sort of night club, before staggering home in the early hours. Niel found Denis quite reserved at this time. I have no doubt that at the Rose and Crown he would have run into C.H. (John) Knott, the redoubtable Tonbridge character who had run the cricket sides in which Denis and I had played. He was a man of few words, but his gruff exterior concealed a kindly heart, and I am sure he would have wanted to know from Denis how he had been doing and what news he had of other former pupils away at the war.

The Regiment was now preparing for its next action, Operation Blackcock, which was designed to advance the line closer to the Rhine. My reunion with Denis was to be brief because I learned on January 12 that I was to attend a course on photo-reading at the School of Military Intelligence at Matlock in Derbyshire. This two-week course was to begin on January 17 and after it I would get two weeks' leave, so I left Holland on January 13 and arrived in England two days later. It still seems unbelievable to me that I joined the army the same day as Denis, but after our period of training, we were hardly ever in each other's company from the moment we arrived at the Sherwood Rangers. Denis had been wounded early in the Normandy campaign and I had been relieved that it was one of those 'nice' wounds which were not serious enough to cause lasting distress, just serious enough to take him out of harm's way for a long period of time. But I deeply regretted the fact that we had had little chance to talk and to share the comradeship of war, except in this very brief period when we discussed all that we had been doing long into the night. I was able to overcome his disappointment in missing the intervening action since Normandy by describing some of the worst aspects of it, and I think that I was able to satisfy him eventually that he had been well out of it. Before I left for England, I had to brief him fully because he was to take over my job as Intelligence Officer. This pleased me since he would be in less danger than in a sabre squadron, but there was quite a lot which I had to convey to him about his work and the people with whom he was likely to come into contact. Then it was some quick goodbyes all round before catching the transport home.

This was my first time in England since all of us had left these shores on the eve of D-Day. I am sure that those relatives I went to visit at Maidstone found me a rather different person to the callow youth of May 1944. In spite of the V1s and V2s, I found a greater spirit of confidence among people generally than when I had left. News from all fronts had improved considerably and there was a feeling that the worst was over. I did not like to disillusion anyone on this score, but I did find some comfort on the few occasions I visited the Rose and Crown in Tonbridge that the bar-chat among the schoolmasters there was more about which boy was likely to get his 3rd XI colours than the war headlines. I cannot remember much about the course itself at Matlock. It was designed to improve my reading and analysis of photographs and there were some interesting practical sessions. Most of it, however, consisted of lectures and it took me back all too readily to school lessons. In a letter to my brother Peter on January 22, I wrote: 'This place is incredibly boring, but I suppose it is rather a rest from Holland, so I can't grumble.' Peter had recently joined the army and was in an OCTU Training Establishment run by the Royal Artillery at Wrotham near Sevenoaks. Much of the letter was rather pompous as I played the elder brother card in trying to persuade him not to volunteer for service in the Far East. 'Don't do anything about India until you've seen me,' I advised.

While at Matlock I also travelled over to Nottingham to attend a regimental welfare party organised by the redoubtable Mrs Kellett, the widow of the former commanding officer of the Sherwood Rangers. Here I had the chance to talk to families of those with whom I had served, some of whom had been killed and some who were still out in Holland. As I entered this party, I noticed a handsome woman whom I felt sure I knew but whose name I could not remember. I sought an introduction and found that she was the wife of Lieutenant A. L. Head, who had been killed with other members of RHQ on June 11 1944 at St Pierre. I still could not quite work out why I seemed to know her, until I suddenly remembered that, while we were at Calshot before D-Day, Lawrence had asked me to do a portrait of his wife from a photograph, which was of course the explanation. The quiet courage of those left at home was very moving and naturally they plied me with lots of questions about everything.

The best thing about Matlock was that I met up again with Jimmy Burridge, a subaltern in the 11th Hussars who was also attending the course. The last time we had seen each other, we were sheltering under a hail of mortar bombs in Normandy near Odenfontaine. Jimmy was a marvellous character who later achieved distinction as the breeder of the great racehorse Desert Orchid, winner of the Cheltenham Gold Cup and four King George VI Chases at Kempton, and became immensely popular with the racing public. He was three years older than me and had been born in Lahore, the son of a sergeant-major in a Sikh regiment. He had been educated at Haileybury, reputedly with his fees paid by his father's success at the gaming tables, and then had gone up to Oxford, where he had played cricket, tennis and squash for the university. His Oxford career was cut short by the war and he had arrived in North Africa in 1942. While commanding an armoured car reconnaissance patrol, he had been the first man into German-occupied Tunis, an experience which he related with a kind of off-hand bravado, although in fact he had had to hold the Germans and growing French crowds at bay until reinforcements arrived. Then he landed at Salerno before his regiment was withdrawn to prepare for the D-Day landings. Here he was mentioned in despatches three times, as the 11th Hussars fulfilled much the same role as the Sherwood Rangers in the subsequent battles, and he was clearly an officer of dash and courage.

Jimmy was a soul-mate in the dull surroundings of the School of Military Intelligence at Matlock. Both of us regarded the course as a chance for a bit of rest and relaxation rather than the next step up the ladder and we spent most of the course in each other's company. Jimmy did not take himself too seriously and we gradually explored the various pubs of Matlock, no doubt earning quite a few disapproving glances from the locals, and rather haphazardly undertook whatever homework was required by the authorities.

When the course ended both of us were due a week's leave, which I spent visiting friends and relations. I saw my brother and sister and went back to Maidstone to see my Aunts Frances and Maude and my Uncle Bernard. At the end of the week I had arranged to meet Jimmy Burridge again at the transit camp near London to which we had both been told to report, and then to travel back to Holland together. We stayed one night in the camp but then found out that we would have to stay there a week before a ship became available to take us back. This prospect did not appeal because a transit camp miles from anywhere in a very cold February is as inhospitable a place as you can find. So we packed our kit, commandeered a three-ton lorry and told the corporal of the guard that we were checking out. Without more ado we made tracks for London and put up at the Mayfair Hotel. Later we contacted Tilbury to find out the sailing times the next day as we were both keen to get back to our regiments. Unsurprisingly, Tilbury would not give us these details over the telephone but did say that, if we turned up at about midday, we should be all right. Armed with this information, we retired to the bar of the Mayfair for an evening of which I can recall little except that I held my drink rather better than Jimmy. I certainly had to put him to bed, not long after he had caused a stir in the restaurant by slumping face-down into a bowl of pea soup.

We duly turned up the next day at Tilbury quay without further mishap and tried to find a ship to board. The embarkation officer had other ideas and told us that we would have to go to a nearby transit camp to collect the right papers and then come back the following day. This seemed absurd and we told him so with some vehemence, but we were nonetheless firmly shepherded back to the quayside. We then collared an inoffensive dockhand, tipped him five shillings to take our kit on board, made a dash up the gangway and went to hide in the lavatories. There we reckoned we would have to stay for a couple of hours until the ship sailed. We stuck this for over an hour, but then Jimmy, somewhat against my better judgement, declared that he was bored and suggested that, if we went to the lounge and mingled with the other officers, we would surely not attract undue attention.

All would have been well if some steward had not asked us if we had a cabin. We told him that we were fine and not to concern himself with the matter, but he insisted on seeing the head steward and it was not long before we found ourselves once more in the presence of the embarkation officer. He was not a man to whom I had taken an instant liking and I am sure the feeling was mutual: the episode recalled those unfortunate moments in the headmaster's study before justice descended. The embarkation officer lectured us sternly and then called the Military Police to escort us off the ship. We were marched ignominiously to the security office, where our identities were checked. All might still have been well, but Jimmy had unfortunately lost his identity card and I was left to reflect that I had not chosen my partner wisely for this little escapade. We were both accused of being deserters, trying to escape from the United Kingdom, and a message to that effect was telegraphed to the GOC South-Eastern Command. Despite our protestations of innocence, we were made to sit in that dingy security office for two hours and told that we might well be locked up in the Tower of London. But this distinction was to be denied us and we were taken off under escort to another transit camp.

This camp consisted of tents in the middle of a field and was a hundred per cent worse than the previous one. It was also another freezing cold February day and night. But this time my luck was in, because, just as I was drawing blankets for the night, who should walk in but Bill Enderby, my C Squadron second-in-command on D-Day, when he had been wounded. If there was one person on earth who could wangle anything, it was Bill. He phoned the GOC South-Eastern Command, whom he knew, and received permission to put himself in charge of the whole draft for the next day and saw that we were on it. I parted from Jimmy after the boat docked to go our separate ways, and then travelled on with Bill to rejoin the Regiment on February 18 at Cleves. As I walked into RHQ, a shell landed outside and damaged the Dingo I had just drawn up in. It was an appropriate welcome back.

CHAPTER ELEVEN **RHINE**

Since I had been away, the Regiment had been involved in plenty of heavy fighting. In late January each squadron had been involved in Operation Blackcock, supporting 52 Lowland Division and capturing Heinsburg and Kirschow in bitterly cold weather and across snow-covered ground. Then in early February it had returned to the Nijmegen area to take part in Operation Veritable, firstly under the command of 2nd Canadian Division and then our old friends in 43rd Division. The fighting had been particularly heavy around the town of Cleve, which was captured a few days before I returned and where the Regiment was now resting, maintaining the vehicles and training reinforcements, of whom there had been a steady stream.

Bill Enderby had a permanent injury to his arm and had been medically downgraded, but he persuaded the authorities to let him back and was now given command of A Squadron. I also was to have a new position, for as the Colonel welcomed me back from my course and leave, he told me that I was to have command of the Recce Troop. This was a position I had long coveted and I had continually pestered the previous incumbent, Ian McKay, to take me on as his second-in-command. Now Ian had gone to B Squadron and the job was mine. I could not have been more thrilled.

I had only a few days to acquaint myself with my new command before we were due to go into action again, so I got down to things as fast as I could. The Recce Troop consisted of about 45 men and, as the name implies, its job was reconnaissance, scouting ahead of the main sabre squadrons to check roads and bridges, observe enemy positions and provide information on what lay ahead. We came under the direct command of Regimental HQ, with the code name '22', so I saw plenty of the Colonel, and in later life he often addressed me as 'Dear 22', although he was known to leave out the 'dear'.

The Troop consisted of eleven Stuart tanks. The Stuart or Light Tank M3 was called the Honey by the British as, when the Americans supplied it to us, they'd said, 'You'll find it a real honey.' Each tank weighed twelve tons, had a crew of four and was armed with a 2-pounder gun and two machine-guns. It was obviously more lightly armoured than the Sherman, but it had a very high top speed of almost 40 m.p.h. and it was wonderfully reliable. HQ Section had two of these tanks plus a Dingo scout car, while the other tanks were in three sections of three, known as A, B and C. My own crew had Trooper Chalky White as wireless operator, Trooper Arthur Hinitt as driver and Trooper Tom Trott as gunner. My Dingo was driven by Trooper Bert Crowhurst, while the other tank in HQ Section was commanded by Sergeant Pothecary (ex-11th Hussars), who was the senior Sergeant in the Troop. Sergeant Weir, a regular, commanded A Section, Sergeant 'Nev' Hinitt (ex-3rd Dragoon Guards) B Section and Corporal Slater C Section. The remainder of the tanks were commanded by corporals and lance-corporals, so I was the only officer in the Troop.

Reconnaissance can be a very hairy business, although there were many occasions when the Germans were wily enough to take no action at all when they saw us in the Honeys or on foot, preferring to surprise those who followed us. I also had to find routes for the Regiment to take when it was moved en masse from one area to another. An armoured regiment on the move comprises an enormous number of vehicles – not only the sixty tanks but also the many soft-skinned trucks and cars of A and B Echelons, all of which stretch out for miles. In evaluating the route, with the help occasionally of the Military Police, we had to check whether bridges could accommodate the weight and width of each vehicle, and try to ensure there was not too much other traffic about. One mistake and we might have been leading the Regiment up a dead end, which would have caused untold confusion for all and definite trouble for me.

The Troop initially did need a bit of pulling into shape, because Ian McKay had left them a little time before I arrived back to take over, but once we had got to know each other, they proved to be a wonderfully efficient body of men to command. There was lots of boisterous good humour, and there were plenty of characters and a general feeling that everyone mixed together well.

The Hinitt brothers were particular characters. Sergeant 'Nev' Hinitt, the elder brother, had been a pre-war regular in the 3rd Dragoon Guards, serving, among other places, on the North-West Frontier of India. He told the story of the time when tanks replaced horses, and the tank driver was guided by his tank commander by means of reins, which were tied to each of the driver's hands. He was dark-haired with a dark moustache, came from Retford and was enormously efficient and brave. I could not have asked for a better senior sergeant and, as well as keeping the Troop in good order, he also became a personal friend with whom I often corresponded when he went to live in New Zealand.

His younger brother Arthur drove my Honey tank and also acted as my batman. He had also served in North Africa and he had been wounded twice while with the Recce Troop. He was dark, handsome and adored by the girls, with whom he used to flirt quite outrageously. He was a joy to be with as he was invariably smiling and enjoyed a good joke. I never heard him grumble and in tight situations he remained cool and unflappable.

Bert Crowhurst was the driver of my Dingo. He had been a policeman in civilian life and he was the finest driver I came across in the army. On a long reconnaissance of perhaps a hundred miles or more to find routes for the Regiment, I would read the map for him along often tortuous roads. Then, when we had finished, I would say, 'Home, James', and Bert would invariably remember the way back without any further help from me. How he did this, often in the dark and without signposts, is still beyond me. He was also highly adept at judging the width of our vehicle, so that he could squeeze through parked tanks on a narrow road at what I thought was enormous speed. On one occasion General Horrocks witnessed this skill, when he was held up in a traffic jam, and commandeered us to drive him back to his HQ. Bert did not say much and had a serious nature, but he was greatly respected by other members of the troop for his attention to detail, his driving skills and his complete integrity.

The other member of the Recce Troop I remember with affection was Corporal Morris, who had joined the 11th Hussars as a boy trumpeter and was a consummate soldier. He was skilled in all the trades of driver, gunner, wireless operator and tank commander, and was also outstandingly brave, so he was usually my first choice when anything dangerous had to be done. He never complained at this and I had particular reason to be grateful to him in an action to come at Issum.

The members of the Recce Troop were my first proper command in the Regiment and I was very keen to do well. I was aware that I had to earn the respect of the men and not ask them to do anything I was not prepared to do myself, but once they had come to know me better and I them, it was clear that I could rely on them in any situation. I may of course be biased, but they really were a first-class body of men, many of whom had had much more military experience than me. We developed into a good team and contributed much to the Regiment's success in the final months of the war, when there was naturally some concern at being knocked out just as the job was finishing. In short, I had immense respect for those I commanded.

When I came back from England, Denis Elmore was away with a touch of flu, but he returned shortly, so the two of us and Dick Holman shared a room together in Cleve. Denis was still acting as Intelligence Officer and Dick was commanding RHQ Troop, so we were all in close touch with RHQ and saw plenty of each other both on duty and off as we prepared for the next phase of the advance.

This began on February 28, when we moved out from Cleve towards Goch to support 128 Brigade of the 53rd Welsh Division in an attack on Weeze. The move-off was hectic because we had little notice, so I was apprehensive about getting my Recce Troop on the road. I felt an extraordinary excitement: it was the first time for about three months that I was going into action and now I had the responsibility of commanding something bigger than a troop of Shermans. The Recce Troop, along with C Squadron, A Company of 12 KRRC and a squadron of 43 Division Recce, were all put under the command of the new second-in-command of the Regiment, Major Basil Ringrose, DSO, and called Robinforce. Basil Ringrose had been with the Regiment before the war but apparently had a quarrel in Palestine with Colonel 'Flash' Kellett, whereupon he was sent off to Abyssinia to work with Haile Selassie. He came back before Alamein, then went off to further staff duties and only now was he returning to Regimental duties.

The job of Robinforce was to flank Weeze and come in from the south. The ground was still so muddy that there was not much for my troop to do, so Basil adopted me as his ADC and most of my time was divided between him and the forward troops, giving him the picture. My own crew were furious as it meant running the gauntlet over a piece of waste land which was under observation and fire from enemy mortars; every time we crossed, the damned stuff came down, but we survived. The fighting was fierce all round: we were having to cope with experienced German parachute troops, who fought tenaciously to cover the German withdrawal to the Rhine.

This period of action lasted about a week. From Weeze we moved on to Kevelaar. The thick woods made progress slow and we were grateful for the support of the infantry from KRRC, who appreciated the dangers that woods held for tanks and acted accordingly. One tank from B Squadron was knocked out by a German Panzerfaust team, and its commander, Corporal Turner, later died of his wounds.

On March 4 the Regiment as a group moved off to capture Issum, along with a battalion of the Oxford and Bucks Light Infantry in armoured tracked troop-carrying vehicles known as Kangaroos. The Recce Troop was out in front, along with the Shermans of C Squadron, who mistakenly opened up on some armoured cars which turned out to be American. Fortunately no one was hurt, but there were profuse apologies and we had to appease them by donating a couple of our tank suits which the American commander coveted. I wanted to get into Issum first and ordered Sergeant Pothecary to come with me, so we entered the town at top speed. No Germans were there but the place was under shellfire and I found that the bridges out of town on the far side had been destroyed. Accordingly I halted my troop and set up a forward HQ, where Denis soon joined me. There was still a lot of shelling, which made things uncomfortable, and once a shell narrowly missed me when I was standing at the window of a house. Both window and wall were shattered and, covered with dust and fragments of glass and brickwork, I dived under an adjacent infantry troop carrier for protection. There was another body beside me seeking similar shelter and, as the smoke cleared, I recognised a familiar face from my schooldays, that of Ernest Delevigne, the driver of the vehicle concerned. I was so surprised that all I could say was, 'What the hell are you doing here?' and I dare say he thought the same. I was mildly surprised that he was not an officer as back in England he owned a Bentley, but it was one of those happy moments when inconsequential chat delayed the renewing of one's duties.

The Colonel ordered up the armoured bulldozer, driven by Corporal Evans, to fill in a shallow part of the river to make a firm foundation for a tank bridge. Evans knocked down a house near the river and then used the rubble as a bridge. By this time I was asleep in my billet, but Frenchie Houghton, the Adjutant, came in and woke me up with a fiendish grin on his face. He then stood there while I dressed to ensure that I did not go back to sleep again. He told me that the Colonel wanted a tank at the next bridge on the road to give the engineers some protection against the danger of counter-attack, because our infantry patrols had reported the Germans were dug in not much further on. I decided to do the job myself and asked Corporal Morris to accompany and drive me. It was not really his job, but there was no word of complaint as he dressed and joined me in the Honey.

Corporal Morris drove and I sat alone in the turret with the wireless tuned to the RHQ net. The bridge concerned was about a mile and a half further up the road and we soon came to it. The engineers were working on it without much enthusiasm or sense of urgency, not helped by some intermittent and at times heavy mortar fire. The scissors bridge was parked at the side of the road, waiting to be put in place. Corporal Morris and I sat there having a cigarette and still somewhat sleepily keeping an eye on things, when suddenly the mortaring increased in intensity and we found the engineers racing back along the road, claiming they were being counter-attacked. I jumped back into the tank and told Morris to pull in to the side of the road, where I clumsily fiddled about with the Browning machine-gun and passed a Bren and some magazines to my driver. I then reported what had happened to RHQ and we waited entirely on our own and with some trepidation. To say that we felt vulnerable would be a considerable understatement, because the Honey was not the best place to be if a German Tiger or some other monster were to start lumbering towards us.

However, apart from some continued mortaring, I could hear nothing and I decided it must have been a false alarm, so I turned the tank round and sped back to Issum to find my runaway engineers. As I arrived at RHQ, I found that Brigadier Prior-Palmer was there with the Colonel and the young white-faced engineer subaltern, who was having to explain to his superiors why he had deserted his post when I had reported that all was quiet. I felt a little as though I was telling tales out of school, for the Brigadier made his displeasure absolutely plain by turning to me and saying: 'Stuart, you will take these engineers up to that bridge again. You will be in command, and that bridge will be ready by morning even if you are counter-attacked by twenty Panzer Divisions.' Without more ado we both saluted and went out, my companion looking rather shame-faced. The bridge itself was finished by first light, with further help from Corporal Evans and his bulldozer, and I reported this over the wireless to RHQ. The Colonel told me that B Squadron would be up soon to cross over and asked would I stay for a while to act as guide.

The tanks were not long in coming, lining the road in one long stream and accompanied by Welsh infantry. The first tank to cross the bridge, a Sherman Firefly, had Corporal Ernie Leppard as its wireless operator. It had crossed and moved on about forty yards the other side when one track was hit by a shell and then an armour-piercing round whizzed perilously close to the turret. The crew baled out under machine-gun and mortar fire, taking cover in a nearby bunker with some infantry. Meanwhile all the other tanks of B Squadron pulled quickly off the road.

Corporal Morris was up by the bridge on foot, so I was left in the Honey sitting right in the middle of the road, which was clearly under enemy observation. I bawled at Morris, who turned and ran back, vaulted into the driver's seat and backed off the road. I felt such relief that I could have kissed him. Meanwhile the bulldozer of Corporal Evans started moving around as though nothing had happened, because Evans had his ear muffs on and could not hear a thing. Mercifully nothing happened and he eventually headed back to Issum. After a further ten minutes of inactivity, I received orders to return too, whereupon I went straight back to my billet and flopped exhausted into bed. Just half an hour later my batman woke up both me and Denis, and Denis, who had slept very soundly and had no idea that I had even been out, stretched his arms and exclaimed: 'What a smashing night's sleep!' I had to resist the temptation to hit him.

After Issum there were two or three more days of action, before on March 7 we were withdrawn from the fighting to prepare for the Rhine crossing. Although I had missed some of the early stages of the Rhineland battle, it had all through been a grim affair because of the fanaticism of the German rearguard as they sought to delay our advance. Canadian casualties to the north had been particularly high, but no formation had emerged unscathed and I was especially grateful to have missed the fighting around Cleve.

We now had nearly three weeks' rest, firstly at Issum for about five days and then in billets at Goch. Dick Holman had now gone back to A Squadron, so I shared a billet with Denis at RHQ while my Recce Troop stayed in three battered houses just down the road. It was here that I was arrested for the second time in a month. During a visit one evening to my troop, I entered one of the houses with my crew to find some cooking facilities and discovered it was occupied by a married German couple with two children. They offered us some eggs and I invited them to join us for our evening meal of tinned meat and veg. As we were in the middle of our meal, the door suddenly burst open and two military policemen stormed in. They told me that I was under arrest for fraternising with the enemy. They then relieved me of my revolver, marched me to their Jeep and drove me to Brigade HQ. There I had to wait for an hour or so before being marched into the Brigade Major's office. He looked at me and I looked at him and we both burst out laughing. It was R. H. (Tich) Haynes, who had stayed with me at Judde House when Bedford played cricket and rugger against Tonbridge in 1941. It did not take long to persuade him to drop the charge.

Denis, Dick and I decided to go into Brussels and travelled down in a Jeep. We stayed in some luxury at the Plaza Hotel, lying in bed each morning until about ten before going across the road for coffee with waffles and treacle in the restaurant above W. H. Smith. Then it was shopping for an hour, followed by a pre-lunch drink or two, and the afternoon was usually spent in the cinema. By 6 p.m. we had become thirsty again, so it was time to return to the bar for a couple of hours before a good dinner, more drinks and a night club until 5 a.m. It was an agreeable regime and it lasted for a few days before the war, rather than our stamina, called a halt. One evening I went to have dinner with a Wren friend of mine, Catherine Hunt (later Lady Sandford), at her mess. In my time at Dorking with the Emtages, I had fallen in love with Catherine's sister, Olivia, the youngest of the vicar's three daughters. This had resulted in my becoming a regular and spellbound churchgoer, though sadly the romance had gone no further than the odd game of tennis. I did, however, regularly correspond with Olivia and it was she who told me that Catherine was in Brussels. After our dinner I invited her to the cinema the next afternoon with Dick and Denis, at the end of which we suggested dinner and a tour of the night clubs. Faced with the prospect of having three thirsty and headstrong subalterns in tow, she was no doubt right to turn our invitation down.

We returned from Brussels to find preparations in full swing for the Rhine crossing, which was to be known as Operation Plunder. The Rhine was about 600 yards across at low tide and considerably more at full tide, so it was the biggest obstacle we had faced since D-Day. This time the leading tank assault regiment was to be the Staffordshire Yeomanry: they would swim the river in the DD Shermans with which they had been training since August 1944. The Sherwood Rangers were to be the Reserve Armoured Regiment, supporting the 51st Highland Division. For a week before the assault we were busy with tank maintenance, loading extra ammunition, rations and jerrycans of fuel to keep us going if the support elements did not get across.

On the night of March 23, 21st Army Group's assault was launched under the covering fire of a huge artillery barrage. In our sector elements of the 51st Highland Division were first across, along with the DD tanks of the Staffordshire Yeomanry in the area around Rees. The tanks swam across successfully, but encountered a lot of difficulty on the far side of the river because of the steepness of the muddy banks. Little opposition was met at first and Rees was occupied by 153rd Brigade, but German counter-attacks developed swiftly and the commander of 51st Highland Division, Major-General Rennie, was killed in the bridgehead early on March 24. The next tank regiment across, the 13th/18th Hussars, were sent in to help consolidate the bridgehead, and then it was our turn.

The crossing was made on rafts, each raft taking two Honeys comfortably. The rafts were timber-built on pontoons pulled across by two wires, which were operated by barrage balloon crews who had volunteered for the job. It took about half an hour to get over and there was some artillery fire: we were uncertain whether to stay in the tank and avoid shellfire or remain outside it in case the raft and tank were hit and sank. The landing point on the other side was treacherous and it was not easy to get up the bank. I was the first of the Recce Troop to go across, along with Sergeant Hinitt and other elements of RHQ, and the rest followed later. We assembled in a field near Rees to await the next day and slept on our groundsheets in the middle of an artillery battery which kept us awake most of the night.

For the next week, the Regiment fought with various battalions of the 51st Highland Division, mainly around Isselburg and Dinxperloo. Our orders were to break a hole in the enemy line to allow the Guards Armoured Division to move through and exploit our success. Somehow it always seemed that the 8th Armoured Brigade did the breaking through and then the Guards Armoured the swanning. Indeed, after Dinxperloo one of our well-known NCO troop commanders was reputed to have called out to a very smart-looking Guards officer as he drove through: 'Mind your paint, sir, as you go, it's been a bit dirty round here.' The only reply he received was a cold stare. To be fair, this is what an independent armoured brigade like ours was intended for and it also explains why the Sherwood Rangers ended the war with more days' actual fighting than any other armoured unit. We fought with very nearly every British division at some time in the campaign, and of course with two American ones as well.

On March 29, A and B Squadrons supported 152 Brigade in capturing the area south of Dinxperloo, and C Squadron and the Recce Troop were then to come through to capture the town, along with 154 Brigade. As A and B did not finish their work until 9 p.m., we were ordered to wait until first light, when I was to recce the two roads leading north out of the town. The night was very uncomfortable and at a candlelit conference I tried to establish from Jack Holman how far I was to recce. He said that orders were for me to go as far as possible, which I could only presume meant until one of my tanks was hit. Such orders always made me cross with higher command because they were difficult to pass on and explain to my men, who rightly made the same deduction as I had.

A and B Squadrons had a tough time because the whole area was littered with mines. Sergeant-Major Hutchinson of A Squadron was killed when he stepped on a mine while parking his tank on a verge and Captain Neville Fearn wounded in the same explosion. Hutchinson was a yeoman farmer in civilian life, had joined A Squadron as a trooper and risen by his ability and courage to the rank of Squadron Sergeant-Major. His was a great loss to the Regiment, but the incident reminded us only too clearly that the enemy was still very dangerous.

We were shelled intermittently all night, and then at 3 a.m. we set off towards Dinxperloo. I led the column myself and went through to the northern edge of the town, where I halted to wait for more light. The small town had been pulverised by our own artillery on the preceding days, something which in later years Stanley Christopherson thought to have been a trifle overdone. For my part, however, I was thankful that it eased our progress. The area surrounding the town was a series of flat open fields and small farmhouses and, with the arrival of dawn, I felt generally unhappy about the whole task and determined to take my time. We all had breakfast and I then decided not to be operational myself, as we had two roads to recce, but to send one section down each and wait myself on the junction to see what happened. I therefore ordered Corporal Slater and one other tank to take the more northerly route, and Corporal Morris the other. I told them to proceed cautiously, advising Slater, who spoke German, to stop at each house to question the civilians about the whereabouts of the enemy. I remained on the junction with Sergeants Pothecary and Hinitt and the rest of the tanks, which would form a large force if there was trouble on either axis.

Very soon a report came through that Slater's tank had been brewed up, so I sent Sergeant Hinitt off to investigate and the Dingo to bring back Slater and his crew. The Dingo returned with Slater and one other soldier, but Slater said in a rather distressed way that Trooper Southam was still inside the partially burning tank and he did not know whether he was still alive. His tank had been taken out by a Panzerfaust at close range and the hulk was covered by enemy machine-guns, whose fire had prevented him going back to look for Southam. Sergeant Hinitt confirmed this in his report, saying that the tank was in the middle of the road and there was no hope of getting past it. Enemy fire around the tank was very fierce and he thought that there was about a company of enemy infantry, dug in with Panzerfausts, 20-millimetres and Spandaus.

I relayed this report back to Jack, telling him that an effort had to be made to see if Southam was still alive, but that my Honeys had insufficient firepower to attempt much. I said that infantry and Shermans were needed and, although he seemed pretty irritated about the whole thing, Jack agreed, saying he would bring the tanks himself. Tanks and infantry arrived about the same time and I reported the situation, as I had by now been up to see for myself what was happening. The infantry company was from the Argyll and Sutherland Highlanders in the 51st

Highland Division and the company commander, Major J. S. Corcoran, as good as called me a liar for exaggerating matters, since he was sure there was little opposition on this road. My eagerness to reply was tempered by the sight of the DSO and MC ribbons on his battledress, while his second-in-command sported the MC and Bar. Together they made an impressive pair, the more so because both were armed only with walking sticks.

The commander told me to show them where the enemy was and we started to walk up the road. Out of their earshot I whispered to Jack that this was bloody silly, because round the next corner we were going to be shot to pieces. I warned the other two but, like Felix the Cat, they just kept on walking. As we rounded the corner, we were met by withering small arms fire and all ended up in the same ditch. From there our two heroes observed the position and ordered up their men to give us cover while we towed the tank away.

Jack agreed to lay on a barrage and I told Sergeant Hinitt that we must get the smouldering tank away at the first attempt to avoid further loss of life and also find out the fate of Southam. We went back to the junction to fetch my Honey, which Jack would use as his command vehicle, and left Sergeant Pothecary there to act as our HQ. Then, as the infantry came up, I decided to tow the knocked-out tank back down the road and I ordered Sergeant Hinitt to back a tank right up behind the other, so that we could somehow attach tow ropes. We reached within fifty yards of the tank when we came under very aggressive Spandau fire which drove us to ground. The infantry gradually worked their way into a supporting position, and Hinitt and I crawled up a ditch on the left-hand side of the road until we were close to the tank. I then spotted a building a little ahead of us which seemed to be some kind of factory, and I told Hinitt that this would be a good place to work from, as it covered both the road and the tank.

We made a dash for it but were spotted and pursued by rifle and machine-gun fire. We threw ourselves at the entrance of the building, but no sooner had we done this than every German in the vicinity opened up on the building with machine-guns, rifles and 20-millimetre weapons. It just happened to be a milk-processing plant, with huge numbers of bottles lying around, and there were the most shattering explosions and unbelievable noise from the breaking glass, which left us both rather frightened.

Smoke shells from the tanks of C Squadron gave us some protection and we were able to dash back along the road, where two men from its other side had by now successfully attached the towing rope to the smouldering tank, which was now being moved back to safety. The tank doing the towing was commanded by Sergeant Pollard of C Squadron, and it was he who had ordered the smoke to be laid down. Hinitt and I still had to make our own escape but we were helped by more smoke shells and we eventually made it back. On my way I passed the Scottish company commander lying on a stretcher with a 20-millimetre shell through his foot. He grinned at me and acknowledged that he had not really believed my assessment about the enemy strength. Trooper Southam, it was discovered, had taken a direct hit from a Panzerfaust and had clearly been killed instantaneously.

The battle now became more of a pursuit as the bridgehead beyond the Rhine widened every day. On April 1 we moved to Rurlo, where a viaduct was held by the enemy rearguard and A Squadron had to deal with it. One troop of A Squadron was cut off for a time, and I went up myself with Sergeant Pothecary to help. The Germans lacked anti-tank guns and their own tanks but their infantry had no shortage of Panzerfausts. Bill Enderby was up there trying to extricate his troop and was glad of our help. He wanted some German prisoners collected from a big white house, and I decided to go myself while Trooper Trott covered me with the Bren. But as I came up to the house, someone took a pot shot at me and I scuttled back. A few minutes later Denis and Dick reported that they already had the prisoners. Bill Enderby had pointed out the wrong house and the other two had nabbed the prisoners first.

Next it was on to Twenthe. The bridge by which we were due to cross the Twenthe Canal had been blown and the Colonel told me to recce another about two miles west. This was at the locks of Wiene. I went on in the Dingo, taking Sergeant Pothecary and Corporal Morris with me. As we approached the bridge, which was on top of a large dyke, I halted the vehicles and told Pothecary and Morris that we would go the rest of the way on foot. I gave orders to the gunners of the two tanks to cover us and open up if we were fired on. There was no cover at all, so we had to walk boldly up to the dyke. The only thing that happened was that a German leaped out of a slit trench at the top of the dyke and disappeared, so we cautiously climbed the dyke and raised our heads over the top. The bridge was directly in front of us; it was not large and it had been blown about halfway across. I knew, however, that the Colonel would not be satisfied with this negative and limited information. He would want to know the width of the gap and if it would take a tank, was mined or covered by enemy fire.

I knew that I would have to walk across the bridge as far as I could. My greatest fear throughout the whole campaign had been to be thought a coward by the men I commanded. I can honestly say that I would have preferred to die than to let that happen, so I knew that this was one of those occasions when I had to take a serious risk. I also knew what the other two were thinking – that if I went forward, they would have to follow. There was no point approaching the task cautiously, since I only had to raise my body above the dyke for it to be seen for miles around. I therefore told them what I intended to do and what they would have to do if I was hit.

I rose to my feet and walked steadily towards the bridge, feeling that at any moment the bullets would start ripping into me. On the bridge itself I stopped at the gap where it had been blown. I could see no sign of mines, but the bridge was clearly no good for tanks, and the only way across was for the infantry to lay planks and walk across them to the other side. Pothecary and Morris had by now joined me and were probably feeling just as vulnerable as I was. A shot suddenly rang out, but missed us by miles. Morris looked up to scan the other bank and asked in an unsuitably matter-of-fact way: 'Have you looked at the opposite bank, sir, because about 200 yards away in those trees I can see about two or three hundred Boche?'

I looked up as he spoke and there they clearly were, so all three of us turned and ran like hell, pursued by a few desultory shots. I can only think that they were keeping their powder dry for a rather better target. I made my way back as quickly as I could to RHQ between Borculo and Neede, where I passed on to the Colonel all the information I had gleaned. The Colonel of the 12/60th KRRC, Lieutenant-Colonel Bill White, and one of his company commanders were with Stanley, and they made me take them back to the dyke to see the situation for themselves. About halfway across the open ground approaching the dyke, we were fired on and ran to a nearby farmhouse for shelter. There we crouched, hot and panting because we were all wearing thick tank suits. This time the fire had come from our side of the dyke and the Germans had clearly twigged what we were up to. From the farmhouse I pointed out to my companions the salient features of the approach to the bridge, and when Colonel White had absorbed this, he said: 'Well, come on, we must be getting back. We'll go one at a time and run like hell.'

He set off first, followed by his company commander, and I brought up the rear a few seconds later. A few inaccurate shots whizzed by, but the only casualty was the company commander, a very large and slow-moving man, who got stuck going through a barbed wire fence and tore his tank suit to shreds as he fought to free himself. He really made a very funny sight and, as I ran, I was roaring with laughter at the spectacle. The infantry then laid on an attack on the bridge, supported by the tanks of C Squadron. The KRRC company involved was commanded by Major Bill (now Lord) Deedes, but as soon as the soldiers came down the embankment towards the canal, four enemy Spandaus caught them in a deadly crossfire. Two officers and two NCOs were killed and twenty-five others wounded, and the attack at that point had to be abandoned. It was the worst day's casualties that company suffered in the whole North-West Europe campaign.

The 43rd Division Commander, General Thomas, now cancelled the direct attack across the canal in favour of a flanking movement through Enschede, not least because weather conditions had grounded all fighter support. Consequently, on April 3 we found ourselves on the road to Enschede and then moving on to Hengelo. The attack on Hengelo was carried out by the 7th Hampshires, supported by B Squadron of the Sherwood Rangers. Later our own KRRC came up, together with more infantry from the 5th Dorsets and C Squadron from the Regiment.

Hengelo was a delightful town, one which I remember with particular affection. We were able to rest here for a few days, billeted in various houses, sleeping in really comfortable beds and being royally looked after by the local people. We were able to see for ourselves in contrasting ways what the Dutch had suffered during five long years of occupation. Jack Holman had set himself up in a house owned by a collaborator, who had been imprisoned by the Dutch, but he had a very attractive daughter who was still in the house and on whom Jack had his eye. One morning she was taken away by a group of resistance fighters and brought back with her hair completely shaved off as punishment for showing favours to the Germans. Later on a Jewish girl of about sixteen was brought out of the attic in a house in the town, where for four years she had been hidden in a tightly confined space by a Dutch family who were unrelated to her. I could not begin to imagine the stress and terror that living with this situation for so long had caused either the girl or the family. It put our own fighting efforts into some greater kind of perspective and also made us starkly aware of the meaning of liberation.

My particular affection for Hengelo rested on the fact that I celebrated my twenty-first birthday there on April 5. The officers of the Regiment laid on a party which was attended by many of my friends, including Denis and the two Holmans. Brigadier Aubrey Coad of 130 Brigade and the Colonel were also there. A band played 'Happy Birthday' and we sat down to a seven-course meal with champagne. Everything on the menu had some connection with me: there was Potage Recce, Canard du Stuart and Les Fruits Collines. I was presented with a rocket, specially made by the fitters in recognition of the numerous ones I had received from the Adjutant, a cheque for £10 from the officers and two silver cap badges by my batman, while Denis gave me his old cigarette tin which I had long coveted. I reflected on the fact that my life had come quite a long way since my last birthday two months before D-Day, but now I had come of age in more ways than one. It was a wonderful evening, and it remains the only birthday in my life of which I have any distinct memories.

I shared a billet in Hengelo with Denis and had plenty of time to talk to him. Both of us were aware that the war was drawing to a close: we knew that the Russian Army was on the outskirts of Berlin and that our own progress was quickening now that we were across the Rhine. Our thoughts were beginning to turn to the future and I remember telling Denis of my wish to stay in the Army, perhaps even transferring to the Indian Army. Denis too wanted to stay on, a decision he had arrived at some time before.

A new officer, Peter Kent, turned up from England. He had an interesting background, for he was in fact a German, of Jewish parentage on one side. He had come to England after his family had been terrorised and become naturalised under an English name. Because he spoke fluent German, he was invaluable as an Intelligence Officer, and that was the role he now took on in the Regiment, taking over the job from Denis, who was due to return to a sabre squadron. I did not like this one bit, because I did not believe he was fully fit. He had only recently recovered from a nasty bout of flu and I believed that the wound he had received in Normandy was still affecting him. I therefore spoke to Hilda Young on the quiet, and he must have done something, because Denis was made Liaison Officer to Brigadier Coad, commanding 130 Brigade, a position which was meant to keep him out of harm's way.

On April 9 we started moving forward again, leaving Hengelo with regret but with many friendships made and shared. Later a street in Hengelo was named after the Regiment, and I have in my possession a recently published and marvellous book by Hans Pol, a Dutch inhabitant of the town with whom I have met and corresponded many times. Hans set himself to tell the story of Hengelo's liberation in quite amazing detail and he has unearthed facts and stories which show us how important was our contribution to this little part of Europe. From his account it is easier to appreciate now than it was then in what momentous and historic times we were living and how much more significant liberation was for those whose countries had been occupied than it was for us.

CHAPTER TWELVE **FINIS**

It was bitterly cold on the morning of April 9 as we passed through Oldenzall, Denekamp and Nordhorn. The River Ems was crossed at Lingen as we headed in the direction of Bremen. On the radio from home and in the newspapers the talk was increasingly of the end of the war being in sight, but our own briefings did not encourage us to think that it was such a foregone conclusion. The Germans still had to be defeated and the fighting at the Rhine and since showed that they would fight for every inch of their homeland. Arthur Phayre, who had commanded the guns of the Essex Yeomanry since D-Day, called in to say goodbye. He had been appointed Commander Royal Artillery in the 11th Armoured Division, which meant promotion to brigadier and a step up the ladder for someone who was a regular gunner officer. He had done much to help the progress of the Regiment in our advance from the Normandy beaches.

Our own advance was slow to start with because we were not leading and there was a lot of congestion on the road. The first opposition was met on April 11 at Hazelunne, when B Squadron bumped into a roadblock. Hubert Beddington, who was leading, dismounted to examine the obstacle and immediately came under shellfire which wounded him and most of his crew. Another officer, Lieutenant Hunt, who had only joined us the previous week, was killed by a Panzerfaust and his crew only extricated with difficulty from their burning tank.

At one place a scout car with infantry markings came speeding up the road. It reached A Squadron at the head of the column and rushed on past the leading tanks, despite all kinds of shouting and waving to try to stop it. Ronnie Hutton, who was now A Squadron Leader, came up on the wireless to announce in his Irish brogue: 'Infantry Brigade scout car has now passed my leading tank and heading into enemy territory. All sorts of good luck to him.'

There was further trouble at Lastrup on April 12 when the village seemed to be clear but the leading tank was fired on as it went through. Later Sergeant Budner and Trooper Young of C Squadron were killed by a high-explosive shell. The Wehrmacht still had plenty of teeth sharpened for the unwary, and even where resistance had begun to fade, it could quickly be re-kindled by fanatical elements who thought nothing of shooting those of their own soldiers who tried to surrender.

On Friday April 13 there were even more casualties at Cloppenburg. The road was frequently blocked by felled trees and removing these was both difficult and dangerous as the approaches were covered by enemy guns. German paratroops were in evidence and there were also plenty of snipers. The south side of the town was only lightly held, but resistance stiffened as we went further in. The infantry kept finding themselves held up, and the tanks of Richard Hyde's troop had an unpleasant time clearing out the offenders. Four men were killed. First the tank of Sergeant Sage, one of the Regiment's oldest and most experienced tank commanders, took a direct hit through the turret from a Panzerfaust; Sage and Trooper Fletcher were killed. Then Troopers Hulland and Snedker were killed by machine-gun fire as they tried to rescue Sage and Fletcher from the burning tank. Four other men were casualties, one of whom, Sergeant Mulley, later died of his wounds.

We were therefore pleased to be allowed to rest from April 14 to the 18th. On the roads there were an increasing number of displaced persons of one kind or another. Quite a few of these were slave labourers who had been employed on German farms and were now looking to go home. Many of them were French and Belgians, and it was also obvious that the German civilians were increasingly worried about the possibility of reprisal attacks by these people. Quite a few German civilians were also on the roads trying to escape from the fighting, and not far west of us was the German concentration camp at Belsen with all its horrors. It had been liberated on April 13.

Since our move on April 9 my role had been to act as an extra Liaison Officer to Brigadier Coad, along with Denis. Coad was a grand chap and we both got along very well with him. There was nothing much for my Recce Troop to do, so I spent my time in the Dingo rushing up to the forward troops and back again so that Denis could pass on information to the Brigadier.

By now the British advance was getting close to Bremen. On April 18 we went into action again in support of the 9th Brigade of the 3rd British Division, with a view to penetrating into the southern suburbs of Bremen. That evening I went to have dinner with B Squadron, as Denis had now returned to them, determined to see some action in command of a troop before the war ended. Ian McKay was B Squadron Leader. As I was leaving after a very convivial evening, Denis was looking for his bed-roll, which had somehow gone missing. As he loved his bed, this was something of a disaster, but I turned to him and said: 'Oh, stop flapping about; it'll turn up in the morning. Now stop being so rude and show your visitor out.'

He stopped his search for a moment and came up to me to say goodnight. 'Look after yourself,' I said. 'Remember what I've told you and don't do anything bloody silly.' 'No,' he said, rather humbly, 'I won't. Good night, little feller.' And then I left. It was a very dark walk back through the woods and I had no revolver, so I sang hymns to show the Germans I imagined to be hiding in the woods around that I was not frightened.

On the next day, April 19, it was C Squadron who started the attack, which was then taken over by A Squadron. One of the troop commanders was Peter Mellowes, whose tank broke out of the bridgehead of the River Issel and headed north-east without encountering much opposition. On the outskirts of Bremen he broke through the German outer defences, advancing with the Royal Ulster Rifles on either side of the road. Suddenly a platoon commander came running back, climbed on Peter's tank, and pointed to a house on a crossroads about 400 yards ahead where he said Germans were dug into strong positions.

Peter took his tanks up to the house, which concealed him from the Germans' view. As he moved forward through a small orchard, he found that he had come round only fifty yards behind them and they were oblivious to his presence. The Germans were dug into a road embankment with anti-tank guns, mortars and machine-guns, and their position extended for 400 yards or so. Peter ordered his tanks to fire and completely wiped out the German positions, killing scores. He climbed out of his tanks to see if there were any survivors and was horrified to find that most of the dead were just boys of sixteen or seventeen, whose lack of preparedness was a sign both of their inexperience and the fact that they had been badly led.

Peter reported back to his Squadron and was told to consolidate his position on the crossroads he had just captured. There he waited for several hours until reinforcements came up, which was at about 4.30 in the afternoon. The first troop to come up was from B Squadron, which had now taken over the advance, and this troop was commanded by Denis Elmore. Denis's tank had a small model aeroplane on the front, with a tiny propeller which was turning slowly in the wind. He listened to a situation report from Peter, then announced that he had been ordered to advance further along this road and set off.

All this time I had been sitting with the elements of RHQ, who were themselves at the HQ of 9th Brigade. I did not have my wireless on because my own troop had little to do and RHQ would tell me if anything was needed. After a while, however, something decided me to go up to the forward troops to try to find out what was happening, and I set off in my Dingo, with Bert Crowhurst driving. As I was racing along the road to the front, Frenchie Houghton, the Adjutant, stopped me and said: 'I'm afraid Richard Hyde has just had it up the road; his tank is completely brewed up.'

My heart was by now racing and I asked for the tank's code sign. 'One,' Frenchie answered. I felt a sinking feeling in the pit of my stomach, as I struggled to digest this simple piece of information. 'That's not Richard Hyde,' I answered, ' it's Denis.'

Frenchie moved away and I told Bert Crowhurst to go further up the road. I could not believe that what I had heard was possible, and I was trying desperately to cope with a whole range of emotions and to hope against hope that there must be some mistake. I saw a tank coming back down the road towards us and for a moment thought that it might be Denis's. On the back it had two or three wounded whom it was taking to the Regimental Aid Post, and I flagged it down.

'What happened?' I asked. 'Is it Mr Elmore's tank?' One of those on the back of the tank replied: 'We were hit by an 88-millimetre, sir, right through the turret. Mr Elmore's had it.' My stomach turned to water. 'Can anyone get near the tank?' I asked. 'No, sir, it's burning like hell and all the rounds are exploding all over the place.'

'So, there's positively no chance of him having got out then?' I asked again. But I knew even before I spoke what the reply was going to be, and the answer came back firmly and clearly, 'None whatever, sir.'

I later found out what had happened. Denis had left Peter Mellowes at the crossroads and disappeared from sight around the next corner. Peter then heard a very loud bang, which must have been the precise moment when the 88-millimetre armour-piercing shell went straight through the turret, where Denis would have been sitting, and the tank started to burn. Denis would certainly have been killed instantly, which was at least some comfort, and two of his crew, Troopers Harkness and

Miles, also died. On the next day Padre Skinner was at last able to approach the smouldering tank and extricated the bodies of Denis and Trooper Miles. He buried them temporarily nearby and then returned to exhume the bodies and re-bury them in the 8th Infantry Brigade cemetery at Fahrenhorst, nine kilometres south of Brinkum on the main road between Bremen and Bassum. Later Denis's grave was moved first to Soltau, which I visited, and finally to Becklingen.

My own feelings, as Bert Crowhurst turned the Dingo round and drove back, can be imagined. Even at this distance in time the memory of that day still hurts and I can still see Denis's cheery face that last evening when we were together. I told Bert to drop me and go back to the Recce Troop billets because I just wanted to be alone. I wandered around on my own for hours, convulsed in tears. The pain and shock were too difficult to bear in any company, however well-meaning. I had already lost so many friends of all ranks and yet had managed to hold my own and keep going. But this loss was much more difficult to cope with because it was so unexpected and so unfairly near to the end of hostilities. If only Denis had not gone back to B Squadron, if only he had not taken the lead with his troop that afternoon, if only ... Then I began to wonder why it should have been him rather than me: I had, after all, experienced many more near misses during those months Denis had been recuperating at home. I reflected on all we had been through in the past – at Tonbridge, at Sandhurst, in the Regiment – and none of it seemed to lead to this point.

I knew, however, that I would have to keep going because others depended on me. My Recce Troop were wonderful and I have never experienced such kindness, both from them and from the officers at RHQ. Dick Holman turned up, also visibly distressed, and so did Hilda Young, the Doctor, who treated me with great gentleness and understanding, bringing along a bottle of whisky to help me forget. But nothing really helped. It was one of those points in life, which we all experience at some time or other, when we know that nothing will quite be the same again. I still think about it now, wondering about the fifty-six years which I have enjoyed since that moment and what Denis might have become and gone on to do, and whom he might have married and what his children would have been like. He was the Regiment's last officer fatality of the war, out of a total of thirty-five.

The incident only served to remind all of us that life could be taken away in a flash, even at this final stage of the war. The Germans did now seem to be more ready to surrender than two weeks previously, but there was still great danger from mines and booby-traps. Even sea-mines were used under the roads, generally set with a time fuse, so that the mine exploded after several vehicles had passed over it – not unlike the tactics used by the IRA in trying to kill our troops in Northern Ireland. Once we saw a Kangaroo blow up on a mine placed under a bridge and completely disintegrate, so that nothing remained of either the vehicle or its occupants.

We were by now well into Bremen, assaulting the northern suburbs despite fire from gun-boats in the harbour. There was street fighting to be done in the city on April 26 and 27, alongside 129 Brigade, and the commander of the German garrison, General Bekker, was captured by a troop from B Squadron. Ian McKay had a very fortunate escape while holding a conference with an infantry company commander when a machine-gun opened up at close range, killing three people, including the infantry officer, and forcing Ian to dive into a ditch. Bremen's dock area had been completely flattened by shelling and RAF bombing, but the wealthier suburbs, which contained some lovely houses, were relatively undamaged. In several of these houses, however, whole families had committed suicide, including the Nazi mayor, his wife and three children.

We concentrated on April 29 to move off towards Cuxhaven further north. News came through of Dick Holman's MC, which was richly deserved. We passed through Bassen to Bucholz, where we met opposition in the form of a German officer who shot the track off

Sergeant Webb's tank with a Panzerfaust before he was himself mown down by the tanks behind. Then it was on to Rhade and Karlshofen, where we came across several large mines in the road.

On May 2 the Regiment suffered its very last fatal casualty of the war, when Trooper Carter of A1 Echelon was killed by a sniper, along with a military policeman to whom he was showing the way. Nearby, the Brigade had liberated the San Bostel concentration camp, where 2,000 out of a total of 22,000 inmates had died in the previous ten days. Conditions there, as at Belsen, were indescribably awful.

On Friday May 4 the Regiment crossed the Hamme Canal. On the previous day Hamburg had surrendered to the British 7th Armoured Division, so we knew that the end was near. RHQ established itself at Karlshoffener in a picturesque old farmhouse which had been spared damage, and soon after we arrived, our old friend General Thomas of the 43rd Division came to tell us of what would be our next operation, the capture of Bremerhaven in support of his infantry. Thomas still remained his fire-eating self and was determined not to let up in his relentless assault on the enemy, even though that implied further casualties at this late stage.

My own Recce Troop had little to do and that evening of May 4 I agreed to drive two of the men in my Dingo down to the echelon so that they could go on leave. It was cold, showery and getting dark as I came back along the road. I looked up and suddenly in the distance saw hundreds of coloured Verey lights and rockets shooting into the air. The sky itself was being further illuminated by many searchlights, and it was an extraordinary sight. I turned to Bert Crowhurst beside me and said: 'That's either a signal for a night attack, or peace has been declared. Step on it and we'll find out.'

We raced back to RHQ, where bedlam reigned. Sergeant Pick, the Signals Sergeant, had a message pad in front of him and I craned my neck over his shoulder to read what was on it. I could not help but notice that Pick's face and neck were slightly flushed and that he and everyone in there were in a state of enormous excitement. The signal had come from Brigade HQ and it said: 'No advance beyond present positions. No further harassing fire. No practical move without further orders. BBC News confirmed. German Army on 21st Army Group front surrenders with effect from 0800 hours tomorrow 5 May 1945. Details as to procedure will follow.'

That afternoon on Luneburg Heath at 6.30 p.m., General Admiral von Friedeburg, the Commander-in-Chief of the German Navy, had signed the Instrument of Surrender of all German forces in the West to Field Marshal Montgomery, to take effect the following morning. What I had seen in the evening sky was the British Army celebrating the end of nearly six long years of war with the only appropriate means to hand. That celebration was to continue all through the night. On the previous day we had been in action and had started to prepare for our next attack on Bremerhaven. Now all that was behind us and the sudden unexpectedness of the end caught me by surprise.

I felt as though I had been engulfed by a huge wave and my first reaction, after the initial excitement had died down, was one of indescribable relief that the killing was now over. Then came a sense of intense exhilaration as I was swept along on the tide of excitement and emotion filling RHQ. Everyone from the Colonel downwards had broad grins and were slapping each other on the back and shaking hands regardless of rank. Confirmation of the message arrived by despatch rider an hour later from Brigadier Coad, and then the search for drinks began. Luckily we did not have far to look because, thanks to some liberation work by the 51st Highland Division, we had a large stock of champagne in the mess truck which was immediately brought in by Sergeant Marshall. Corks were popped with a noise resembling gunfire, but the champagne tasted good and we vied with each other to fire the flares from Verey pistols as far into the air as we could.

After half an hour or so of drinking and wild excitement, the reaction set in. I thought back six years to when I had been a fifteen-year-old schoolboy at Tonbridge and reflected how far I had come since that time. I thought of my parents in their prison camp in Hong Kong, from whom I had not heard properly for so long, and wondered if they were even still alive. I thought of my brother and sister and other relatives back in England, not knowing if the news we had received had yet filtered back home. I thought of all those men with whom I had served since that fateful Sixth of June and how many of them had not been lucky enough to make it this far. In particular, I thought of Keith Douglas and Johnnie Mann, Ted Cooke and John Holmes, Doug Footitt and Geoff Storey.

But the real sense of aching was for Denis, who had shared so much of my life at Tonbridge and in the war over the last eight years. It just seemed so unfair that he was not here to enjoy this moment, which he had done as much as anyone to deserve, but instead lay in the cold earth a few miles back along the road we had liberated. To be cut down so near the end, when he had so much to live for, was sadness itself and I could not get him out of my mind as the champagne lost its fizz. Quietly I put down my glass and slipped away from the celebrations to my bed. I just wanted to be alone with my thoughts and to reflect on what might have been.

I awoke the next morning to find the sun streaming through the window. Derek Colls from the KRRC was in the bed beside me, snoring away and probably suffering from an even bigger hangover than mine. This was the morning, I thought, for which we had all waited and fought for so long. No more death, no more shooting, no more burning tanks or loud explosions. I could rise from my bed and go to breakfast without worrying whether I would be blown to bits that day. Everything which had for so long held us down and ruled our lives had now been taken away in an instant and we were free and at peace. It was time for me to get on with the rest of my life.

AFTERWORD

When I am asked these days, especially by the younger generation, what it was like to fight in a war, I get some odd looks when I deliberately understate that 'it was pretty stressful'. I accept their rather baffled and puzzled expressions and acknowledge that I am being something of a tease in using a word which now has a wider interpretation and which many children use in simply describing their lives at school. They are, of course, quite right; stress affects them as it does doctors, nurses, teachers and many others, some of whom receive financial compensation for their sufferings. But I do believe that stress in battle has rather more substance. Only those who have been through it will understand why, although something can be learned from the reading of personal war experiences through the ages. Those thousands of schoolchildren who now visit the First World War battlefields of the Somme and Ypres with their peaceful fields and beautifully tended cemeteries must find it very hard to visualise what it was really like. But if they read Siegfried Sassoon's *Memoirs of an Infantry Officer*, Vera Brittain's *Testament of Youth* or even an evocatively constructed novel such as *Birdsong* by Sebastian Faulks, then they can begin to realise what those generations lived through and what war is really like for those young men and women who have to experience it.

I know that war is a distressing, ghastly, harrowing, horrific, fearsome and deplorable business. How can its actual awfulness be described to anyone? I have done my best.

BIBLIOGRAPHY

PUBLISHED SOURCES

Stephen Ambrose, *D-Day* (Simon & Schuster, 1994)

– , *Citizen Soldiers* (Simon & Schuster, 1997)

Keith Douglas, *Alamein to Zem Zem* (Oxford University Press, 1966)

–, *Collected Poems* (Faber & Faber, 1966)

Sidney Keyes, *Collected Poems* (Routledge, 1945)

T. M. Lindsay, *Sherwood Rangers* (Burrup, Mathieson, 1952)

Barry Orchard, *A Look at the Head and the Fifty* (James James, 1991)

Hans Pol, *Our Forgotten Liberators* (Stichting Oald Hengel, 2000)

Countess of Ranfurly, *To War with Whitaker* (Heinemann, 1994)

Arthur Reddish, *Normandy 1944: from the Hull of a Sherman* (Ken Ewing Publications, 1995)

William Scammell, *Keith Douglas: A Study* (Faber & Faber, 1988)

Leslie Skinner, *The Man Who Worked on Sundays* (Privately published, 1996)

Sherwood Rangers Casualty Book (Privately published, 1996)

Tom Staveley, *The Boyhood of a Poet: Sidney Keyes* (*The Listener*, January 1947)

The Tonbridgian Magazine

George Taylor, *Infantry Colonel* (Privately published, 1990)

UNPUBLISHED SOURCES

Stanley Christopherson, War Diary

Stuart Hills, War Diary

Letters to author from former members of the Sherwood Rangers

Letters written by the author to family

INDEX